Digital Advertising

Digital Advertising

2nd edition

Andrew McStay

Reader in Advertising and Digital Media,
Bangor University, UK

First published 2016 by
PALGRAVE

Palgrave in the UK is an imprint of Macmillan Publishers Limited, registered in England, company number 785998, of 4 Crinan Street, London, N1 9XW.

Palgrave Macmillan in the US is a division of St Martin's Press LLC, 175 Fifth Avenue, New York, NY 10010.

Palgrave is a global imprint of the above companies and is represented throughout the world.

Palgrave® and Macmillan® are registered trademarks in the United States, the United Kingdom, Europe and other countries.

ISBN 978–1–137–49433–7 hardback
ISBN 978–1–137–49434–4 paperback

This book is printed on paper suitable for recycling and made from fully managed and sustained forest sources. Logging, pulping and manufacturing processes are expected to conform to the environmental regulations of the country of origin.

A catalogue record for this book is available from the British Library.

A catalog record for this book is available from the Library of Congress.

Printed in China

Contents

Illustrations

Images

1   Digital: The Capacity to do Things They Never Could Before

The aim of this second edition of *Digital Advertising* is to understand the scale and nature of the digital advertising industry; to appreciate the role of creativity; to recognize how media are being used in diverse and fascinating ways; to chart the scope of change at both analytical and creative levels; to comprehend the insights into our lives being gathered by audience researchers; to understand the implications of artificial intelligence for advertising; to comment upon the seeming schism between technologists and artists in advertising, and to suggest means of theorizing all of these developments. For a sense of change, the first edition of this book was written in 2006–2007 and published in 2008. At this time the ubiquitous pop-up was still very much in use, viral advertising was new, we were plagued by spam, Twitter did not have a revenue model, and, while social media were rapidly being adopted, few had worked out how to monetize it. Here's the big one, though: we didn't even have smartphones! This is by far the most important change since the first edition of this book. Other key changes are that social media is a norm for early adopters *and* parents alike; behavioural advertising is the prevalent means of targeting people online; the most creative online advertising is akin to media engineering; we now talk of ecologies of interconnected advertising content to reflect our insatiable appetite for screens (PCs, tablets, phones and watches); and we have ads that not only target people without human intervention, but that select their own visuals and choose their own words.

The volume proceeds on the basis that to try to capture a breaking wave by means of a book is misguided. After all, new ad campaigns arrive daily, new killer apps and online services emerge online monthly, and new hardware that changes what is possible enters the market annually. As with the arrival of smartphones and wearable devices, new technologies that disrupt everything emerge approximately every five to ten years. Tracking surface changes to advertising is largely pointless and such an endeavour is better suited to online media that has a faster turnaround in terms of writing, reviewing and speed of publication. See outlets such as *Campaign, Advertising Age, TechCrunch, The Conversation, Wired, Engadget, The Economist* and *Guardian Tech* for what is happening day by day and week by week. Indeed, students would profit by simply typing #digitaladvertising into Twitter to find a plethora of contemporary case studies and insights from industry figures. So why a book? Because a book has different properties and requires something different of both the writer and reader. A book-length study allows us to consider the nature and scope of digital advertising in depth. Although I read all of the above publications and have written short articles for some, they are fleeting pieces of a whole that is difficult to picture. This book offers an overall view and allows us to interrogate, theorize, understand, connect different practices, contextualize and bring together the various actors that make up the practice of digital advertising. It grants us holistic understanding and not just fragmentary glimpses of a whole we cannot comprehend. To mix metaphors, I am less interested in breaking waves than the actors, forces and currents that drive the digital advertising environment. Much can be learned from historical awareness, tendencies, contexts and in-depth assessment of contemporary case studies. This book is also unusual in that it does not belong to any one discipline. While *about* advertising, the book draws not just on advertising studies but media studies, business studies, law, policy, information science, social theory and cultural studies. These are all necessary if we are to get to grips with digital advertising – a curious assemblage of psychology, business strategy, artistry, hardware, software, industrial practice, policy, law and regulations. My "product offer" or Unique Selling Proposition (USP) is to provide the reader with a strong sense of the practical make-up of digital advertising, but also with the theory to understand its history and where it is going next.

What is digital advertising?

Digital advertising is an expression used to refer to advertising that involves computational networks. Strictly speaking, the 'digital' prefix refers to 0s and 1s. This is binary, which means numbers that are presented by two symbols. In physical terms a "0" is an uncharged electrical state and "1" means charged. All digital information sent across networks involves patterns of on/off electrical charges that are recompiled by a receiver. However, it is more useful to think of digital media in terms of connectivity, feedback, interactivity and increased levels of information both in terms of that which is available to us, and that which we generate about ourselves. For advertisers, the term 'digital advertising' serves to cluster a range of types of media and strategies, including web, mobile, tablet, social, locative, wearable and other networked devices capable of contributing to advertising experiences. There are three dimensions that we might consider when we hear the term digital advertising:

1. Innovation in the means by which advertising is displayed and the creation of new advertising experiences;
2. An increase in the quantity of information used to target advertising at people;
3. Greater interconnection between devices through which advertising is displayed and through which information about behaviour is collected.

As digitality has embedded itself into the communicating strategies of virtually all companies interested in advertising, is there much point in examining digital advertising in isolation? My answer is yes, not least because companies of a digital nature are changing the very nature of advertising. Although the term remains problematic because one might rightly say that digital is no longer new and has been the status quo for some years, there are a few reasons why I argue we should keep the term. Firstly, because the advertising industry is more or less comfortable with the notion; secondly, because the award shows that confers prizes on the advertising industry use the term; thirdly, because it indicates ongoing development in how advertising might be displayed; fourthly, because it involves connecting different devices in order to serve more complete advertising experiences; fifthly, because of intensification of data gathering about people; and sixthly, because the first edition of this book was titled *Digital Advertising* and I would like to retain the expression!

However, it is not only digital advertising that is a problematic notion, because the principle of advertising is also being questioned. A search of websites of the top ten advertising agencies in the world reveals that none describe themselves as advertising agencies, although they all continue to make advertising. This is exemplified by one senior creative I interviewed who said that during his time at Dentsu (one of the big conglomerates) the word "advertising" was actually banned from use. This was an ideological exercise in defining how they see themselves, although they continue to produce much award-winning advertising. The question of self-definition is not a new one. Seeds of self-doubt began to take hold in the 1990s when ad agencies began to offer *integrated* marketing activities. This means that rather than just being concerned with advertising, they also offered sales promotion, direct response and public relations expertise. This saw large agencies attempt to become one-stop shops. This book does not comprehensively cover digital marketing, but it frequently strays into its territory because the distinction between digital advertising and marketing (along with public relations) is unclear. Traditionally marketing had more to do with purchase-related activities and the retail environment; in contrast, advertising had more to do with the media. In digital environments this distinction is far less clear than it used to be. As mentioned, flux seems to be the order of things.

Lastly, although agencies may be distancing themselves from advertising, this does not mean they are not in the business of advertising. Although plainly a major part of the story, agencies do not get to define what is, and what is not, advertising. This becomes significant when we think about how ads are regulated. It is important that we have a clear sense of what is regular media content and what is paid-for content aimed at influencing people. The separation of advertising from wider media content is important so we know when someone is being paid to sell to us. This allows us to weigh up the merits of the sponsored communication and, if entertaining, enjoy the ad for what it is.

What does this book address?

The next three chapters provide a basic overview of the digital advertising environment. Readers with an understanding of the advertising business and its media will want to jump ahead to Chapter 5, where the richer and more novel content of this book begins. Others should appreciate the clear summary of the industry in Chapters 2 to 4, what digital advertising encompasses and how it works. Chapter 2 explains that globally, online advertising is currently by far the fastest-growing advertising medium and that as online advertising grows in popularity, it requires us to reconsider what we mean by advertising. Many on hearing the word 'advertising' will think of glossy images in magazines, television commercials and billboards. Clearly these exist, but they are not as popular as they once were. Search advertising (hereafter called 'search') is particularly pertinent as it is worth roughly 60 per cent of the entire amount of money spent on digital advertising. As will be depicted later in the book, this leads us to ask whether it is not only that forms of advertising are changing, but whether the very nature of advertising itself is mutating. To understand digital advertising today it is prudent to have a sense of its origins and roots. I begin with both the web (1991) and the first online advertising to establish the technical, industrial and cultural logic that today still informs online practices. I then progress to delineate the practice of digital advertising, the scope and make-up of the industry, what it does, how it works and who its key players are. I then briefly consider some of the key debates being discussed in the advertising industry (or what I term 'Adland', subject as it is to its own culture, practices, body of knowledge and set of formal and informal rules), many of which will be revisited in later chapters. These include the question of accountability, the rise of automated advertising, privacy, convergence and promotional culture, the role of social media and the backlash against digital media.

Chapters 3 and 4 continue by means of offering the novice reader an overview of digital advertising media. I divide these into 'standard' and 'non-standard' digital media. Although new devices, formats and ways of delivering advertising are emerging, things do not move quite as quickly as you might think. While the technology press can lure one into believing that everything changes on a daily basis, this is not true. For example, since the first edition of this book was written in 2008, advertisers continue to spend most of their money on web advertising. As Chapter 3 explores, the proportions of spend on web advertising remains similar with search at 55 per cent; display at 30 per cent; classifieds at 14 per cent; and other formats at 1 per cent (IAB, 2014a). These are what we can term 'standard' digital advertising formats. However, the direction of media travel is clear, and although at the time of writing mobile only represents around £1 out of every £6 spent on online advertising, the fact that people spend so much time with phones dictates that advertisers will continue to gravitate in that direction. So far for mobile, display advertising is the most popular format with advertisers (if not consumers). Chapter 4 pays attention to non-standard media, or formats and platforms not ostensibly designed for advertising. The most popular of these are gaming and social media. Towards the end of this chapter we will also consider the merits of earned media, as opposed to the paid-for media that is synonymous with the history of advertising.

Chapter 5 moves in another direction to explore a very different dimension of advertising. Here we pay attention to creativity and its role in digital advertising. I first provide an overview of the history of creativity in advertising and then progress to assess creativity today, particularly in a media and communicative environment where the only certainty is change. While this is true, the traditional role of stories and narratives remains. Indeed creatives, at both traditional agencies and digital hotshops, agree that creativity and storytelling go hand in hand. This is less about "once upon a time" than under-standing of archetypes, aspiration, desire, creation and resolution of tension, narrative, characters, and the ways that each of these can be subverted to provide an interesting and memorable twist that leaves a favourable brand impression.

As we will see, creatives continue to be obsessed with *ideas*. All crea-tive practitioners from every type of agency I spoke to stress that this principle remains important – if not sacrosanct. Further, the role of ideas is not diminished in the digital era, but is foregrounded. This is because human insights that sell should translate across all media. The principle of ideas involves turning advertising strategy (what message is to be communicated and to whom) into a memorable, convincing, palatable and potentially enjoyable advertising experience. The best of these are insightful in that they reflect basic truths of lived life. Historically they have assisted in building brands (or what is left of a company after the removal of all of its production-related assets) and generating monetary value. Examples old and recent include: Apple's *1984* (this positioned its main competitor IBM as George Orwell's Big Brother and cast all other machines as boring and monochrome); Nicorette's *Quitting Sucks* (this displayed brand empathy with what consumers are going through); Nike's *Just Do It* (this utilized a sport-sperson's mentality to separate Nike products from sports gear as fashion items); and Dove's *Real Women* (this attempted to generate intimacy with women by being on their side in an airbrushed world). The point behind each of these campaigns is a strategic thought that can shape entire companies in relation to their competitors. However, the chapter also discusses what I phrase 'small ideas'. This concept reflects feelings within the industry that strategy is too slow and what is required are tactics, i.e. the capacity to be reactive to what is taking place today. In an era where the average phone user checks their phone 110 times per day, there is brand kudos to be won by taking advantage of events unfolding daily. The chapter unpacks these industrial dis-courses and practices by articulating creativity in terms of experience, sensation, situation, combinations, culture hacking, playfulness and subversion. As we head towards the chapter's conclusion I progress to define creativity by raiding multiple disciplines including philosophy, psychology, history and aesthetics.

Chapter 6 brings together earlier interest in media and creativity to understand *non-interruptive* approaches to advertising. Although advertising has changed enormously in terms of how media are used and how companies interact with consumers, many core principles remain the same. As the millennial generation (20–30 year olds) gives way to the next (those born between 1995 and 2002), we see hardening of social attitudes towards corporations and renewed interest in non-digital experiences. In other words, what these consumers seek is authenticity. Ad agencies have responded to this with advertising that no longer looks like advertising. This involves what is termed 'native advertising' and 'branded content'. This is diverse and involves use of YouTube influencers, documentaries using multiple social media, sponsored BuzzFeed stories, films, games, viral content and earned media (where people share interesting advertising content).

Although advertising remains intimately associated with ideas and storytelling, historically the industry has underappreciated the role of media. It has used media as channels by which to communicate information. What this conception of media misses is exploration of the medium itself, but more significantly how non-standard media forms can be used. In Chapter 7, the expression I use for this is *media hacking*. I unpack this principle by paying particular attention to B-Reel, a firm who are neither a traditional advertising agency nor a media production company, but who act as creative partners for agencies and clients. The chapter ends by assessing a range of examples through which storytelling can be improved with hacked media.

Chapter 8 focuses on threats to the digital advertising and publishing industries. Increased use of behavioural advertising has led to the development of widely used adblocking software. The term is slightly misleading (I did not create it) because it only blocks a certain type of online advertising – those that are placed by third parties. However, this is proving to be a challenge because many of our favourite websites have come to rely upon behavioural advertising revenue. This chapter explores key actors, ethics and reasons for growth in adblocking. I also address the role of click fraud, or when an advertiser's digital advertising campaign is sabotaged by a person or machine repeatedly clicking on their ads and driving up costs.

Chapter 9 addresses the ethics and practices of advertising to children in the digital environment. The regulation of the advertising industry is varied but comprises a balance of self-regulation versus legislation. I pay particular attention to UK regulatory arrangements, but many principles and topics in this chapter are common to other countries and legal jurisdictions. To illustrate the regulatory situation, I examine a policy review in the UK on whether advertising and the media are forcing children to grow up too quickly. I also examine video blogging (vlogging) and how the Committee of Advertising Practice (CAP) dealt with sponsored content that is neither regular advertising nor independent media content.

A key development in advertising is the use of analytics, or the way in which data is collected, analysed, put to work to better understand audiences, and used to target advertising at people when they will be most receptive. This is not a new idea, but digital media provide new opportunities to collect more information from different sources, and to use this to create and target advertising in real time. To this end, Chapter 10 considers the role of 'big data', analytics and profiling practices in advertising. The term was coined by an industry analyst named Doug Laney who, while working at a technology and research firm now called Gartner Incorporated, outlined ways in which our information processing techniques are developing. He referred to three characteristics: first, an increase in *volume* of data; second, the *velocity* by which data moves and needs to be reacted to; and third, the *variety* of forms it comes in. The chapter works through case examples of the types and variety of data collected. It progresses to assess the relationship between advertising, identities and profiling in greater depth. Again, we will work through specific examples of *very* large companies (that I'll wager the reader has never heard of) to examine the sorts of information that the data industry deals with. Notably this is not just about what we have clicked, bought, done or said, but also about emotions and feelings.

Chapter 11 continues the interest in mood and emotions, but rather than focus on analytics it highlights how emotionally aware advertising is being used out of the home. Here I will introduce two concepts. The first is *emotiveillance*, or the practice of monitoring emotions to influence and manage people; the second, *empathic media*, is an expression I use to identify technologies used to assess emotions. I use these principles to diagnose the ways in which digital outdoor advertising is using sensors and cameras to get closer to people by means of reading our emotions and behaviour, and to examine advertising that improves itself on the basis of biometric and behavioural information. This investigation requires that we understand the nature of emotional analytics, the practical terms in which these are being used, and automation and the growing use of artificial intelligence (AI) in advertising.

Our love of content and social networking has to be paid for somehow. The question is whether we have the right funding models to generate this revenue. As will be made clear throughout this book, increasingly media content is paid for by advertising technologies that monitor our behaviour. This entails a massive range of information types from online and offline sources, and even data from our bodies to infer emotional states. This rightly raises questions about privacy. Although this is a word we hear a great deal about, it is badly defined. The aim of Chapter 12 is to provide an understanding of what privacy actually is. We begin by doing a practical assessment of how readers (i.e. you!) are being tracked and progress to recognize that although the word "privacy" is used a great deal today, it is a premise that is poorly understood. Worse, it is often framed in negative terms regarding "having something to hide". This chapter exposes this fallacy and argues that privacy has more to do with personal control, choice, informed consent, choosing who to be open with (and when to be more reserved) and the right to be respected. When we start to look at privacy this way around, we see that privacy is about dignity, agreed values and what I term 'privacy protocol'. The ad industry is acutely aware that privacy is a sensitive matter, not least because of threats from national and transnational regulators. It is not just a social matter, but a business one too, with all parties (industry and critics) agreeing there has been a breakdown of trust in the commercial online environment. The chapter explores why this is the case in reference to Google Android's free apps ecology.

Chapter 13 concludes the book by reconciling two seemingly opposing tendencies in advertising: the creatives and the data acolytes. The chapter works through practical examples to illustrate what I call the 'data sublime', or belief in greatness beyond that which is calculable. I also examine creatives' response to this situation that, unsurprisingly, appeals to the heart and intuition over correlation. However, under closer inspection, this divide in Adland is a mere manifestation of philosophical and intellectual/creative rumblings that have gone on for centuries. This chapter briefly provides some context about this so we can better understand the terms of the debate. The chapter also defines criteria for AI enhanced non-human creativity. Its final thoughts, however, are reserved for people and respect for their rights to control data about them. As a business that considers itself agile, innovative and creative, can advertising do business in a privacy-friendly fashion?

Finally, please see the A–Z of Key Terms for definitions of theories and terminology that I have generated as a result of examining the contemporary state of digital advertising. This will help keep you on track if you meet words you are unfamiliar with. Also, at the end of each chapter is list of questions. If you use these in the classroom or write essays based on them, I'd like to read what you find and conclude. Feel free to tweet me at @digi-ad with an online link.

2 The History and Business of Digital Advertising

All who study or practise digital advertising have trouble keeping up with developments because there is so much going on. Whereas television, press, radio, cinema, direct mail and outdoor media are relatively simple to understand, "digital" is a catch-all label for a wide range of formats, approaches and areas of industrial expertise. This chapter will provide a panoramic view of digital advertising in terms of its history, what it is, who makes it, who uses it and what the key debates are in Adland today.

History

To understand the history of digital advertising, we begin our narrative with the inception of the World Wide Web in 1991 and the understanding that the web is a set of interconnected documents published on the internet, negotiated and navigated with a web browser. At the heart of the web is Hypertext Markup Language (HTML). This is a relatively simple computer language that can be used to create webpages that include links, graphics, multimedia components and, importantly for us, online digital advertising. Note that they are called web*pages* that in turn are produced by *publishers*. This gives us a sense of the roots of web-based media and its connection with traditional print formats.

It is inspirational to read the original proposal for the web to obtain a sense of the essence of the web and how it was envisaged before it physically existed, particularly the links between media and connectivity. The proposal *WorldWideWeb: Proposal for a HyperText Project*, written by Tim Berners-Lee and Robert Cailliau (1990), describes hypertext as 'a way to link and access information of various kinds as a web of nodes in which the user can browse at will' and to provide people with a single interface with which they can access a range of information types. Both in 1990 and today, this information is organized by servers and clients whereby our own machines equipped with web browsers (clients) request and display information from other remote computers (servers). By means of the web browser, people would navigate hypertext pages where 'pieces of text which refer to other texts' reside, with this 'network of links ... called a web'. Notably, too, the *'web is also not complete'* (my emphasis). This is an important point because unlike other media (books, television, radio etc.), the web had the capacity for growth built into its DNA. Although Tim Berners-Lee developed the web, it really began to catch on in 1993 when a freely available web browser called Mosaic was publicly released. Mosaic went on to become Netscape Navigator that in turn became Firefox (a popular browser owned by Mozilla). Another historical point to note is that in addition to being able to write and read webpages, the web was social from the beginning.[1] By means of the web, thousands of communities, special interest groups, cultures, fan groups, discussion boards and forums formed. Although people had used the internet before the web to group and communicate, the technical and visual ease of the web interface meant this was accessible to many more people. Notably, these early users and communities were fairly hostile to advertisers and marketers who were quick to see new opportunities to reach a wealthy demographic.

By the early 1990s, the business and mainstream press carried stories foretelling new futures, modes of communication and life on the "Information Superhighway". There was a *Back to the Future* character to all of this in that the introduction of any new communication technology tends to elicit similar social reactions.[2] Needless to say, these were heady times, and in the development of early online advertising we see the interaction of forces of ownership, investment and, perhaps most importantly, mixed ideological outlooks on what the web should become. For some, it was a new stage of humanity and frontier of knowledge, communication and experimentation. For others, it was a gold rush – a new means of publishing, making revenue, marketing, selling advertising space and a litany of get-rich-quick schemes.

The early 1990s leading up to 2001 is known as the dotcom boom era. It involved economic opportunism, venture capitalism, high rates of return for relatively small investments and start-up costs, attempts to grow companies as quickly as possible and massive overvaluation of what e-company stocks were worth. This was the textbook definition of an economic bubble inflated by hype. The belief that the future was inexorably digital arose from a number of influences, not least a libertarian frontier mentality realized by a longstanding technology culture in the San Francisco "Silicon Valley" region. However, although many rash investment choices were made, on the whole investors are not stupid. They understood that they would lose money on many start-ups that gave a convincing pitch, promised big returns, but delivered little. The reason why this happened and why it was sustainable is because these losses were significantly offset by the investments that really made it. After all, the web promised something new: an easily accessible global marketplace. The trick was to get there first and not to miss *the* investment that really makes it. Between the years 1997 and 2000, the web was, for many, the site of the future of global commerce. New dotcom companies entered the market at an exponential rate and confidence in the "New Economy" was at an unprecedented high. Although the epicentre of web activity was the US, like the growth of the web itself, the web industry boom was global. This was a period driven by massive excess, euphoria, youth, unfounded valuations of companies, losses, many losers and some big winners. It is out of this environment that Amazon, eBay, Facebook and Google, the online giants of today, emerged. In 2000, the bubble popped – or more accurately, it went BANG! One has to remember that much of the investment in new companies was made on the basis of what they *might* become. This absence of real returns, viable business plans and most importantly the collapse of confidence in the sector meant that in financial terms the dotcom industry quite literally collapsed and fell in upon itself. This downward trend began on 10 March 2000 as the stock market peaked, declined and crashed. This slide of web technology firms continued for another two years.[3]

Digital advertising: a matter of scale

As Calcutt (1999) notes, early countercultural users of the internet were desperate to keep the online environments free from commerce, while at the same time marketers, venture capitalists and traditional businesses were equally bent on turning it into a global marketplace. This was not helped by a less-than-subtle approach to advertising. Pop-ups, floating screen-based advertising and banners were irritatingly popular with advertisers. The commonly accepted beginning of web advertising comes from AT&T and their advertising on the pages of *HotWired* in 1994, a digital offshoot of *Wired* magazine (Doubleclick, 2005). *HotWired* charged clients a fee of around $30,000 to place ads on its website for 12 weeks. Other initial sponsors included MCI Communications Corp., Club Med, Adolph Coors Co.'s Zima brand, IBM Corp., Harman International Industries' JBL speakers and Volvo

Cars of North America (Advertising Age, 2003). Even at this early stage of digital advertising, online agencies were tracking the "click-through" rates for their clients. Due to the success of *HotWired*, online service providers that had a large amount of users attracted advertisers to their sites. In 1996, the effectiveness of this type of advertising began to be audited by Millward Brown (an organization that assesses the success of advertising, marketing and branding) that evaluated the success rates of *HotWired*'s banner advertising. They pronounced *HotWired*'s campaign a success and that banner advertising was effective, even on first viewing.

However, the dotcom crash led advertisers to re-evaluate where they spend their money. After the promise that the web would lead to the demise of traditional mass media, the implosion of the digital commerce seemed to prove the doubters and naysayers right. As the 2000s progressed, the online advertising marketplace matured into one where traditional advertisers were increasingly comfortable placing digital advertising as part of their communications programme. This tallied with companies developing their web presences, traditional news providers having online outlets, and the understanding that the web was here to stay and that this would be a commercial environment. Widespread adoption of social media was still a few years off (beginning around 2005). In the UK, by 2003 the online sector held 3 per cent of the total advertising spend across all advertising media (television, radio, press, direct mail, outdoor and cinema). By 2005, this had grown to a media market share of 7.8 per cent, growing at a rate of 65.8 per cent year on year. Indeed, this growth was so significant that it drove the expansion of the entire advertising media market. Since the early 2000s, the online advertising industry has grown exponentially and is now the fastest growing advertising medium, growing faster than any other marketing/ advertising channel. All market reports (UK and global) assessed for this book point to upward growth for the foreseeable future. Today this growth is largely attributable to the continued rise in search advertising, but also to increases in mobile and smartphone access, tablets and use of video and display advertising on social media sites. For the UK, the Internet Advertising Bureau (IAB) offers up-to-date statistics on advertising spend so I will not linger on statistics about 2015 when this book was written (you can search 'IAB ad spend' for yourself). The IAB also has outposts in most mature advertising markets, so have a look at the regional site for your own country/region. The historical trend, however, is interesting and noteworthy. For a sense of scale, digital advertising was 3 per cent in 2003, but ten years later in 2013 represented 35 per cent of what in the UK was a £17.9 billion market. By the end of 2013, other media ranked as: television at 25 per cent; press at 18 per cent; direct mail at 12 per cent; outdoor at 6 per cent; radio at 3 per cent; and cinema at 1 per cent. Again, have a look at figures for your own country in your own year and see whether the rate of growth is comparable. Certainly in the UK, a key reason for this growth is innovation in both hardware and how we access digital content, but also the quality of digital content itself. This also returns us to the principle of scalability and the web discussed earlier: because the digital environment is not complete and has *scalability* built into it, new content, systems, platforms and ways of doing things will continue to emerge and amuse us.

The global picture of digital advertising practice

Although I promised not to bombard the reader with statistics, a modicum will be useful to obtain a snapshot of the state of the advertising industry. I include how much is spent on advertising, understanding of who is advertising, who the largest agencies are, who the key digital players are and which mega-companies own these agencies.

Advertising Age (2015) offers a range of useful statistics that helps us understand the scope, size and types of advertising markets across the world. As of 2015, **the world's largest markets** (expressed in $ billions spent on advertising) are: US (182.7); China (50.3); Japan (45.6); Germany (24.9); UK (24.3); Brazil (17.3); France (13.0); Australia (12.5); South Korea (12.4); Canada (11.5); Russia (10.3); Italy (8.8); Argentina (8.5); Indonesia (7.9); and Mexico (7.3).

The world's largest 15 advertisers are (expressed in $ billions spent on advertising): Procter & Gamble Co. from the US (11.4); Unilever from Rotterdam/London (7.9); L'Oréal from France (5.9); Toyota Motor Corp from Japan (3.4); General Motors Co. from the US (3.3); Volkswagen from Germany (3.2); Nestlé from Switzerland (3.1); Coca-Cola Co. from the US (2.8); Mars Inc. from the US (2.8); PepsiCo from the US (2.7); Sony Corp. from Japan (2.7); McDonald's Corp. from the US (2.7); RB (Reckitt Benckiser Group) from the UK (2.5); Ford Motor Co. from the US (2.4); and Nissan Motor Co. from Japan (2.1).

In terms of **the world's largest advertising agencies**, *conglomerates* increasingly own these. This means that many of the agencies you will be aware of and know in your own country will be owned by the same parent company. These are Interpublic, Omnicom, Publicis, WPP and Dentsu (that bought another giant, Aegis, for $4.9 billion in 2013). The following list details both the world's largest agency networks and the conglomerations that own them:

1. Young & Rubicam Group owned by WPP
2. McCann Worldgroup owned by Interpublic Group of Companies
3. Dentsu (Japan) owned by Dentsu Inc.
4. DDB Worldwide Communications Group owned by Omnicom Group
5. BBDO Worldwide owned by Omnicom Group
6. Ogilvy & Mather owned by WPP
7. TBWA Worldwide owned by Omnicom Group
8. Publicis Worldwide owned by Publicis Groupe
9. Dentsu Aegis Network owned by Dentsu Inc.
10. J. Walter Thompson Co. owned by WPP
11. Epsilon owned by Alliance Data Systems Corp.
12. Leo Burnett Worldwide owned by Publicis Groupe
13. Havas Worldwide owned by Havas
14. FCB owned by Interpublic Group of Companies
15. IBM Interactive Experience owned by IBM Corp.

Digital context

ZenithOptimedia, from whom the *Advertising Age* (2015) report draws much of its data suggests that the internet will account for more than one-third of US ad spending in 2017. Similarly, it expects the internet's share of worldwide ad spending to top 31 per cent in 2017. In the UK, the IAB (2014a) reports that spending on digital advertising is already over a third of the total advertising media market. To rank: digital = 39 per cent; television = 25 per cent; press = 17 per cent; direct mail = 10 per cent; outdoor = 5 per cent; radio = 3 per cent; and cinema = 1 per cent. One reason why digital is so popular is because it is a diverse set of formats.

I do not ask the reader to remember the precise numbers or even the geographic regions, but rather the rate of development, the pre-eminence of digital, the relative size of the ad markets (still over-whelmingly dominated by the US) and the fact that many agencies are owned by a few conglomerates.

Digital agencies

The 1990s saw the rise of specialist agencies dedicated to the digital environment. Many advertisers were keen to try these new exotic boutiques, although the big agencies reacted and created niche spin-offs dedicated to serving digital wants and needs. Adland's interest in digital was not just about making ads for new media channels, but also dealing with database marketing and managing interactivity. Where advertising had been based on one-directional communication, they now had to address and develop opportunities for multi-pathway communication and track people's engagement with the advertising. Initially the digital sector was represented by interactive agencies, which originally meant working with the web. Boundaries, however, have become blurred. As digital becomes more mainstream it is growing increasingly difficult to say that one agency is digital whereas the other is traditional. This is natural as digital is no longer an offshoot but the status quo. Digital and interactive agencies operate in a similar fashion to traditional agencies, although they focus on interactive and digital advertising services. Like traditional agencies they offer general services such as strategy, consumer insight, creativity, design, management, media and tracking of consumer engagement with advertising. More uniquely digital and interactive agencies may be involved with brand development, developing potential online custom (lead generation), creating digital communications strategies and working out ways of reaching digital audiences and delivering advertising to them, developing rich media advertising campaigns, online video, mobile applications, social media, virtual environments, email communications, search engine marketing and optimization, designing websites, data mining, assessing advertisers' return on investment and bespoke projects. Judged by creativity, strategy and effectiveness, **leading digital agencies** in 2015 are 360i New York; R/GA New York; Proximity Toronto; FRED AND FARID Paris; Razorfish New York; OgilvyOne London; VML Australia; Proximity Bogotá; Proximity Barcelona; and Possible New York (Warc, 2015).[4] One cannot help noticing the US domination of this list, but it is also worth noting the non-Anglocentric countries too.

Leading digital media

In the UK the most popular formats for digital advertising break down as: search = 55 per cent; display = 30 per cent; classifieds = 14 per cent; and other = 1 per cent. Along with other forms of digital advertising, we will discuss these in some depth in the following two chapters. **Search advertising** is the leading form of digital advertising. Unsurprisingly, Google is the number one provider, as it is by far the largest search engine and the world's number one website in terms of global traffic (Alexa, 2015). What is notable, however, is that the barrier to entry is very low both in terms of cost and knowledge required to use search advertising. Whereas advertising in the past was prohibitive because the cost of accessing above-the-line media was high, search advertising allows smaller organizations to advertise too. Notably too, its advertisers only pay if users click on an advertisement or call a telephone number. In Chapter 3, we will look at search more closely but for now it will suffice to recognize that Google offers two forms of advertising. The first is *Adwords* that works by placing advertising next to search results. The advertiser chooses a set of words or phrases that best relate to its business. Advertisers may also bid on words that will positively associate with the advertiser and its brand. Google also offers *Adsense*, a form of behavioural advertising that displays advertisers' advertising to people with relevant interests and profiles. Behavioural advertising will be discussed in greater depth in Chapters 3 and 10.

Display advertising is the second most popular format. As explored in Chapter 3, this is a diverse medium but typically involves ads on the top and sides of webpages. In the UK, the IAB (2014b) reports that display advertising is dominated by the consumer goods industry (18.1 per cent); finance (13.7 per cent); retail (12 per cent); entertainment and the media (10.7 per cent); travel and transport (9.8 per cent); technology (7.6 per cent); telecoms (7.6 per cent); motors (7 per cent); business and industrial (6.4 per cent); government and political organizations (3.7 per cent); leisure equipment (1.4 per cent); property (1.3 per cent) and gardening and agriculture (0.7 per cent).

We will unpack advertising media in greater depth in Chapter 3, but to end this section we should be aware that **classifieds advertising** is the third most popular format. This entails sites where people post their own ads. The most popular classifieds sites are for cars, property (renting and buying real estate) and jobs. The key growth area to be aware of is **mobile advertising** which is dominated by consumer goods, entertainment and the media. To rank in order of use: consumer goods industry (24 per cent); entertainment and the media (22 per cent); retail (11 per cent); telecoms (9 per cent); technology (9 per cent); finance (7 per cent); motors (7 per cent); travel and transport (4 per cent); government and political organizations; (2 per cent); business and industrial (2 per cent); leisure equipment (1 per cent) (IAB, 2014b).[5] **Tablet advertising** is also increasingly popular because tablets are often used to search, review and purchase goods.

Key debates taking place in Adland

Many themes of forthcoming sections will be returned to throughout the book. I have collected and presented them here so the reader has a snapshot of key debates taking place within business publications such as *Campaign* and *Advertising Age*, at conferences and within agencies. These include the question of creativity versus data-driven advertising, industry convergence, adblocking, the "death of advertising" and the role of privacy online.

The automation in advertising: what about creativity?

A debate that has rumbled on since the professionalization of advertising is the role of creativity. We will address creativity in Chapter 5 but suffice to say that the industry is split between those who see analytics and technology as the future of advertising, and those who argue that human insight and intuition is the most important driving force behind advertising. Although cooler heads draw attention to the fact that data can be used in novel and interesting ways, new analytical technologies are causing much disquiet in Adland. The split between analysis and creativity is one that dogged advertising throughout the twentieth century. Scientific methods employed have encompassed statistical, psychoanalytical and motivational approaches to understand consumer and audience behaviour. Today we see a different type of scientism in the form of big data processes. This entails the use of large amounts of information about people to target them with the right advertising, at the right time and in the right place. It also has predictive capacities because by understanding market trends (what people have bought, looked at and said), machines can offer suggestions about what we will want. Indeed, we may not even know that we want it until it is put before us! For example, mid-income bracket males of 30–40 years of age that use Apple computers, drive a Volkswagen, ride mountain bikes and enjoy outdoor sports may well be interested in grinding their own coffee beans. They may not have done this before, but ownership of electric coffee grinders fits the demographic well. The automated study of consumer behaviour to serve advertising entails ability to collect large amounts of data from multiple sources and to process this quickly so generating relevant advertising. This is not just about the targeting of advertising, but also the creation of advertising. To caricature the situation, the concern among traditionalists is that if data-driven advertising processes that make use of artificial intelligence have enough information, this will rid advertising of the need for people to create advertising. While I suspect few actually believe that creatives in agencies will be out of a job anytime soon, the reality that machines can create ads has certainly caused a stir in Adland.

Adblocking

The use of software to remove ads placed by third parties is increasingly popular among younger people. Adblockers do not remove all advertising from web and mobile experiences, but those that are placed by third parties who serve advertising on web publishers' behalf. Further, as explored in Chapter 8, users' resentment focuses on ads that contain animations, sounds, non-skippable video content and which take over screens. Adland argues that adblocking damages the advertising business and the capacity for publishers and service providers to give us free content, and that it chokes off vital revenue for start-ups. Adblocking companies and those who sympathize with them point out that they do not block all ads, but just the most irritating sorts. They also highlight that people have a legal right not to be tracked by third parties if they do not wish so, and that adblockers are one means of expressing this preference.

Privacy

Another key theme for the advertising business today is privacy. This has not always been the case and while advertising has always had critics, abuse of privacy is a relatively new criticism. Before the web was launched in the 1990s, the idea that our advertising might be watching what we do, following us, tracking us and reporting back would have been laughable and sinister. It is of course the norm today as advertisers track online behaviour and the sites we visit. The digital advertising industry is keenly aware of privacy issues. It is faced by four situations: the first is that information about people is valuable so it can better create and target ads; secondly, its own surveys point out that people are not happy with being targeted by means of their online behaviour; thirdly, regulators around the world pay close attention to any privacy-invasive behaviour; and, lastly, regulators are willing to exercise powers and therefore the ad industry is understandably keen not to generate further stringent regulations.

Promotional culture

Although this book is about digital advertising, it is important to recognize that, from an industrial point of view, advertising sits within a broader context of the marketing mix; and that from an academic and lay perspective, advertising sits within an environment rightly identified in terms of promotional culture. This refers to the idea that it is not just the promotional industries (advertising, marketing, PR and media) that promote, but that today we all seem to be at it (Davis, 2013). Be this in politics and media management, academic self-promotion on Twitter, students cleaning up their Facebook accounts before they go looking for work or just clothes selection for the day, the idea of promotion permeates modern societies. This book has opted to consider advertising in its own right but as new media forms (particularly those that involve sharing, linking, posting and recommending content) continue to evolve, the distinction between advertising, marketing, public relations and even personal promotion are not clear (after all, personal management of social media accounts requires audience understanding, strategy, knowing what to filter out and creativity in how content is presented).

Convergence

Increasingly our attention time is earned. Whereas historically advertising has often relied upon media scarcity to ensure we cannot miss its wares, today's diverse media environment means that advertising has had to up its game and improve. Due to this fragmentation, advertisers are working harder to earn our attention. The principle of earned media belongs to public relations (PR) because PR practitioners typically do not buy media space (and attention time), but they seek to generate positive conversation, writing and buzz around their clients. Historically PR is the practice of managing reputations. This involves an arguably greater diversity of target stakeholders than advertising (e.g. decision makers, politicians, business leaders and employees, as well as everyday potential customers). For example, the Chartered Institute of Public Relations (2015) defines publics as 'audiences that are important to the organisation. These include customers – existing and potential; employees and management; investors; media; government; suppliers; opinion-formers'. As a result PR typically sees communication as a two-way process. The point about 'relations' is key in that public relations entail nurturing relations with significant individuals and groups to steer them towards a strategically desirable outcome for the client.

The need to earn attention now applies to advertising, particularly because the popularity of social media has forever utterly changed the nature of PR. Historically, advertising has largely been linear and one way, or *at* people. As the media environment has developed, this principle is less assured. The blurring of advertising and PR has developed because advertising is taking greater interest in types of promotion that do not require off-the-peg formats (as with what used to be called above-the-line media (or mass media and impersonal communication)). Conversely, PR has developed a greater interest in using media to communicate and engage with target stakeholders. This may involve creation of short online videos, photos and websites, and other online content to best position a client. From an advertising point of view, this has required new skills because designing and managing social media campaigns is different from traditional media. They are inherently conversational and often run live and in real time. It is also content that is frequently shared or forwarded, so making use of non-linear distribution channels. Lastly, both advertising and PR are increasingly mapping the effectiveness of their own endeavours. This is achieved by monitoring press releases; tracing conversions (getting someone to click, buy or read something); assessing injections of ideas and positions into debates; success/failure in handling negative comments; responding to events in a timely manner; engaging in conversations; and counting shares, retweets, reblogs, likes, posts, Vines and so on. The need to trace and deliver numerical accounts of return on investment is something typically associated with advertising.

However, advertising is changing too. For example, a search of the About pages on the homepages of the top five agencies in the UK in 2013 reveals that few actually like to call themselves advertising agencies any more. To list:

1. AMV BBDO refers to itself as a 'communications agency';
2. McCann positions itself with the line 'Truth, Well Told';
3. RKCR/Y&R positions itself through 'Ideas before advertising. Ideas beyond advertising' (but not advertising!);
4. BBH says that it 'evolved from a renowned advertising agency into a communications business equipped to lead in the digital age';
5. Adam and Eve/DDB defines itself in terms of 'effective communications' and 'brilliant work that works'.

Although all agencies display advertising work they have done on their websites, they seem less keen to be defined by it. The reason for this is that they seek a more expansive definition of what they do, they do not wish to be pigeonholed (and lose business to marketing communications companies) and they certainly do not wish to be considered as outdated or irrelevant. What is clear, then, is that these longstanding agencies still exist, they are still doing advertising work, but that linear one-way advertising is not only what they do. All are keen to see themselves as creative communications organizations able to respond to any communicative need.

Being social

When I wrote the first edition of this book in 2008, there was much ado about "Web 2.0", the rise of social media and the general sense that people were participating more actively in their own media experiences through posting, commenting, liking, friending, sharing and so on. This principle is still important because it reflects the fact that media culture is not something provided for people, but that it is in large part generated by us. After all, what would Instagram be without our images? Media culture today is intrinsically participatory in the sense that we create our own profile pages, create and manage reputations and promote ourselves on platforms such as Facebook, Twitter, LinkedIn, Instagram, Periscope and the rest. This invites two observations: (1) the well-understood principle of user-generated culture; but also (2) that in the so-called Web 2.0 *we* are the source of information.

After all, as we will see in the course of this book, we disclose a great deal of information about ourselves online. Whereas historically market researchers have had to find out information about people, where they live, how much money they have, what they like, what their views are, what brands they like/dislike, what they do, who they do it with, what they feel about topical matters, where they go on holiday, what they buy, what they look/sound like, who their friends are, and so on, we now willingly (if not always knowingly) self-generate this information. Historically speaking, this fact is a strange but lucrative outcome for the market research industry.

The digital backlash

Before we conclude this chapter, we should reflect on industry perceptions of digital advertising. Adland is split on this, with those from creative departments bemoaning the lack of branding capacity. They have a point because when compared to television, digital has arguably not yet delivered mass audience brand experiences. Given that the world's largest spenders on advertising are looking to build brands, reputations, perceptions and values, they need media that can deliver scale. Conversely, digital media companies promise enhanced targeting and lack of waste in reaching people who are not interested. Although targeting seems to work well in theory, in practice studies are finding that many digital ads are not reaching their target audiences. A study by Google, for example, found that over 56 per cent of digital ads are not even seen by their target audiences (Google, 2014).

Conclusion

My aim for this chapter was to provide an overview of the rise of digital advertising, key historical developments, agency trends, markets and the type of media used. The latter half of the chapter highlighted some of the ongoing discussions about digital advertising in Adland today. These are as diverse as the digital media environment itself, but include the value of data analytics, adblocking, privacy, earning rather than paying for attention, suspicion of targeting technologies, the utility of digital for branding, and that many digital ads are not even reaching their target audiences.

Think points and questions

▸ Although the internet bubble of the late 1990s is most well known, this is a sector still prone to much excitement, fast growth and exuberance. Read the leading technology news sites and answer: will these technologies, apps and platforms still exist in two years? Importantly, why do you think this is the case?

▸ A point often missed in advertising studies is the macro-environment: understanding of who the big players are, what they own and where they are located. Spend some time searching through the homepages of the businesses listed in this chapter, read and follow *Advertising Age* to obtain more recent statistics and identify who the trade associations are in your own country as these will provide you with the local picture.

▸ Check ad-spending statistics in your own country by visiting the trade association for digital advertising in your region. If you are outside the UK, do they differ proportionally from the UK? If so, why?

▸ Have a search of the leading advertising companies (i.e. those who produce famous advertising!) and examine how they define themselves. If we are "post-advertising", what is the nature of this persuasive communication? Or is it a case of advertising is dead, long live advertising?

3 How it Works: Standard Digital Media

In the UK in 2015, digital advertising comprised 39 per cent of the total advertising market. This means that of all money spent on advertising, nearly 40 per cent is on digital media. This breaks down to search at 55 per cent; display at 30 per cent; classifieds at 14 per cent; and other formats at 1 per cent (IAB, 2014a). These types of advertising are carried through three types of screens: *online* (display, search and classified for desktops and laptops); *mobile* (display, classifieds and search that has been optimized for the small screen); and *tablet* (display that has been optimized for the medium-sized screen). Industry analysts agree that there is much further to go with mobile, particularly because of its locative potential. For example, in London, advertisers can use beacon technology (based on Bluetooth) on buses to push targeted offers and content to commuters as they travel around the UK capital. Similarly, retailers are also exploring how to communicate with a shopper's smartphone in the hopes of detecting nearby smartphones and sending ads, coupons or supplementary product information. They can also be used as point-of-sale systems and to collect information on those consumers – particularly how consumers move throughout stores. Tablets have also proved to be a key opportunity for growth, particularly because of the amount of browsing and purchasing that takes place on them. The value of tablets to advertisers is illustrated by the rise of cyber-shopping days such as "Black Friday"[6] and "Mega Monday" (which have spread from the US to other shores).

This chapter continues work started in Chapter 2 that outlined the size, structure and make-up of the digital advertising industry. I proceed by first assessing the scope and nature of search, display and classifieds to provide understanding of the key financial drivers of online media. I also unpack the significance of each of the "three screens" and the ways by which behavioural and programmatic advertising promises to link these together in order for screen owners to be targeted across each.

Search advertising

As mentioned, search dominates digital advertising and (as of writing in 2016) has never had less than 50 per cent of the total amount of money spent on digital advertising. It is also dominated by Google – the world's number one website. In the UK Google maintains a popularity rate of around 88 per cent, Bing of around 6 to 7 per cent, Yahoo of around 4 per cent and others of around 1 per cent. Results for mobile searches are even higher at around 92 per cent. Google does not lead in every country (China, Russia and South Korea, for example, have different popular search engines), but seen globally it is by far the front runner, so I will focus my discussion of search on Google. Despite today being a verb (to Google) and the most popular engine, Google has not always existed and it was not the first search engine. In 1997 AltaVista was the number one search engine, handling more than 25 million queries per day. It was not until 7 September 1998 that Google launched. Other search engines popular in the mid-to-late 1990s include Lycos, Excite, Infoseek, Inktomi, Northern Light and Yahoo!.

Ironically, back in 1998 when Google launched, its creators had very little interest in advertising and were deeply suspicious of blending advertising with search results. What set them apart from the other sites such as AltaVista is that the others were portals. This means that search was combined with email, news, stock prices, celebrity gossip and banner advertisements. By contrast, Google's was an exercise in minimalizing clutter. It was utterly focused on its primary function, which was to help its users search for content. Another reason for this stripped-back approach is that Google was keen not to slow its service down with extra loading time which provided users with speed as well as attractive simplicity. Despite higher bandwidth speeds today, this purist approach continues, as the Google search browser remains uncluttered. In the 1990s this came at a cost because although today Google (and the broader Alphabet business) appears invincible, up until 2001 when it got involved in advertising the company was struggling to find a business model that would generate any revenue. It is deeply ironic that a business whose founders disliked advertising so vehemently would make billions from it and reshape the nature of advertising and more.

Google today clearly rules the roost. It is difficult to see how its preeminence in search-based technology can be challenged. The success is driven by key principles. The first is *relevance* that can be bench-marked against germaneness to the search query and the context in which the search is conducted (for example place, time and the nature of information being sought). This connects with *usefulness* to people and reduction of irrelevant information about products and services they are not interested in. This is a system that is intended to work for consumers and advertisers alike in that potential customers do not want irrelevant results and advertisers only want to reach people who might be interested in their products. Google offer two services for advertisers:

1. *Adwords*: this provides ads on desktops, laptops, tablets and mobiles when people use the Google search engine. Ads are placed above natural search results. For example, typing 'coffee London' provides a list of coffee shops in London but at the top flagged with 'ad' is an ad for Nespresso, the coffee capsule maker. The ad buying mechanism is very simple, allowing the smallest of businesses as well as corporations to use Adwords. It targets by region and shows how many people notice the ad (expressed in clicks), the percentage that click through to visit the website or call and, with the tracking tools Google provides, it can display sales the website is generating as a direct result of the ad. It also allows its users to tweak ads, try new search terms, pause the campaign and re-start it. Successful Adwords campaigns are based on the degree to which advertisers can predict the search term users will employ. For example, if a boutique business sells titanium bike frames, it would include 'titanium bike frames' as part of its keywords, it would have it in the text of the ad and it would show titanium bike frames that people can buy on the website that they are being asked to click through to. The closer the fit between the search and the advertiser, the higher ranked the ad is, the more clicks it receives. Google ranks this by what they call a Quality Score that uses the ad, keywords and landing page (the advertiser's website) as criteria.

2. *Adsense*: this allows publishers of small and large websites (measured in terms of users visiting the site) to earn money by displaying behaviourally targeted ads (or ads targeted by the sites we visit, interests, online habits and purchases). This works by web publishers making ad space available, the space being auctioned by Google to the highest and most relevant bidder, and then payment to the publisher. Google's algorithms decide the winner on the basis of

relevance of ad to consumer and the type of site the consumer is visiting. For publishers the scope and reach of Google provides access to a large number of advertisers that in turn generates more relevant advertising expressed in terms of site content and the type of people visiting.

The key reason why Google has been so successful is the simplicity and ease of its advertising product. It allows small and large players access to large and hyper-targeted markets (expressed in terms of product type and/or geography). For a rather unglamorous example, I live in the Welsh mountains and on needing to replace my septic tank I searched for tank installers. This led to a slew of tank vendors and installers occupying ad spaces as I navigated the web for the next few days. (Ironically, I'd bought one and had someone to install it so was no longer interested!)

Search engine optimization (SEO)

No discussion of search is complete unless we mention the practice of marketers altering their websites to improve search engine results. This is the process of making websites as "Google-friendly" as possible. Tweaking the code behind websites, or *optimization*, is done because people are more likely to click results closer to the top of the results page. Further, because these Google search results are natural (and not flagged as an ad) they enjoy a higher trust status and are considered more authentic than paid-for advertising. Strictly speaking this has more to do with marketing than advertising but, as highlighted in Chapter 2, the distinction between advertising, marketing and public relations (PR) is blurry. Google's (2010) *Search Engine Optimization Starter Guide* offers a large number of recommendations. Below is an overview, but see Google's recommendations if you have a special interest in optimizing web and mobile sites to enhance search results. Key factors are as follows:

▸ Have the topic likely to be searched for in the <title> tag of the HTML document.[7]
▸ Create different title tags for each webpage within a site to reflect its content.
▸ Use relevant <meta name=description> tags that say what the page is about (bearing in mind the *relevance* principle).

- Use simple URLs that are informative such as www.madeupforDigitalAdvertisingbook/Chapter3.com rather than long URLs with information that is meaningless to people, such as www.madeup forDigitalAdvertisingbook.com/1234S1a24uwnirpldvoua3df3jk2/.
- Generate buzz: ensure that the website is actually interesting so people refer others to the site.
- Make sure hyperlinked words within a site say something about the content of the link's destination.
- Embed the subject of the page (and potential search terms) in all headings and file names used to design the site. For example, do not just use 'image 1' but call the image file 'Creative advertising' if the site is about advertising.
- Restrict access to parts of the site you want to be readable to search engines (crawled). This is done by entering robots.txt files that tell search engines/web robots that they should not visit all pages on the site.
- Particularly with sites that allow commenting, add 'nofollow' to links or use blogging software that does this automatically. This means that reputations are not ruined by spam links.

Google uses a system called PageRank[8] for sorting the importance of webpages. This works by assessing the format and content of pages (and language embedded in the HTML), and the amount and quality of in-bound links to webpages, because these function as endorsements. Webpages are more important if other important pages point to them. A page with more recommendations from in-links will be more important than a page with fewer. Quality also plays a part. For an offline example, a personal endorsement from a university professor for a job application is worth more than ten from your friends. However, if the professor is free and generous with recommendations or links, the importance of these will drop in significance.

Understanding how people read and search results gets geeky. Marketers, for example, are interested in where the focus of our gaze is on a screen. Over the years this has developed as we have begun to use more screens. For example, a report by Mediative (2014) on eye-tracking shows that attention on desktops and laptops is drawn to the search results starting in the top left of the search results page, where people expect the first organic listing to be located. People read horizontally before moving their eyes down to the second organic listing, which they read (horizontally), but not quite as far along. Today, scanning is more *vertical*, as people try to get to the desired content quicker, view more search results listings during a single session and spend less time viewing each result (1.17 seconds in 2014 versus 2 seconds in 2005). This increase in speed is a result of being conditioned by mobile devices to scan vertically more than horizontally and to take the fastest path to the desired content. The importance and consequence of this becomes apparent when one considers how many purchasing decisions involve Google searches and that the attention paid to results is just over one second. Although being the number one organic result still matters, an outcome of the eye-tracking study is that people *do* look further down the page and are more likely to click lower links than in 2005.

Display advertising

You might think it a paradox, but online display advertising arrived before the web itself. For example, in the mid-1980s, Prodigy (a dial-up online service from IBM and Sears) offered its customers access to news, weather, shopping, bulletin boards, games, polls, expert columns, banking, stocks, travel and a variety of other features. These pre-web internet pages also featured banner-type ads that were forerunners to what we now know as online display adverts on websites; 25 October 1994 saw the birth of web display banner advertising with AT&T's *You will* campaign, the first ever online banner hosted on *HotWired* (Wired's web pages from the 1990s). The first interactive ad arrived in 1996 for Hewlett Packard (HP). This featured a banner that allowed users to play the game 'Pong' within it.

Today, in the UK, display represents around 30 per cent of the amount of money spent on digital advertising. It shares similarity with the press and magazine publishing industry in that the basic idea is that advertisers are able to display their advertising on a page. As with press and magazines, there are numerous formats used to do this. The Internet Advertising Bureau (IAB) promotes specific guidelines on types of display ads, shapes, sizes and formats. This helps people who create, plan, buy and sell interactive advertising speak a common language about what display ads are. The formats and technical specifics are too many to list, but visit the IAB and its recommended Display Advertising Guidelines.[9] The most popular standard formats used on websites are banners (across the top of websites), skyscrapers (vertical and usually run down the right hand side of a webpage), and mid-page units (MPUs) that are used by advertisers for static advertising, and rich characteristics (such as moving parts, video and audio). The IAB also promotes standards for mobile that include static images, rich media and dynamic advertising that slides into users' screens and may be scrolled up or down (like a reel of film with different frames). The need for standards on mobile is important because consumers are even less keen on mobile advertising than web advertising. Other considerations are load time, the type of data connection users typically have (currently Wi-fi, 3G or 4G) and the amount of power that an ad requires from a person's device to load.

Although digital display advertising has roots in the press and magazine industries (not least because advertisers buy spaces from web *publishers*), the ways by which these ads appear on our web and mobile *pages* are very different from paper-based industries. After all, with the exception of inserts and leaflets, in advertising in press and magazines content is placed on a page, printed and distributed. There are a variety of ways that display ads can be served on web and mobile pages. These include: buying direct from publishers; buying from entities called "ad networks" that serve advertising on the basis of our online behaviour; and what is called "programmatic" advertising. The last is the newest approach and is discussed throughout this book because it promises to reshape the advertising industry. We will progress to account for this in terms of *programmatic logic*. Whereas behavioural advertising is about our online behaviour, programmatic advertising is based on the premise of using data from all sources possible (online and offline) to deliver advertising *and* create the advertising content. It is early days for this approach but the principles of this method are causing a great deal of heated discussion within Adland. Below are accounts of display methods. I unpack how digital ad space may be bought directly from publishers, via ad networks, through exchanges, but spend most of this section dealing with programmatic and real-time bidding techniques.

Buying direct

This is by far the simplest method because it entails buying advertising space directly from an online web publisher. The value for advertisers is that they know exactly what they are getting for their money and they can be sure that their advertising will not be placed against inappropriate content (potentially harming their brand and reputation). Notably, as mentioned in Chapter 2 and explained in Chapter 8, these ads are not obstructed by adblockers.

Advertising networks

Buying direct is useful if an advertiser knows which sites it would like to advertise on. Clearly, however, the web is a big place and if advertisers want to reach more sites and potentially people, ad networks exist to offer a large collection of inventory so marketers can buy ad space and *impressions* more easily (impressions is the unit for how many times an ad is served). The value of ad networks to publishers is that they give them a way to profit from their ad spaces without having to go to the effort of selling slots to advertisers.

Some ad networks focus on reach and quantity (how many publishers) while others boast of the quality of the stock they sell. The principle for both is the same, in that they save marketers and agencies from having to sift through thousands of publishers' sites as they compile potential ad slots (otherwise known as *inventory*) from many publishers and sell opportunities to appear in these spaces at a profit. Ad networks are intermediary companies that advertisers (or their agencies) use to place their online advertising on a wide range of websites. This means ad networks are businesses that sit between web publishers and advertisers, or their agencies. The success of ad networks is judged by the extent to which they can marry available inventory from web publishers with demand from advertisers for spaces in which to place their advertising. Another way of phrasing this is that the size of an ad network can be measured by the percentage of internet users the network reaches. For context the leading network, Google's Doubleclick, reaches over 90 per cent of internet users worldwide. Ad networks collect and use information when an internet user visits a website participating in that particular network. Through their product, the Display Network, Google, the largest of all advertising networks, uses information that a user has made by means of web searches. Ad space is typically bought on a cost per thousand impressions basis. Although advertising served by ad networks can be useful in terms of maximizing reach, advertisers relinquish some control over where their advertising ends up. From a publisher's point of view, although they save themselves from having to manage the advertising process, they have little control over who is advertising on their sites.

Another product that ad networks offer is *retargeting*. This is the automated act of carrying out specific follow-ups (typically with emails and targeted banners) with web users who have visited a website and not purchased a product or service. The idea of retargeting is to convert window shoppers or those who changed their mind about buying into buyers. This is a popular but aggressive means of advertising (akin to in-store browsing, declining to purchase and then being pursued through the streets by a salesperson). Facebook is a good example, as many ad networks (such as Ad Roll and Perfect Audience) use Facebook ads to retarget products and services that a person may have browsed, but did not buy.

Buying through an ad exchange

Ad networks and ad exchanges are related and often confused. An ad exchange is similar to a stock exchange in that it auctions impressions to the highest bidder. Also, whereas ad networks sell bulk amounts of ad spaces (bundled to be appropriate for specific age, gender, geography and interests), the advent of ad exchanges has brought technology that allows buyers and sellers to value inventory on an impression-by-impression basis that are bid for in real time. This means that theoretically publishers have a better sense about who is buying and at what cost. From the advertiser's point of view, they receive feedback on how each impression has performed.

Buying through programmatic and real-time bidding (RTB)

Ad exchanges initiated the principle of real-time bidding (RTB). This breakthrough allows buyers to determine the potential merits and value of an online ad space in the time it takes a webpage to load. This is decided by data about the type of user and their interests. Machines, not people, do this. They establish the right user for a specific ad, on a given medium, at a price the advertiser is willing to pay. This approach entails the *automation* of buying and selling advertising space on a *per-impression* basis. As with ad exchanges, this is done by *auctioning* ad space in *real time* so advertisers bid for slots in which they would like to place their advertising. The ad stock includes display, rich media, video, mobile, tablet and social media inventory. This is somewhat different from eBay (there is no person waiting until the last second to buy!), because it is automated and done by computers. Andy McNab, UK Managing Director of the programmatic firm Rocket Fuel, comments:

> Ultimately a shift has taken place in the mind-set of brand marketers. The focus has shifted from buying publisher placements in the hope of reaching your audience, to audience guarantee buys. This is

not only a first in digital, but in advertising. Marketers realise that the importance of digital buys does not rest on content alone but with the consumer. It's the who, not the where. (IAB, 2014c: 38)

The bidding principle came from search advertising where advertisers enter the price that they are willing to pay to reach a customer with the profile they are looking for. As there are multiple advertisers looking for the same customer at the same time, RTB exchanges hold real-time auctions to decide who is the best fit with the potential customer. The winner of the auction and the price of the ad space are determined by *context* (relevance of the site to their product/service/organization type) and *audience* (how good a match a viewer is for the advertiser). The chain of events is that:

1. If an advertiser wishes to advertise online they will decide how much they want to spend and what they want to achieve. They (or an agency acting on their behalf) will log on to an advertising exchange. They do this through a demand-side platform (DSP) to access available inventory held by the ad exchange.
2. By means of the platform, the ad exchange will display available spaces, with this information about spaces coming from the ad networks that hold the publishers' inventory. The ad network then serves the advertising on publishers' websites to reach an audience with relevant interests.

The latter point about audiences is key. Historically cookies and clicks have been highly unreliable in establishing *attribution*. This is the attempt to understand and quantify what aspects of advertising influences us, when influence occurs, and to what degree. The problem harks back to John Wanamaker, the Philadelphian merchant who in the 1870s famously commented, 'I know half my advertising is wasted. The trouble is, I don't know which half' (Economist, 2006). Attribution is complex because it involves the attempt to work out when, where and by what combination of content people are influenced to click. Although it is likely that a conversion (for example a click-through to the website of a particular washing machine manufacturer) is the result of a series of display ad exposures, which ads should get the most credit for the conversion? Advertisers talk about attribution in terms of what they term the *marketing funnel*, or the path from awareness of a product to purchasing it. What advertisers and marketers are interested in knowing more about is the decision-making process and chain of events that lead from awareness to conversion. For example, this may involve clicking on ads, going to the product website, researching competitors, reading reviews and other things we do when researching medium- to high-priced items. Attribution is thus the endeavour to work out what is most influential, why this is, and to help decide when and where to allocate marketing resources. This is a flawed effort because although clicks and journeys can be traced, the insight data currently offers is limited. Despite claims to accountability, the picture for advertisers is less clear than proponents of RTB suggest. Indeed, although critics (from my own field of media studies) worry about the exponential data generated for advertisers, advertisers would very much like the powers that critics attribute to them! However, the intentions of advertisers and the direction of travel are notable because attribution analysis will only improve in forthcoming years.

Programmatic

Since the advent of digital advertising it has promised increased personalization and relevance (Peppers and Rogers, 1993), and in this manner programmatic is no different. It is automated in the sense that when we program something we give it parameters, a task and methods to achieve this. Programmatic advertising is the same in that it allows advertisers to automatically target consumers based on certain metrics that are obtained through algorithms. It differs from behavioural advertising in that it uses a greater range of data sources to target advertising and it also allows the opportunity to use automated means to create advertising. Programmatic ad serving is very similar to RTB in that it typically (but not always) uses real-time exchanges to buy ad space. The only significant difference is that whereas RTB is a specific way to purchase ad space (by means of auctions held as a webpage loads), programmatic is a method to determine if the inventory space is right for the advertiser who wants to purchase it. Although this may be bought via RTB methods (and often is), it is not always the case because programmatic ad buys can involve purchasing ads that have a fixed cost (rather than bid-for ones that have a changeable price). Ad spaces, for example, might be purchased direct from *Time* magazine so the inventory and price is agreed and fixed. The programmatic part of the transaction that differentiates it from a traditional direct sale is the automation of the ad-serving process on the *Time* webpage.

The significance of both RTB and programmatic is twofold. The first aspect is that by automating the ad space buying/selling enterprise this removes a lot of discussion between ad companies and publishers, telephone calls, emails, person hours, paperwork and expensive executives. The second is that programmatic logic requires a great deal of information about users. The impetus behind programmatic logic is to know more about the person clicking's viewing and motives. Seen another way it is the logical progression of behavioural advertising as it uses more data points about consumers derived from their clickstream, demographic and behavioural information. This range of information sources makes programmatic different from behavioural advertising because the latter is reliant on our interests expressed through web activities. In contrast, programmatic draws on a wider range of sources. A promotional report from Rocket Fuel highlights that: 'Traditional segment-based buying may define segments with just five to ten attributes like age, gender, income, geography, education, mindset, and interests' but 'the best programmatic buying systems can evaluate millions of data features all in real time' (Siebelink and Belani, 2013: 4). This is achievable because information about people comes from a variety of origins, including website publishers, database companies and businesses that collect as much information as legally possible from both online and offline sources.

Another way in which programmatic differs from behavioural advertising is through *dynamic creative optimization*. This is the automatic altering of an ad to fit the viewer and context in real time. Programmatic companies, for example, claim that 'Machines can test thousands of variables in a fraction of the time required by humans to conduct the same tests' (ibid.: 10). Programmatic also promises improved retargeting (the process, mentioned above, of targeting consumers who visited a publisher's website but did not buy or fulfil a desired action). It also claims to be sensitive to the context in which advertising takes place (for example: content that appears next to the ad, device on which the ad is delivered, day-part, day of the week and environmental factors such as news that is being reported, sports results or celebrity events).

Beyond the automated serving of display advertising, programmatic also promises to assist in campaign management. From the point of view of both inside the industry and outside, this is the most significant point because programmatic involves: simplification of creating and serving ads; new buying mechanisms and efficiencies of RTB; and data management for all involved parties (excluding the consumer).

Due to increased understanding of users, we will theoretically see campaigns that flow more seamlessly between different devices, and be served ads that are context sensitive and relevant to our actions and histories. The *logic* of programmatic advertising is one based on increased use of artificial intelligence and "big data" techniques in advertising. We will progress to discuss big data in Chapter 10 and artificial intelligence in Chapter 11, but for now consider the range of data sources feeding programmatic ad buying, serving and tracking:

▸ First-party data: information which is collected and aggregated directly by a given web publisher (for example purchase behaviour and how people behave on their websites). This is the most reliable, and therefore most valuable, data.

▸ Second-party data (or the trusted other): this involves an unusual business arrangement where a partner (company A) is willing to share customer data with company B (and vice versa). For example people interested in stargazing might visit the partner company's site about telescopes and be tagged with a cookie. When they leave the publisher's site, the cookie anonymously follows users to serve them ads wherever they travel on the web.

▸ Third-party data: information that is bought and sold in an open market environment to build a rich and comprehensive view of consumers. Companies that do this are known as data management platforms (DMPs) or data aggregators. They typically purchase data on a large scale from web publishers. The benefit of third-party data is the sheer volume of user data advertisers can access in order to gain a big-picture view of users because the third party has relationships with a large number of websites (by means of cookies and IDs on mobile phones). However, this data is also widely accessible to competitors, so companies are not gaining unique audience intelligence when they use third-party data resources. Notable examples include organizations such as eXelate, Lotame and Bluekai. When selling this data, they typically charge a cost per thousand people for the use of the data. Third-party data can come from a range of places including online tracking, registration data, public records and offline transaction data such as loyalty cards.

Note that first- and third-party data can be used in tandem. Lotame, for example, promises marketers that it can marry a company's own data (on past campaigns, traffic through website and applications it might own) and then use this with demographic and behavioural insights derived from third-party data sources (such as MasterCard, BlueKai and Kantar).

From an advertiser's point of view, many advertisers and marketers within the industry find the lack of control they have over where their advertising is placed problematic. This is a concern because ad exchanges, RTB processes and programmatic techniques help publishers sell off less desirable inventory on the basis that it can target 'who' (types of people) rather than 'where' (types of sites). While the capacity to target types of people wherever they may be is a good thing for advertisers, the concern is that if an advertiser's ad lands on the wrong sites, it can do more harm than good to the brand. A UK newspaper, *The Sun*, vividly illustrated this in April 2015 when it revealed that ads for major British and international brands appeared on websites devoted to paedophilia, incest, bestiality and racism.[10]

This is a matter of what the ad industry refers to as *brand safety*, or the attempt to protect brand image or reputation. As *The Sun* exposé makes clear, the problem is that programmatic advertising means that brands do not always know where their ads will appear. The problem can be subtler than unwanted advertising on violent sites. For example, an ad for NatWest (a UK bank) promoting its personal loan service was shown alongside a web article on vulnerable borrowers and irresponsible lending. This is damaging in terms of upset caused to consumers reading the site, but also in terms of reputation if picked up by the media and used to accuse the bank of irresponsible lending. This is a problem of context, association and reputation. Although programmatic *promises* greater understanding of audience members (expressed in terms of online profiles and past interests merged with offline data), creativity-on-the-fly according to who is viewing, and sensitivity to the context in which ads are being served, the lack of quality ad stock remains a concern for brands. However, as this book argues, the principle behind programmatic is extremely interesting and one to watch over future years, which is why I refer to it as programmatic logic.

Mobile display

In 2015 mobile was worth 20 per cent of the total digital advertising market, with this figure predicted to rise to 39 per cent by 2018 (IAB, 2014a). This increase in spend by advertisers is understandable as smartphones are increasingly used to access the internet. In the UK 57 per cent of the population in the first quarter of 2014 used their smartphones to access the internet. This was up 8 per cent from 2013. This figure will only grow, so Adland is keen to know how these users can be reached. Indeed, it is fair to say that mobile will become the number one medium, not least because our phones are always with us. This has a number of implications. Many news agencies, for example, have struggled to straddle digital and paper versions, but mobile ads are providing much-needed revenue to traditional vendors. The overwhelming means of access for many news companies is through mobile media (apps, platforms and web visits). In the retail sector, given that a large portion of advertising is dedicated to getting us in stores and consuming, phones are of special interest to marketers. The problem is people do not like to receive ads on mobiles, because we see them as intrusive and distracting. However, we are more receptive than we used to be. This is evidenced by industry research conducted by research firm Nielsen that points to a drop in respondents' complaints of intrusiveness (from 64 per cent in 2013 to 56 per cent in 2014). Similarly, on whether mobile ads are 'helpful', the research records an increase from 19 to 31 per cent (xAd/telmetrics, 2015). Although this may seem implausible, the rise is more believable if we consider relevance and being able to receive the right offers, time saving, free content and discounts. The major benefit that mobile platforms offer is location sensitivity and the capacity for mobile to boost offline sales. Whereas PCs/laptops and tablets help to generate online sales, mobile is different because mobile shoppers use their devices to look for nearby locations to visit as part of the purchase decision. Such activity might involve searches for a restaurant, movie times, goods prices, store addresses, coupons and checking reviews of items/places.

The mobile advertising market breaks down into search, display and "other". These are respectively worth 54, 45 and 1 per cent of what in the UK is business worth £707 million (IAB, 2014a). Although mobile display advertising involves banners and video ads, it also encompasses *native content* or what is more clearly understood as sponsored content (see Chapter 6 for a full account of native advertising). The bulk of display advertising occurs within apps. This means that 58 per cent of mobile display advertising occurs within apps themselves and 42 per cent of mobile display advertising takes place within mobile browsers (such as Google's Chrome or Apple's Safari). As mentioned, a key virtue for advertisers is location sensitivity. This awareness is achieved by understanding both the online behaviour of the mobile device and the real locations of the device. This is done by means of IDs for advertising. Both Apple and Google have their own approaches to this:

Apple iOS

Until 2013, Apple iOS used UDID, or Unique Device Identifier. This was a *permanent ID* that allowed ad networks to trace phone IDs and their users across multiple apps to build richer profiles of what people are interested in. Ad networks could then sell their databases to other advertising companies that were able to compile a detailed picture using their combined UDID databases of what that iPhone was used for. Under pressure from privacy activists and the media, Apple changed its approach. With UDID, users had no way to turn off the ad tracking, but today users have more control over whether they are being tracked. The key change is that the ID is not tied to the device, because the user can reset the ID that they are being tracked by. Today, Apple recommends developers create a unique user identifier for their applications. The problem for mobile display ad networks is that they desire access to different devices, apps and sites. They require IDs that work across devices/platforms. This effectively means that ad networks can no longer track users across multiple apps. Going further, Apple told third-party App Store developers to either stop tracking or be banned from the App Store. Today Apple uses IDFA (Identifier for Advertisers) that provides users greater control over ad tracking (there is a switch that can be accessed through Settings>Privacy>Advertising (as in Figure 3.1).

Google Android

When Apple changed its ID methods from UDID to IDFA, Google followed suit. Prior to 2013 it employed Android_ID, a 64-bit number that is given when the user first sets up the device and should last the lifetime of the user's device. This allowed tracking across Google Play services and apps. From 2013 Google's Advertising ID (for apps) grants tracking and ad targeting without relying on the identifier uniquely married to the device. As with Apple's, this is best understood by opening an Android phone and clicking on Settings>Accounts>Google>Ads (as in Figure 3.2) where the user can opt out of in-app behavioural targeting and reset the advertising ID, as can be done with Apple's devices.

Apple and Google have different approaches to apps. Adding to its strictness on tracking, Apple is now choosy about who may use its App Store and all apps must abide by a stringent set of principles.[11] These are informed by the general approach that developers should not be 'creepy' or cross the line (Apple says it will know this line when it sees it), and that app developers should not cheat the system (for example, they should not 'steal data from users'). Specifically this means that

Fig 3.1

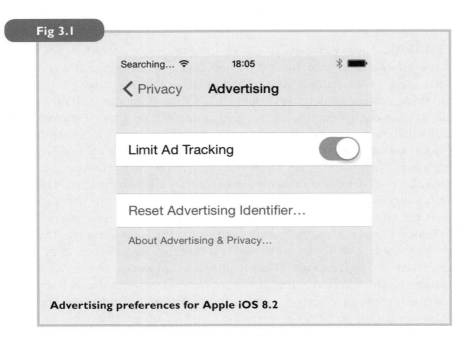

Advertising preferences for Apple iOS 8.2

Fig 3.2

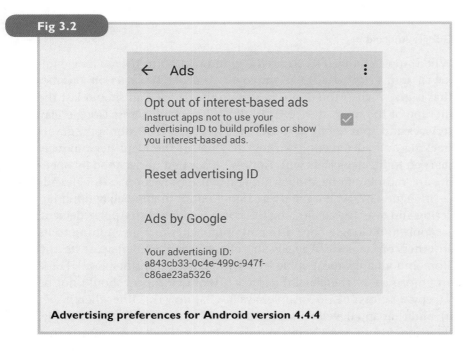

Advertising preferences for Android version 4.4.4

apps should not require personal information to function, apps cannot transmit data about a user without upfront consent, and all apps must have a privacy policy. Android has a much looser set of regulations that primarily focus on keeping out malicious applications.

Classified

So far we have discussed the pre-eminence of search, the ubiquity of display and the rise of mobile. The reader might be surprised to read that the third most popular format with advertisers is "classifieds". For those of you who grew up without reading local newspapers, you are forgiven for not knowing what classified ads are. Classifieds represent 14 per cent of the total amount of money spent on digital advertising. It is a form of advertising most commonly associated with local newspapers where *readers post their own ads*. It is called classified advertising because it is generally grouped under headings classifying the product or service being offered. Online, classifieds are dominated by three sectors: cars, property (renting and buying real estate) and jobs. Large notable sites in the UK include the new and used car website Auto Trader, property websites such as Zoopla and Rightmove, and jobs websites such as Monster. Like search advertising described above, classified advertising represents an opportunity for smaller advertisers to announce their wares and services. It also allows large advertisers to target regional markets. For sense of scale IAB/YouGov (2014) research found that 47 per cent of their sample of the UK public (n=2,214) had looked online for a car, job or home in the last six months. The majority of searching across all these sectors takes place in the evening. Key factors for people when using classifieds websites (and what marks out the most successful sites) is ease of navigation, relevant ads and trust of the website. Curiously there was a notable difference in the IAB/YouGov study between men and women, as men were more likely to respond to ads than women.

Conclusion

Along with Chapter 2, the intention of this chapter has been to present background information and insights about digital advertising. As has become clear, digital is not one medium but an increasing set of media that are networked and based on multi-pathway connectivity. Although social media and native advertising receive a great deal of attention, it is useful to understand the financial shape of the digital advertising media market. Followed by display and classified, search advertising continues to lead. This is an important observation because it tells us something about the character of digital advertising media in that it entails customizability for advertisers, personalization for users, low mediation (targeting is more important than flashy graphics), automated buying mechanisms, content not getting in the way of users' experiences of web and mobile media, and extensive use of our behaviour. Related, this chapter also introduced the principle of programmatic logic. The reason for phrasing programmatic in terms of logic is because the idea is bigger than the actuality. In some ways programmatic advertising is yet to be realized. In conceptual terms, it is the use of artificial intelligence to understand our behaviours, communications, histories, friend networks, postings (text and images) and demographic background, so to provide targeted advertising in real time. For scholars of advertising this may appear identical to behavioural advertising, but it is not. It is conceptually and practically different in that behavioural advertising simply refers to cookies installed on web browsers, whereas programmatic entails a much more diverse set of information types derived from online and offline means (including cookies). Further, these ads are not just served in real time, but created in real time in accordance with contextual information users. This provides a heterogeneous visual fluidity to our media experience.

Think points and questions

▶ What are the key modern digital media trends today and how do they inform the practice of advertising?

▶ The advertising industry has understood for some time that mobile offers rich opportunities, but also that mobile is a deeply intimate medium where advertising can be perceived as intrusive. Can mobile advertising be done in a way that benefits mobile users and advertisers alike?

▶ What is the difference between buying inventory directly from web publishers, ad networks, exchanges, and through programmatic and real-time bidding techniques?

▶ What are the future opportunities for advertisers using programmatic logic?

4 How it Works: Non-Standard Digital Media

Chapter 3 provided an overview of the most popular digital advertising formats used by advertisers: search, display and classifieds. This third foundational chapter pays attention to other formats typically used by advertisers. Although routinely employed, I have dubbed these as non-standard media because they were not designed with advertising in mind – although each medium has matured to offer advertisers bespoke services. We will examine gaming and social media, and progress to explore case examples of how media space and attention can be "earned" as well as "rented".

In-game advertising and advergaming

Gaming is strange in that it is one of the largest, but often most forgotten, media. Indeed, on average, the global games industry is increasing revenue by 5.7 per cent per year and is predicted to rise to $93.18 billion by 2019 (PWC, 2015). For sense of scale, *The Economist* (2011) judged the gaming industry to be: twice the size of the recorded music industry; a quarter more than the magazine business; and equivalent to three-fifths the size of the film industry (including DVD sales as well as box-office receipts). On popularity, in the UK there are more game players than non-players. The IAB (2011) reports that: 82 per cent of 8–65 year olds play digital games; 98 per cent of kids (8–15 years) play games; 77 per cent of adults over 25 play digital games; the gender split is roughly equal at 49 per cent for females and 51 per cent for males; and games are popular with all social grades and occupation types, with C2DE at 46 per cent and ABC1 at 54 per cent.

The overall prevalence and interest in gaming might be surprising. However, when one considers the range of games available, this begins to make more sense. After all, Nigel Mills, a UK Conservative MP, admitted to playing Candy Crush[12] on his iPad while in a parliamentary committee meeting. Games are not only played on dedicated games consoles, PCs and laptops, but also through social networks, apps and handheld screens (phones/tablets). Game formats include:

games consoles; PCs/laptops; handheld consoles; mobiles/tablets; social networking games; and internet browser games. In addition to the range of platforms, the broad adoption of games is attributable to the fact that the most popular games do not involve shooting zombies. Puzzles, board games and quizzes are the most popular forms followed by social networking games. When gaming is seen this way, the cross-generational and demographic appeal is more understandable. Indeed, massive multiplayer online games are the least popular. The IAB report on gaming also details that despite the anti-social reputation of gaming: 72 per cent of all game players have played games with others; 81 per cent of games console players have played with friends or family in person; 54 per cent of social networking players have played with friends or family online or over a network; and 41 per cent of internet browser games are played with unknown people online or across a network.

In-game advertising

There are three key ways to recoup costs and profit from building a game. A user can be asked to pay to play or download; they can download for free but pay for extra content and levels; or the game developers can make use of advertising to sponsor content development. The first in-game advertising arrived in 1978 in the guise of Adventureland by Scott Adams, who inserted an advertisement for his then forthcoming game, Pirate Adventure (Edge, 2006). Brands also featured in early Sega racing games for the Atari 2600 console that featured Marlboro display advertisements on the raceway. High profile early 1990s titles such as Zool (a rival to Sonic the Hedgehog) and the FIFA International series contained advertisements for Chupa Chups (a lollipop manufacturer) and Adidas, respectively. Historically advertising within games has presented advertisers and marketers with a problem because: a) ads had to be embedded in the game when it was being designed; and b) there could be a long period of time between deciding to place ads in games and actually seeing them on screen. Of course, once the ad was in the game it could not be changed, updated or easily measured. The introduction of *dynamic in-game advertising* has resulted in a flexible, updatable and creative alternative for advertisers looking to access multiple niche audiences. Similar to how a website rotates different display advertisements through the same fixed space, dynamic in-game ad space can change the messaging on the same billboard in a game. Marketers can now serve their advertisements into a game in real time and select the type of game and placement they require. For example President Obama's 2008 campaign used in-game advertising, including online modifiable games such as Guitar Hero, Burnout Paradise and Madden 09. These were employed in "swing states" such as Ohio and Florida. Advertisers can specify the number of impressions that should be served. Further, units of advertising can be tracked close to real time so advertising placement companies can determine how many times a character walks past or interacts with an advertisement. They can also ascertain the quality of viewing and whether users position themselves so they can see the advertisement more clearly, the distance at which it is viewed and whether a viewer pauses to look at it. Agencies and networks involved with in-game advertising include: Rapidfire, GameHouse, Playwire, Zynga, and Matomy. From a game publisher's point of view, the games industry is broadly keen to involve advertisers to offset development costs.

Advergaming

Advergaming began as a relatively insignificant medium primarily featuring on desktops and PCs. Given the rise of gaming among a broader audience, smartphones, tablets, apps and social networking, this picture now looks very different. Advergaming is different from in-game advertising in that it requires an entire game surrounding a specific product or brand. The benefit to brands is that it prolongs exposure of brands to their target audience. Whereas traditional advertising offers at best a minute or two of brand engagement, games can deliver significantly more depending how sticky the game is. Although many advergames are simple in format, companies have created or augmented their own to reflect their brand values. The vacuum cleaner company Dyson, for example, a company that markets itself on principles of innovation and quality, uses mentally challenging games involving telescopes and potting balls. Due to the blurring of entertainment and advertising, advergames stand in an ethical crossfire given their obvious appeal to children (see Chapter 9 for more on children and ethics).

Gamification

This is more of a tactic than a medium, but all areas of the technology industry seem to be making use of the noun *gamification*. By encouraging fun, competition, challenges/successes, improvization, patience, skill and point scoring, games-based thinking can encourage engagement with sponsored communication and advertisers. Although the principle encompasses in-game advertising and advergaming, it is different because it can be applied to other advertising and marketing campaigns that are not ostensibly games that involve controllers or points. The ALS Ice Bucket Challenge of 2014 (discussed in Chapter 6) is a good example in that it involves challenges, successes and forfeits in a domain with rules known to participants.

Social media

The relationship between social media and advertising can be seen a number of ways. Principally, advertising funds social media. As we do not pay (with money) to use social media sites, we have to pay through other means. We do this through providing information about ourselves that allows social media companies to gain revenue by selling space and our attention time to advertisers. Social media companies also allow marketers, analytics firms and audience researchers to use information about us to understand how their brands are performing. Some social media companies also track their users as they navigate the rest of the web. Facebook, for example, does not just track within its own site, but it embeds cookies in users' computers to understand what sites they are looking at elsewhere. Facebook in particular has come under fire for aggressively pursuing users, even when they have opted out of being tracked.[13] However, in addition to targeting and delivering advertising, social media can also be used to earn attention and media space. By this I mean that if the content is interesting enough, people will forward, share, repost and disseminate sponsored communication on behalf of advertisers. This wins brands more attention and saves them from having to pay for media space.

Advertising on social media

In more traditional approaches to advertising on social media, these sites allow advertisers to deliver their advertising through multiple ad formats. There is good reason to advertise on social media, not least popularity. Readers will be able to find statistics for their own country by looking at the webpage of their media regulators or governmental bodies set up to chart media usage. In the UK this is Ofcom, which reports that three-quarters of adult users (16 and older) have a social media profile. For sense of scale, the Ofcom (2015) report remarks that back in 2005 it did not ask about social media because there were so few users. This contrasts with the report today that offers a granular breakdown of the UK's favourite apps and websites (most notably Facebook, Twitter, LinkedIn, Instagram, Tumblr, Snapchat, WhatsApp and Pinterest) and usage (the move to mobile media and multiple visits per day). Each social media site provides advertisers with a range of opportunities and services. These break down as follows:

▸ *Facebook* allows advertisers to create targeted adverts for different audiences. Usefully for advertisers who may be advertising to a niche audience or a highly localized one, it allows them to establish a budget and measure the results across the devices that people use. Static or video ads are displayed in the stream of information people view on Facebook by means of the web or mobile. People are targeted by: location; demographics (such as age, whether they are parents or if they have just received a degree); interests; purchasing history and behaviour; the devices they use; and the types of friends and connections they have.

▸ *Twitter* allows promoted accounts, promoted tweets and promoted trends for desktops and mobile. What is particularly useful about Twitter for advertisers is the capacity to manage who is engaging with an advertiser's tweets, who is clicking through a website, who is clicking and installing apps marketed through Twitter, the capacity to grow followers (assisted by 'Who to follow' suggestions) and to allow people to email direct if they are interested in a product (such as a 'Sign up to enter' or call-to-action link). Notably, when people sign up for Twitter it only asks for a name, username and email or phone number. Without gender, age, wider demographic information or interests, it is difficult for advertisers or Twitter to accurately target the people they want to reach.

▸ *Instagram* is owned by Facebook, but it does not push its advertising services as aggressively. However, given the visual nature of Instagram there are clearly high creative opportunities. Brands, for example, can have their own galleries of branded content. Lexus cars invited selected Instagrammers to a special event to launch a new car in California. Participants used their mobile devices to take and edit photos before sharing them on Instagram. PayPal similarly asked Instagrammers to re-imagine money and take over its Instagram account. Both resulted in attractive, creative and engaging content that worked well with the Instagram community. Instagram also offers ad content that is flagged with 'sponsored', where the time stamp would usually be. These are targeted at people with relevant interests. At the time of writing this was a new development, but one can reasonably assume that ads will be targeted by what both Instagram and Facebook think people like.

▸ *Tumblr* also allows sponsored posts that appear just like regular Tumblr posts, but instead they are made more prominent and visible, and are targeted at users based on gender, location and interest. It allows static, animated gifs and video imagery, and (for an extra fee) capacity to place sponsored content in prominent places on the page (typically just above the middle on the right hand side).

▸ *LinkedIn* is a network used by professionals and people (often students) seeking to join a profession. LinkedIn's advertising services are limited, but allow advertisers to create and place ads on the LinkedIn.com website so members can click on the ads and visit an advertiser's website. Members can be targeted by job title, job function, industry, geography, age, gender, company name, company size or LinkedIn Group.

▸ *Google+* makes use of Google's Adwords service (see Chapter 3 on search advertising). It also allows brands to link their YouTube videos, and even use Google's Hangout platform, to interact with customers in real time. The UK high street retailer Top Shop, for example, used Google+ to generate interest in the brand during the 2013 London Fashion Week. This involved backstage and red carpet hangouts, and use of mini-cameras by models to see events from their perspectives.

▸ *YouTube* is owned by Google and makes use of its targeting technologies and processes. It allows advertisers to target video ads by gender, age, interests and location (such as men in North Wales between 35 and 40 years of age interested in mountain biking). It also allows advertisers to only pay when someone actually watches the ad on any screen type. The analytics behind the advertising is also useful as it allows advertisers to monitor who is watching, what is working and what is not, to be able to tweak the advertising for next time. There is also a community dimension as marketers and advertisers build their followings.

▸ *Snapchat* is accessed via smartphones. Ads are served vertically (rather than horizontally as with television and desktops) and appear in the context of premium or curated content. Notably, too, ad serving does not use of high levels of profiling and targeting, but relies on the quality of the ads and appropriateness of the context in which they are being delivered. Also, in 2015 *Snapchat* introduced customizable sponsored geofilters. McDonald's, for example, became the first company to pay Snapchat to run a geofilter advertising campaign. This will allow users to brand their shared snapped memories.

A few themes should be becoming clear. These are the capacity to target highly refined audiences, simplicity of use, the ability to only pay when someone interacts with the ad, a relatively wide range of ad types and the capacity to use social media to not just display ads, but to build a following.

Paid-for advertising versus shared/earned media

As highlighted, although social media can be used to formally buy space and display ads, it can also be used in more interesting and "earned" ways. A key means of understanding the range of digital advertising options is whether media space is bought or not. Historically advertising has been defined in terms of *paying for space* in newspapers, on billboards, in cinemas, in radio programming, on television and elsewhere. However, if digital advertising is engaging enough people will share content on social media, and forward within their own networks of online friends and associates, for it to become earned media. Although advertising that uses paid-for media space is by far the most popular in terms of money spent, many campaigns that use shared media have been highly successful in branding products and services. We will return to earned media in our discussion of creativity in Chapters 5 and 6, but it is also worth highlighting some notable campaigns and features in this chapter. In the case of advertising, characteristics might include one or more of the following:

▸ Multi-pathway communication where advertisers will respond to users and engage in dialogue;
▸ Behind-the-scenes views of products or advertising production;
▸ Engagement with "amateur"[14] reviewers (bloggers/vloggers, often with huge followings);
▸ Attempts to use influencers in a two-step flow manner (consumers may be suspicious of companies but trust respected opinion leaders);[15]

- ▸ Recognition of "media democracy" and the premise that information technologies are able to empower individual users and give them greater control over their advertising experiences;
- ▸ Potential for brand loyalty, reduction of distance between producer and consumer, and potential for perception of intimacy and authenticity (the gold standard of branding);
- ▸ Understanding of how brands (and competitors) are really perceived (particularly on Twitter, and through reviews in blogs and on YouTube);
- ▸ Co-productive creative opportunities and harnessing of interest in brands (such as inviting the community to create ads);
- ▸ Use of more compelling content (whether produced by advertisers or consumers);
- ▸ Rewards for loyalty (for example fans willing to do something, or share or create content);
- ▸ Capacity to play games both online and offline, and merge the virtual and the real;
- ▸ Multiplier effect, electronic word of mouth and virality.

As is clear, use of earned media works differently to traditional media, not least because advertisers must not be seen to be targeting social media users. As detailed in Chapter 6, it is by definition a non-interruptive approach to commercial influencing. The advertising needs to be interesting because there is very little point in trying to wear an audience down through banality and repetition. For example in 2013 Dove allowed women to take control of online advertising. This echoes earlier work in the 2000s that sought to unmask and raise media literacy about image manipulation and the amount of work that goes into creating portrayals of women in advertising (Zeisler, 2008).

In the online context they did this by buying up ad space that may have been previously occupied by negative adverts with headlines such as 'Lose weight now', 'Get a bikini body in 6 weeks' or 'Want bigger boobs?' The campaign allowed users to replace these ads with compliments. Dove's social media campaign, *Dove Ad Makeover*, made use of a Facebook app. This allowed women to select their own message (for example 'Your birthday suit suits you,' 'Everybody is beautiful' and 'The perfect bum is the one you're sitting on'), and use behavioural segmentation to aim their positive message at women reading about love, careers, travel, beauty or fitness. The ad then appeared in Facebook ads with the first name of person posting and the Dove graphic.

Dove subsequently said that 'A huge 71% of women we spoke to after the Dove Ad Makeover said that they felt more beautiful as a result of the campaign: an incredible step towards enabling women everywhere to realize their full beauty potential' (Dove, 2015). The campaign is laudable, but one should be under no illusion about the motive behind it. Targeting bodily dissatisfaction and unhappiness with a media environment that promotes idealized and unachievable representations of women is deeply strategic. With this campaign, Dove sought to gain competitive advantage through the appearance of sincerity and empathizing with "real women". Indeed, feminists have critiqued the campaign strategy, arguing that it is even more insidious than ads that make use of "perfect bodies" in advertising (Holliday, 2015). This is because it makes use of dissatisfaction with unrealistic representations of women to sell beauty products. It also reinforces obsession about the body, albeit including some different shapes and skin colours. If the reader thinks I am too cynical, note that Dove's parent company Unilever also owns Lynx (also known as Axe), a brand not known for its positive work in female representation; for example Lynx's advertising featuring celebrities such as Kelly Brook (well known to readers of lads' magazines) in their television advertising, and Keeley Hazell and Jessica-Jane Clement (both also glamour models) in their Facebook campaigns. This invites an ethical question: do these types of campaigns (also see #LikeAGirl, from Always and Sport England's *This Girl Can*) represent a moral step forward or an amoral marketing strategy? Further, does it matter? If they are opening up social discussion about advertising and negative representations of women, do the ends justify the means? Readers interested in pursuing this question should see debates surrounding 'post-feminism' and 'commodity activism' (Banet-Weisner, 2012). These topics invite two overarching questions: first, is it right that we turn to consumerist logic, brand culture and advanced capitalism for positive social change? Second, is it acceptable for feminist logic to be appropriated by the beauty industry that for so long has portrayed unrealistic images of girls and women to further its interests?

As an example of how social media can be used the Dove campaign fulfils many of the criteria listed above because it: built a community through its Facebook page; grew numbers of fans and followers; generated interaction with its brands; made use of co-productive media (users wrote the ads); generated sociality; and made use of credibility from peers and "real women". The broader point is that Dove was able to leverage a powerful ongoing social discussion about representation, self-image and bodies and media culture. This allows the brand to "own" this discourse because Dove was the first brand to engage in this discussion. This is a powerful sentiment to own because, as with many leading brands, it is able to lay claim to a human truth and powerfully felt sentiment. The success of Dove is amplified because of the community dimension and because it is built on participation (a defining characteristic of social media). This stands in contrast to representational advertising where values are presented *at* people. Of course, it is no coincidence that Dove had its brand logos placed across sites where Facebook ads are carried!

Conclusion

This chapter has provided a brief overview of some of the non-standard media routes that advertisers use. Although Adland does not spend as much money on these as it does on search, display and classified, they are important routes. We began by considering gaming and its surprising popularity with a wide range of age groups and demographics. As advertising media, gaming breaks down into in-game advertising and advergaming whereby entire games are dedicated to brands. We also began to attend to social media. Each social media site offers advertisers a range of services. We paid attention to Facebook, Twitter, Instagram, Tumblr, LinkedIn, Google+, YouTube and Snapchat. What conjoins each of these services is the ability to target highly refined audiences. In addition to standard routes by which social media can be used, I introduced non-formal methods. These entail shared and earned media techniques, which stand in contrast to paid-for media that define the history of advertising. Although earned media are typically associated with PR, the Dove case study served to highlight that Adland has unique production and media skills by which to engage people.

Think points and questions

- ▸ Why is gaming useful for advertisers?
- ▸ How can the principle of gamification be applied to advertising?
- ▸ What is earned media advertising and how can it be done successfully? How might the principles described in this chapter be applied to other brands or organizations?
- ▸ Brands are increasingly adopting the position of activists to campaign for social change. Is this a positive development? Develop arguments both for and against.

5   Creativity

In 2015 *Campaign*, the newspaper of the UK advertising industry, asked judges of the international Design and Art Direction (D&AD) awards what creativity in advertising means to them.[16] Answers were mixed, and some were long and others short. Rei Inamoto from AKQA said it is a 'force'; Greg Hahn of BBDO, 'a small point of light in a dark room'; Mark Bonner, President of D&AD, 'It's my friend, and I love it'; PJ Pereira, Co-founder of Pereira & O'Dell, 'it feels like a free-spirited attempt to match things – thoughts, ideas, references ... then finding what you can do with them'; and Eric Kallman of Goodby, Silverstein & Partners, 'A place where you can't be self-conscious and you don't worry about what you should look like or act like or be'.

There are lots of creative industries, but no other industry claims to have creativity in its DNA quite like advertising does. Indeed, some readers may be studying for creative advertising degrees (as I did), or already work in creative departments of agencies. The importance of creativity to advertising is not just the view of agencies, but also the view of its clients who come seeking transformation and new ways of looking at their longstanding brands, and to make something exist that was not there before. This "something new" might be profit, awareness, donations, persuasion to a political point of view, enhanced reputation, repositioning of a brand, or possibly maintenance of market position in the coming financial year. This is achieved through the capacity to produce engaging content that fulfils a strategic objective. Creativity serves another role because it is an advertising agency's calling card, and it is also creativity which wins awards, and thereafter agency and career progression. Indeed, awards play a central, if somewhat mixed, role in advertising. Jeremy Bullmore (2003), adman and leading commentator on advertising, is scathing of awards, arguing that the intensity of interest in these, and the impulse to produce work that is an artistic end in itself, promotes self-indulgent advertising that is irresponsible to clients. John Hegarty (2011) in some contrast, but not disagreement, characterizes agencies as addicts, with winning being the cocaine of the industry. Key recognized awards include the Art Directors Club, Cannes Lions, Clio, Cresta, D&AD, The One Club and the Webby Awards (among many others: see IPA, 2011).

By the end of this chapter you will understand creativity in advertising from multiple perspectives. It is less a chapter on how to make advertising, but more about what creativity actually is. Although I summarize industry perspectives on creativity, my intention is to push beyond these to explore the nature of creativity in greater depth. My motives for writing this chapter are personal, conceptual and practical. In the early 2000s as a creative advertising student and after having had my work shredded in 'crits', I and my art director asked (in more colourful language): '*What is creativity, how is it assessed and what makes one ad creative and another not?*' It seemed to us that although creativity was clearly important, industry discussion of the topic tended towards hyperbole and there was nothing in academic books available at the time that satisfied me. But it was clear that creativity in advertising exists because the best work really did possess quality, impact and capacity to surprise. What is it that makes one piece of work stand out from the rest? This chapter provides today's student with some answers.

We begin by assessing creativity from an industry point of view (self-conceptions and what the industry values), but progress to appreciate it from a non-industry point of view. Why? The answer is that we seek to deepen our understanding of creativity; strip the term of hyperbole (industry insiders surely agree there is much hot air around "creativity"); assess it in reference to psychological, philosophical and aesthetic theorization; and return back to advertising practice with renewed understanding. A snappy line from the philosopher Alfred Whitehead sums my approach up best: 'seek simplicity… and then distrust it' (the irony of the simplicity of this line is not lost on me!). Before we get going, I should add that in this chapter I draw extensively on another book I wrote (*Creativity and Advertising: Affect, Events and Process*, 2013), so if you like the approach adopted here – or have an essay to write on creativity and advertising – read that too.

Industry context

Everyone in Adland recognizes that creativity and advertising go hand in hand, but the regard in which it is held varies across the industry. In 1916 Stanley Resor, who helped develop the J. Walter Thompson agency into the advertising giant it is today, remarked that the creative part of advertising comes first and that 'everything else is plumbing' (cited in Jones, 2004: 141). Others understand that it plays a role, but should not be fetishized. This is exemplified by David Ogilvy (1985), another founder of modern advertising, who paints a down-to-earth and instrumentalist picture of creativity as a highbrow word for everyday work. Describing the 'C' word as hideous, he goes on to point out that while agencies might win awards for work, there is no necessary connection between prizes and a rising sales curve. Ogilvy also cites Leo Burnett, another titan of advertising history, who similarly advised against originality for its own sake, quoting an unspecified ex-boss of his: 'If you insist in being different just for the sake of being different, you can always come down in the morning with a sock in your mouth' (ibid: 201). Creativity in advertising thus operates within specified parameters and eschews the bizarre in favour of what is *both* original and useful. This does not necessarily mean being boring or playing safe. Raymond Rubicam, for example, on retiring from Young & Rubicam in 1944, left the agency no rules of practice, but instead the aphorism 'resist the usual'. This continues to be the agency's mantra to this day (Y&R, 2016).

Creativity in advertising history is dominated by the figure of William Bernbach and the US agency Dane Doyle Bernbach (DDB), and their work from the 1960s and 1970s. The full story of DDB in the US, and Collett Dickenson Pearce (CDP) in the UK, is very well documented (see Tungate, 2007; Cracknell, 2011) so I will not dwell on this agency folklore, but it is worth highlighting a few points. To sum up, Bernbach's influential attitude is that research kills creative ideas and renders, at best, mediocrity. The influence of the man and the agency is due in part to the originality of the work, but also their working practices. DDB was first to introduce copywriter and art director teams. It also introduced: new formats and layout styles; greater simplicity to communication in advertising; greater consideration of tone of voice and mode of address (less paternalistic, or one might say patronizing); and humour (the capacity to *share* a joke with audiences). Much of this continues to apply today to ad-weary audiences, in that DDB's stated modus operandi was honesty, authenticity, inclusivity, intelligence, humour, intuition and, sometimes, even provocation. The point about authenticity is worth holding in mind because it is a word frequently used today in relation to how advertising should communicate with younger audiences (a point explored in further depth in Chapter 6). Bernbach recognized the influential power of mass media and suggested that creators of advertising could either brutalize society or raise it to another plane. Creativity and intelligent communication thus provide an interesting twist to debates on the role of ethics in advertising. Rather than communicating *at* people, the suggestion is that advertising may speak *with* people.

For many practitioners, creativity is the atmosphere that attracts, feeds and sustains them. Obsession with this vague principle will seem odd to a reader without an overt interest in advertising. To the insider, it is fundamental. The character of creativity in advertising is of a highly *romantic* orientation in that exponents draw upon the language of excess, irrationality, radical individualism, empathy and the importance of authenticity. Ideas about creativity in advertising have not developed significantly since the 1960s. For proof, identify any leading creative practitioner in advertising today and compare their pronouncements about creativity with those from William Bernbach in the 1960s.[17] To this end it is worth considering the discursive construction of creativity in the 1960s that contributed to such profound changes in advertising practice. The creative oeuvre of DDB reflects the social norms that it grew out of. As a decade the 1960s took pride in being highly moral (ideological) and immoral (disruptive of accepted norms), anarchistic, revolutionary and countercultural. Particularly in the US, the rejection of the status quo was in part a denunciation of capitalism and its promotion of materialism (that in relation to capitalism means happiness through acquisition). The creative turn in advertising was not just a reflection of the times but it was a strategically appropriate one, to reflect a greater sense of authenticity (away from homogeneity, sameness, and the wish for comfort and security established as a result of the Great Depression). Ironically the rejection of capitalism tallied with a rise in Gross Domestic Product and low unemployment rates. With advertising being the public face of capitalism, and therefore itself a symbol of disillusionment, what is dubbed the Creative Revolution in advertising was perhaps born from necessity as well as opportunity. Advertising agencies are populated by people who live in the real world (and are themselves disdainful of crass advertising offers), so it is too strong to say that authenticity in advertising is entirely posture. What *is* reasonable to argue is that agencies are mindful of scepticism towards materialism and that a semblance of intimacy provides opportunity to create goodwill towards brands. The Dove example in Chapter 4 crystallizes this perfectly.

On occasion, romantic constructions of creativity in advertising are taken to the level of pastiche. Paul Arden (2003), for example, best known for his work whilst a creative director for Saatchi & Saatchi, argues that people in advertising should rely less on safe decisions that go only to familiar places than that they should opt for unsafe options that generate reaction and achievement. Underpinning this is recognition that what is new and valuable cannot come to be without change, and change always brings with it uncertainties. Arden's call to action invokes recklessness, fearlessness, anti-conformity, childlikeness, originality, and avoidance of the reasonable, steady and middle path. We can also add a dash of subversion. The latter point is key in that the history of creativity is littered with transgression and morally ambivalent characters.[18]

Although much of the creative revolution in advertising derives from economic and social changes taking place in the 1950s and 1960s, there is also a much deeper impulse from the past that influences ideas about creativity today. In romantic terms, these are the real and fictional lives of artists, libertines, debauchees, heretics, perverts, and those who deliberately departed from accepted doctrine. However, there is a slight paradox here because although the discourse of creativity in advertising draws on radical individualism, this needs to be balanced against the fact that advertising is a collective activity. This is a mistake found in much thinking about creativity that draws upon romantic conceptions (not least the outsider and the tortured artist syndrome). Although creativity in an organizational context very much involves excellent individuals, the creative output in advertising is a collective effort. For further evidence, it is notable that many creative "superstars" on leaving one agency often fail to reproduce their excellence at the next. Creativity in advertising is co-creative in that:

1. Creatives tend to work in teams.
2. Work is subject to the verification and production skills of a wide range of actors, along with internal and external pressures (such as the constraints of clients, marketing objectives, budgets, the advertising brief, hierarchical approval of creatives' work and collaborative constraints).
3. Although new ideas are certainly possible, they always emerge as a result of ads, ideas, innovations, styles, symbolic practice, cultural trends and practices to have taken form elsewhere (although for creative advance to occur there has to be an element of something new, or what is definable only in terms of itself).

In researching this book, a number of interviewees from small agencies that I spoke with described their organizational and creative arrangements as 'agile'. This is an extension of co-creativity as it is an attempt to create a more horizontal working environment, as opposed to a top-down managerial structure served by clear-cut sales, strategy, creative and media departments. The consequence is that multiple actors may make ideas and improvements at different stages of the process. To theorize, this means creativity entails collective output from a dynamic context (where many actors contribute valuable parts to the final whole). While it is fair to say that some parts are more equal than others, the overall culture of an agency matters (in terms of what is collectively valued, what it stands for and how it treats its staff).

As to what creativity in advertising is, it is the process of communicating the strategy of an advertising campaign in an attractive and influential manner (for discussion of creative process also see Bullmore, 2003; Mazzarella, 2006; Hackley, 2007; Hegarty, 2011). Strategy consists of knowing the target market, how the advertisement should speak to the target market (for instance, tone of voice), and the media best suited for reaching that target market. Strategy, in essence, is '*what* do we want to communicate' versus '*how* are we going to communicate it'. Typically, the most valued advertising by both creatives and management is that which is original and stays on strategy. It typically also involves the need to 'do more with less'. From writers' and designers' perspectives this is crystallized in John Hegarty's maxim: 'Write less, say more' (2011: 7). This economy is based on the fact that ads and sponsored content need to capture attention quickly, and maximize impact. Agencies approach strategy differently (both in its creation and the extent to which it is adhered to), but in general strategy is important to the final outcome as well-written strategy helps guide creatives on the tenor and nature of the advertising. Not all agree with this. Dave Trott (2009)[19] for example somewhat brutally describes those who plan advertising strategy as out of touch with popular culture and everyday life, and that creative briefs (the document that crystallizes advertising strategy) harm the creative process. Ironically this point is well made by a former chief marketing officer for Heineken. Writing for *Advertising Age*, Lesya Lysyj (2015) opines:

> You know that no matter what you give the agency, it changes when the creative team is briefed, right? So don't worry about the template, the boxes and all the window dressing. Just get to the seven to 10 words that the creative team is going to create from. Sometimes a creative brief is right on strategy but not going to net good ideas. Look the creatives in the eye like you're Larry David and make sure they actually like it. The brief for the now famous 'Gorilla' ad for

Cadbury chocolate (which grew the business by 8%, by the way) was 'Make me feel how I do when I'm eating Cadbury chocolate.' And it wasn't even on paper.

Creative briefs differ between agencies but will typically contain media requirements, background to the client, reason for advertising, target audience, campaign objectives, consumer insights, a proposition (the key thing the advertising should communicate), the desired consumer response and reasons why consumers should believe what they are being told. This for Trott, as an outcome of consumer research, places excessive limits on creativity. Although these prescriptions might involve the correct strategy, the danger for Trott is that briefs can lead to formulaic and uninspiring work. Seen otherwise, rather than limiting it clarifies the nature of the message to be communicated and opens up possibilities for imaginative expression of the strategy. This is a loud echo of William Bernbach. Others, influenced by David Ogilvy, see the value of research and strategy as about the basic constituents of what to say in advertising.

Ideas (big and small)

Advertising is obsessed with *ideas*. An idea is the answer of how to turn advertising strategy (what message is to be communicated and to whom) into a memorable, convincing, palatable and potentially enjoyable advertising experience. Ideas are solutions to challenges. In the case of advertising they also provide expression, shape and value, and act as points of recognition. The most successful will stand out and become what David Ogilvy (1985) dubbed 'Big Ideas'. These are campaigns that become iconic, popular with consumers as well as industry insiders, and crystallize a human insight so well that the idea translates across all media, however different their properties are. In other words, they are brand builders in that they generate financial value through non-physical means. Further, they are intangible, but most certainly exist in the minds of actual and potential customers. Recent and older examples of *big ideas* include:

1. Nicorette: *Quitting Sucks* (smoking cessation)
2. Nike: *Just Do It* (sportswear)
3. British Airways: *To Fly. To Serve* (airline)
4. Dove's Real Women: (skin/haircare)

Each of these is a long-term strategic vision of a company. They are Trojan horses in that although each of these big ideas is clear and understandable, they are suggestive and come bundled with a legion of positive and desirable associations. Thus, while it is true to an extent that a big idea is simply one message conveyed well, this belies complexity that sits behind simplicity. Particularly in communication, any statement or utterance draws upon a much wider matrix of meaning. Nike's 'Just Do It', for example, is not just a message to tell us to put on a pair of Nike trainers and go for a run, but it is a philosophy, a network of values, a world outlook or an ideology. In Nike's case this is one of self-discipline, personal maintenance, growth, strength, autonomy, freedom and self-reliance. In addition to personal values, they are also political values (that in the US connect with primacy of businesses, deregulation, privatization and neoliberal attitude). Notably the best ideas resonate with us individually. By this I mean they have a characteristic within their construction that communicates with us at a personal level. Given that these messages are simultaneously translated to millions of people, this is impressive. Nicorette's, for example, empathizes with quitters because stopping smoking is hard. Nike's goes further and becomes a participant in our internal debates on whether we go for a run (it's raining), should we bother with the gym on the way home (it's been a long day) and the internal to-ing and fro-ing about whether we should do any exercise today. The magic here is to be able to communicate personally through broadcast means. This can be contrasted with the majority of advertising that presents brands in general terms that people cannot personally relate to. This combines reach with personalization – a powerful, affective and effective combination.

Small ideas are less about strategy than tactics. Sometimes called tactical ads, they are more immediate, grab popular attention, make use of events taking place now, or play with our media habits in some way. This reflects a feeling within the industry that strategy is too slow and what is required are tactics, i.e. decision making that is reactive, takes place in real time, plans for a shorter period of time and takes advantage of current affairs. In an article for *The Drum*,[20] Kevin Roberts, Saatchi & Saatchi's Chief Executive Officer, is quoted as saying:

> Strategy is dead. Who really knows that [sic] is going to happen anymore in this super VUCA [volatile, uncertain, complex, ambiguous world]? The more time and money you spend devising strategies the more time you are giving your rivals to start eating your lunch.

This is a call to tactical arms. Whereas strategy tends to be big, broad and long lasting, *tactics* may be part of a strategy, narrower and more focused and grounded in the present. They are reactive and able to engage in real-time, fast-moving, fluid life. This is something public relations has always been required to do, but in a media environment in which new developments can trend in a matter of hours (minutes?), advertisers also seek to tactically capitalize on breaking events. In different ways, each of the following is an example of *small ideas*:

1. Snickers: in 2015 Snickers dispatched a box of 48 bars of their nutty chocolate to the Top Gear studios following revelations that Jeremy Clarkson had punched and ranted at a producer after being denied a hot meal at the end of a day's filming. This used the campaign line developed by AMV BBDO: 'You're not you when you're hungry.' (A zeitgeist tactical idea as part of a bigger strategy.)
2. Lastminute.com released a tactical ad using clips of Nigel Farage on the eve of the European elections in 2014. The agency, Adam & Eve/DDB, created an online spot, which mashed up footage of Farage to make it appear as though the UKIP leader was advocating cheap holidays to the continent. (A zeitgeist tactical idea that played on Cassetteboy's[21] comedy, politics and cut-and-paste aesthetic.)
3. Geico: a well-known but under-discussed truism is that no one likes pre-roll advertising YouTube clips that require the viewer to watch for five seconds before they can press 'Skip Ad'. A pre-roll commercial by Geico addresses this issue. Before five seconds, the voiceover says: 'You can't skip this ad, it's already over.' Then the family at the dinner table freeze, but the family dog punctures the ending by climbing up on to the table and eating food from the plates. There is a compelling strangeness created by the textual style (reminiscent of lurid Americana and the 1950s perfect family) and, instead of skipping, one is inclined to watch till the end. (Media tactic.)
4. Greenpeace: with the help of Dutch animation company Studio Smack, it edited out all the fauna from the opening sequence of Disney's *The Lion King* to illustrate human impact on the environment. (A disruption of popular culture.)

Storytelling

If you ask a creative about creativity in advertising today, they are likely to respond that storytelling is still paramount and that we should not fetishize technology and media. Given the creative advertising industry's championing of storytelling, one could be lulled into thinking creativity and storytelling are synonymous. This is not true because there are many domains of creative endeavour not based on the creation of stories. The connection between storytelling and advertising is well told by Tham Khai Meng (2015), Worldwide Chief Creative Officer at Ogilvy & Mather. He says that facts are poor persuaders, so these details need to be written up into memorable narratives that move us. To quote:

> Stories are emotion delivery vehicles. That's how they weave their magic. It's why we pay good money to cry at movies. Emotion is the engine that moves people – just ask any fascist dictator. They don't waste time giving the crowd facts and figures about the country's GDP. No, they rouse the mob to a fury with a story about the paradise that awaits them all once they have killed the enemies of the state.

Seen this way, creativity in advertising involves translating facts, benefits and points of difference into markers of aspiration, desire and happiness. Creation and resolution of tension, archetypal stories, injection of emotion, character development, empathy, play and subversion of cultural conventions help to achieve this. Another key point is that creative interest in storytelling is typically media neutral. This means that ideas and stories are privileged and media technologies are simply tools to help tell better stories. Secondly, storytelling also involves an intuitive (but practised) grasp of basic emotional principles and how to stimulate those in people. For practitioners, this understanding does not derive from a handbook about what motivates people, but from empathy and intuition. The first, empathy, is an understanding of other people's points of view and their emotional condition; the second, intuition, is non-verbalized knowledge from experience. This is similar to doing maths sums without showing working out. It is insight derived from experience rather than explicit knowledge that can be written down and easily replicated for others to follow. Understanding of storytelling, drawing people into narratives, myth, character and (importantly) how archetypes can be subverted by contemporary norms, beliefs and styles is central to creativity. This is because creativity facilitates change in how we think about brands and products. Jeremy Bullmore (2003: 204), a stalwart of the advertising industry (copywriter and ex-chairman of JWT and the Advertising Association), highlights that a good creative:

[...] can bring freshness to old promises; they can engage people's minds and self-interest; they can develop a narrative; they can forge connections through visual and verbal metaphor. And they do all these things and many more not just for the sake of it but as a calculated means to a clearly understood end.

Wieden + Kennedy's *Old Spice Guy* embodies this principle. This featured Isaiah Mustafa (actor, former NFL player and man with desirable body) asking women whether they would want their men to smell like him. Winning the Grand Prix at the 2010 Cannes International Advertising Festival, this campaign famously made excellent use of social media (including Facebook, Twitter, and YouTube). This alone would put the campaign on the prize list, but the way in which it took Old Spice, an aftershave for men over 60, and repositioned it, forged new semiotic associations with the product, and recast the nature of the brand is testament to the role of creativity in advertising. Note too that the campaign quite literally speaks *with* rather than *at* people, and shares a joke with its audience about masculinity and even the Old Spice brand itself (a brave move for the company). Although all creatives typically caution that we should not fetishize technology at the expense of storytelling and strong ideas, there are some formal differences between traditional advertising and digital storytelling, not least that the latter is more interactive and participatory.

Despite industry obsession with telling us stories and spinning yarns around products and brands, this is not the only creative means of advertising. For example, the iPhone is one of the best selling products of all time and Apple is the world's most valuable brand, but agencies working on its behalf do not roll out stories about the brand. Indeed, Apple's agency encourages us to *tell our own stories*. This is echoed in Apple's (2015) Grand Prix-winning work 'Shot on iPhone 6' by TBWA/MediaArts Lab that that features users' own stories to communicate the quality of the product. Related, in 2014 AKQA and Nike+ also helped us create our own stories by making use of wearable data collected from running. 'Your Year' used information about our year, location, weather, distance run, minutes trained, field points earned and best times. AKQA and Nike+ partnered with Mcbess, a renowned French illustrator, to create animation forms through which our own stories would be told. These were sent to runners in time for New Year with a view to generating personal, relevant and motivating stories (and to intensify emotional bonds between Nike and runners' own endeavours).

To make the consumer storytelling point more forcefully, Coca Cola are using happiness as its branding strategy. Interestingly Coca Cola used the research[22] it conducted as the marketing communication. In a slide show, prominently placed on its website, it points out that: European teens say that being happy is more important than anything else in life; they say that they are not a "me" generation but a "we" generation; family and friends come first; happiness is "down to you" to make the choice to be happy; happiness is not candy coated, but it's authentic; pressures of life mean one should have fun and be goofy, embrace joy, live in the moment and take risks today to develop skills for tomorrow; and happiness is contagious because of digital networking. Coca Cola's #choosehappiness consumer storytelling campaign is a reaction to this research. The outstanding paradox is that the appeal to authenticity and happiness is a brilliantly executed marketing strategy. Coca Cola's website also contains sections such as 'The Happiness Project' that encourages us to use the hashtag #choosehappiness and share our stories, pictures, videos and texts with the world by means of our preferred online channel (such as Instagram, Facebook, Twitter or Vine). Using our own "happy" stories, this assists in generating authenticity (because the content comes from us), yet it allows Coca Cola to capitalize on this exceedingly basic emotion in order for Coca Cola to be synonymous with happiness. The website features tweeted photos and Instagram shots of Cola drinkers' cute puppies, artfully decorated finger nails (in Coca Cola red and black), of people on holiday in Ireland, hugging at a festival, photos of London, and crafted shots of the classic bottle and the Coca Cola logo. In addition to the images, other hashtags are used such as #summerdays, #friends, #flaneur, #millingaround, #selfie, #boy, #girl, #yum, #streetstyle and many more popular hashtags that Coca Cola will be keen to associate themselves with.

Fine, fine, I now see that people in advertising think it is important, *but what is creativity?*

This brings us to the second part of this chapter. We now understand the extent to which the advertising industry values creativity and thinks of it in terms of storytelling, character, human insight, humour, provocation, emotional resonance, strategy and tactics, resistance of the usual and winning awards, but much less about what *it* is. This is the focus of the second section of this chapter. I will unpack a range of approaches to creativity, including: experience and disclosing; sensational and affective conceptions; situation and placement; and combinations, playfulness, exploration and transformation. Understanding of these will allow us to: theorize creativity; provide a language to articulate why an ad (or something else) is creative; and also allow practitioners to understand how creative work can be improved and pushed to the next level.

Experience

The first approach is the argument from experience. This involves understanding products and services in the richest levels of experiential detail. As noted above in relation to intuition, this is the search for stories and ideas within the product or service itself and how it might fit within a consumer's life. Within this is a big point: *creativity is a means of disclosing.* This sounds very philosophical (and to an extent it is), but it connects well with industry accounts of creativity in advertising.[23] DDB (2012) provides a quote from Bernbach speaking to his copywriters:

> You've got to live with your product. You've got to get steeped in it. You've got to get saturated with it. You must get to the heart of it. Indeed, if you have not crystallized into a single purpose, a single theme, what you want to tell the reader, you CANNOT be creative.

The 'heart' of the product that Bernbach refers to is its experiential essence. This is found by using it, eating it, gazing upon it, touching it, manipulating it, testing it, taking it apart, and understanding the object (be it a thing or service) in both physical and immaterial dimensions. By understanding it at an experiential level, one is able to comprehend it in terms of *quality*. By this I do not mean excellence, but the fabric of experience. Once this is grasped, believable communicative ideas are more easily developed. The idea of creativity as disclosure is not just found in advertising, but in art too. It is about depicting what might be thought of as commonplace in refreshed ways. Consider still life painting that emerged in the late sixteenth century and its painting of apples, teapots, pipes, flowers, plates, glasses and other items from domestic life. Creativity seen this way is about highlighting, renewing vision, bringing into focus, perceptual shifts, making exotic, enlarging and intensifying experiences of objects, to reflect or create particularity. The best advertising also does this. Reading creativity in advertising this way, it has less to do with puns, wordplay, clever visuals, or even making the familiar strange/ strange familiar, but the overall effort on revealing and disclosing. By this I mean that creativity involves recognizing the lived thing *in itself* and imposing this consciousness on others.

Sensational and affective conceptions

In *Creativity and Advertising* (2013) I argued that creativity is not just representational but sensational. By this I mean that creativity is not just about words, images and what they signify, but the nature of the experience that advertising may foster. *It has less to do with what we think than how we feel.* Budding creatives might consider this: how should people feel as a result of seeing your work? One way to think about this somewhat abstract idea is to think about creating a meal for which we select a range of ingredients (some similar and others bitter, salty, sweet and contradictory). We do this caringly and for a purpose – to intensify flavours, and to stimulate an experience for a given end. Only at the worst dinner parties do cooks choose ingredients to be clever. (Some celebrity cooks use the weirdest ingredients, but only on the basis they will surprise, delight and stimulate.) To reach back into advertising history, a classic example of this is David Ogilvy's Man with a Hathaway Shirt from 1951 that featured a man in a shirt also wearing a black eyepatch. This is a delightfully simple combination used to stimulate a specific feeling and affect. It inspired curiosity, intrigue and a large rise in sales of Hathaway shirts. Although we might subsequently intellectualize the ad (what happened to this aristocratic gentleman that resulted in the wearing of an eyepatch?), this tells little of the arresting nature of the advertisement and the sensational ways in which we might be affected without knowing why – even after reflection. Intellectual enquiry also misses the fact that there is sensational power to be found in discordance, imprecise meaning, polysemy, open-endedness and contradiction. Similarly, while brands and advertising are certainly in the business of logos, symbols, imagery, wordplay, meaning and significance, creativity exceeds the intellect because it is interested in quality, aesthetics and affecting emotions. We might, too, note that despite our bias towards the visual senses, this involves *all* image-making systems (aural, olfactory and tactile as well as visual). A sound is just as much an image as a picture.

Although messages clearly matter (an ad has to say something!), creativity seen through the lens of sensation is concerned with quality, texture and experiences that are tangible. Put otherwise, advertising has more to do with moods and feelings than logical thought. (And this is why advertising is not in the business of persuasion, but influence.) This may appear vague, but the need to stimulate emotions connects the origins of advertising, contemporary neuroscientific applications in market research, and tomorrow's interest in understanding more about our emotional lives through our media devices and environments (more on this in Chapter 11). Artists and poets are well aware of the physicality of communication, particularly when the sign (for example speed or noise) has no obvious meaning that we can easily put into words. To draw upon Bill Bernbach once more: 'The fragile structure of logic fades and disappears against the emotional onslaught of hushed tone, a dramatic pause, and the soaring excitement of a verbal crescendo' (DDB, 2012).

Empathy, situation and placement

This *affective* understanding of advertising invites questions on engagement and interaction with the world. After all, we do not consume ads in labs, but on the Tube, during the Super Bowl, while waiting in doctors' surgeries, standing in the middle of the world's metropolises, while waiting for YouTube clips to load, on electronic displays at grocery checkouts, on leaflets as we pick up enveloped mail, via links on Facebook, during the drive to work and while munching on popcorn in cinemas. These environments are each imbued with significance and environmental factors that affect how we engage with advertising (such as temperature, proximity to others, whether we are seated or standing, other advertisements and media content, or which country and culture we happen to be in at the time). The introduction of location, environment, circumstance and coordination of social factors means that advertising experiences are better thought of in terms of materiality of involvement, kinaesthetics, participation, interaction and immersion in the world. As experience of everyday life tells us, we never see things, objects or ads in isolation, but as part of a wider mix of sensory and meaningful information. Communication that can empathize, display understanding of where and when a person is, and understand likely moods, will be more resonant and effective.

A personal anecdote about Evian water might help. The headline 'Welcome to our Factory' is not an especially intriguing one, but its significance was amplified by the fact that the ad was placed on a chairlift tower halfway up a French Alp in the Portes du Soleil. While one might reasonably say that this is an invasion of the great outdoors, it made me smile and it felt appropriate to the product. Also, kinaesthetic and environmental factors greatly enhanced my impression that Evian is somehow more pure than other waters. My theorizing of situational creativity is the utter opposite of abstract. After all, media planners and buyers go to great financial lengths to ensure that their client's advertising is engaged with in the right places, times, situations and contexts. Although the "kinaesthetic flow of everyday life" may not be foremost when media buyers are trying to secure the best deal with owners of billboard spaces, this principle sits behind the motive to acquire the best spaces (in addition to high amounts of people actually seeing them in the first place!). On this point, it is worth reflecting on where most of a marketer's advertising budget is spent. Although we tend to think of advertising as being about ads, in financial terms it is overwhelmingly about where they are placed. In addition to empathizing with where a person may be seeing the ad, the best work also empathizes with where and how the product is being consumed.

Culture hacking: combinations

What I term combinatorial creativity involves taking different elements and mixing them together so to create something new. While not an especially radical or difficult idea (many other writers on the creative industries make similar arguments),[24] it has consequences for both creating advertising and how to analyse it. In James Webb Young's *A Technique for Producing Ideas*, first published in the 1940s, Young observes that ideas for advertising are 'nothing more nor less than a new combination of old elements' (2003: 15) and that the ability to bring old elements into new combinations depends on the ability to see relationships. This is akin to what Arthur Koestler (1970 [1964]) terms *bisociation*, or reaching across different domains and places, finding elements of use, and then combining these. Applied to advertising this includes typographic styles, illustration, photography, media formats, linguistics, art history, music, literature, cultural politics, current affairs and more, and blending these elements together for novel, but

70

considered, effect. This is *culture hacking*, or the manipulation of languages (visual and written) beyond what those signs were originally intended to depict. For a non-digital example, *Fatty, Nerd*, for UNICEF by Prolam Y&R Santiago in 2014, depicted kids aiming their phones, firing-squad style, at classmates in an anti-cyberbullying campaign from Chile. The copy reads: 'One shot is enough. Cyberbullying represents one of the main causes of depression and suicide among kids at school. If you have a smartphone, use it wisely. Don't kill anyone's self-esteem.' Another non-digital favourite example of mine from the year 2000 is the work of Leo Burnett (the advertising agency) for the canned tuna company, John West. Titled *Fishing*, this used a close-up of the top of the tuna tin to look like ripples of water. This provides a sense of calmness, integrity and quality to give the impression that the company's fish is carefully line-caught by a real person. What makes this ad work is originality derived from unusual combinations to provide a jolt, an "aha", a smile, surprise, entertainment, reward and playful intimacy between ad-maker and ad-viewer.

As mentioned, bisociation and culture hacking may involve combinations of a variety of visual, linguistic, cultural and political domains. Droga5's 2014 *I Will What I Want* for Under Armour (a sports apparel brand), made use of debate around gender politics by teaming with model Gisele Bündchen. Typically known as a masculine brand (for rugby players and American footballers), Under Armour received national level news coverage in the US on publicizing the fact that Bündchen would be working with the brand. Droga5 recorded the comments from mass media and social media, and used these comments in their television campaign released two days later. Featuring comments such as 'Gisele is just a model', 'Under Armour WTF!' and 'Is modeling now a sport?', the ad also featured the model in a bleached warehouse environment beating a punch bag. Droga5 subsequently collected comments from social media about the model and the brand, and analysed sentiment in terms of haters and supporters. This was artfully visualized to have Bündchen working out in the background and snowy red spots on the left for haters and blue on the right for supporters. Assisted by strong PR, the campaign subsequently featured on Fox, in *Time* and during television appearances where Gisele discussed the campaign and female athletic aspiration. The work subsequently positioned Under Armour into the second largest sports apparel brand in the US. In semiotic language this is the principle of *transference*, or how positively received signs are used to propagate another sign.

Exploration

Margaret Boden's (2010) book *Creativity and Art* discusses an approach similar to what has been termed here as combinatorial creativity. Boden goes a step further to offer two more characteristics of creativity. These are *exploration* and *transformation*. Whereas combinations involve original juxtapositions of elements, *exploratory conceptions* of creativity involve seeing things differently. This may have to do with technique, materials or noticing something about what is possible that no one else has spotted or discovered. In a sense it is a bigger form of creativity because it involves testing the nature and boundaries of a discipline. This is important for digital advertising because media experimentation is altering the ways that we think about advertising and how it is done. Where the first form of creativity (what I have called culture hacking and combinatorial creativity) involves symbolism and combining elements for a given purpose (but still using traditional formats with which to present these combinations), an *exploratory* understanding involves an expansion of what can be achieved with different forms of media and participatory practices. To define this point more clearly in relation to advertising, we can say that combinatorial creativity involves play with signs *within* a given medium. By contrast, exploration is about play with either the medium itself or how that medium can be used to communicate. The Dove campaign discussed in Chapter 4 is a good example of this because it plays with the medium itself to enhance its message (female empowerment and rejection of negative online ads on Facebook that push diets and breast enhancement products).

Transformation

A transformational approach to creativity in advertising is even bigger. It entails thinking of something that is not possible out of a given set of elements. For this to occur, the pre-existing order of things must be changed so to allow new possibilities, combinations and horizons. In *Creativity and Advertising* (2013) I argued that this has only happened twice in advertising – and that we are living through one of these instances now. The first was in the 1960s as DDB changed how advertising was done. They redrew the very principles of practice and redefined the communicative nature of advertising (from talking *at* people to talking *with* people). They also recreated the format of advertising, working practices and agency culture. Our contemporary period is seeing similar changes in practice – although these are not to most practitioners' tastes. Reviewers of this book and those within creative departments will disagree, but I argue that behavioural targeting, programmatic and artificial intelligence (AI) represent the next creative development of advertising. Indeed, there are already moves in this direction, as the Cannes Creative Data Lions[25] were created to recognize campaigns using data 'as a catalyst for creativity'.

This is because advertising augmented by data is altering audience understanding, targeting, message creation and the understanding of how people respond to these messages (at biological, behavioural, emotional, cognitive and communicational levels). These are game-changing and transformational developments, although I appreciate this is an unusual reading of creativity. This innovative trend represents not only bisociation of computer science, profiling and personalizing experiences of advertising (heterogeneity), but more centrally involves the transformational creation of a new order, structure and paradigm in which advertising is done. This does not mean it is necessarily preferable, but newness is not inherently good or bad, it just is. There are two ways to read the development of AI-enhanced programmatic logic:

1. Transformation of the whole industry itself (data gathering, processing, buying, targeting, creation and serving);
2. The appeal to context: although for a long time the ad business has commissioned extensive research on audiences, the capacity to use incoming data in real time to create contextually aware advertising is a remarkable proposition.

If we consider the entire output of the advertising industry (and not just that which wins awards), the logic and practice of AI-enhanced programmatic promises to be transformational. There is much scope for development in this field because, as mentioned, people need to code and tell the machines what to do. This requires new skills, tools, partners, working practices and expertise, particularly at the level of algorithms and computational filters. Rather than seeing automated algorithmic advertising as inhuman, new creatives should see algorithms as the codification of human values, biases, leanings, preferences, and potentially even of our cultural and artistic histories. One can see the lack of appeal to creative agencies, not least because the emphasis on being measurable disavows the interest in affect and how ads make people feel. As will be developed further in Chapters 10 and 11 on analytics, quantification and feeling are not totally separate. The task for the advertising business is how to merge *experiential creativity* (the first sort detailed) with the optimization granted by automation. The answer lies in creatives, programmers, designers of algorithms and consumer profilers working together. Indeed, this may encompass *combinatorial and experiential creativity* and the selection of commonly understood signs from a common cultural context held within a database.

Conclusion

This chapter has outlined industry approaches to creativity in advertising, highlighting that there is little difference in how leading creative practitioners today and the leading practitioners of the 1960s understand it. This leads one to ask: is this because that is what creativity actually is (maverick, authentic, anti-establishment, humorous, provocative and – for most – also strategic)? Or, might it be that this is only one historically and culturally situated form of creativity? I think it is the latter and suggest that creativity involves wilful acts in situations that are unfamiliar, new and without clear determinates that we can hold on to. It is the opening of new possibilities and embracing of challenges, and seeing opportunities for playfulness and redrafting the rules. This requires inventiveness as well as intuition. Creativity in the emergent media sector requires craft skills and understanding of new tools of the trade, but it appears that those in the creative department have been caught napping on the job.

Distillation of creative principles

1. Originality for its own sake is of little use for advertising because creativity in advertising operates within specified parameters. The bizarre should be eschewed in favour of what is *both* original and useful.
2. Communication works best when it is more than a one-way process.
3. Honesty, authenticity, inclusivity, intelligence, humour, intuition and provocation matter.
4. Individuals can achieve a great deal, but creativity tends to be a collective effort. What could others help you with?

5. Write less, say more: how can communication be reduced without negatively affecting meaning?
6. Big ideas are Trojan horses based on strategy and genuine insights on the human condition that are subsequently used to sell products.
7. Small ideas are tactics to be used in real-time battles.
8. All in creative advertising seem to bow to the storyteller.
9. Creativity deals in qualities to intensify experiences.
10. Creativity is less about what we think than how we feel.
11. Creative advertising empathizes with who, what and where we are.
12. Hack media and culture: use technologies and signs in unexpected ways.
13. Transformation: over to you, but this involves a change of fundamental principles.

Think points and questions

▶ What, if anything, conjoins the work of the world's leading agencies known for creativity? Use understanding generated in this chapter, or develop concepts of your own.

▶ You have been asked to give a 20-minute talk on what creativity is. What would you say and which campaigns would you show?

▶ What is bisociation? Can you think of examples of this in advertising? Can you construct a campaign that consciously makes use of bisociation?

▶ Write a manifesto for creativity today.

6   Beyond Interruption: Attention, Authenticity and Being Native

Looking back, one would be forgiven for thinking that advertising used to be easier: it was the business of selecting the best ways of reaching people and designing messages that would influence them towards a given objective. This might be buying goods, thinking a certain way, voting for a party, giving to charity or subscribing to a service. There was less concern about what people would do with those messages, because media provided little opportunity to either respond to the message sender or to publicly discuss these messages. By the 1990s and 2000s the range of media content available to people had expanded exponentially and interactive media had become the norm. Today of course we do not just respond, but we ourselves are media content producers. This does not necessarily mean keeping popular blogs, sharing homemade music or having millions of followers on YouTube, but that most people today post updates, reviews, tweet, like, forward, repost, share images or just search. This means that we collectively engage and participate in creating our own media experiences, and they are not simply provided for us.

For advertising, a related consideration is that people's available attention time is scarcer than it used to be because it is spread more thinly. Paradoxically, as attention time becomes even more meagre because of seemingly limitless media services and content (but with limited time), those seeking to gain our attention have had to redouble their efforts to obtain it. My point is not that young people have less capacity for attention, but that young and older people immersed in the contemporary media environment soon learn to employ filters to assess whether something is worth their time. Agencies and brands have cottoned onto the fact that being loud and overtly interruptive is not the best method to engage us. The magic trick for advertisers today is to grab attention without being seen to do so and in a way that we find credible and believable. A tall order! What is required is better targeting, and creative and sponsored communication that people might actually want to engage with. In addition to shrinking attention span is the requirement of *authenticity*. This is key because trust in brands is at an all-time with low young people.[26] With principles of increased engagement with media (where we create, share and post), decrease in attention time and a crisis of credibility in mind, this chapter assesses advertising and marketing communications in the social media domain where attention has to be earned. We will consider: the history of audiences and trends towards interactive audiences; native advertising; how agencies engage with successful owners of YouTube channels; attempts to nurture authenticity; and the rise of branded entertainment.

Audiences

To understand audiences today, it is instructive to return to the 1970s when professional media researchers began to ask questions about what people do with media, rather than what media content might do to people. This was a key development because both popular and academic research was previously more concerned with the power of media to overtly influence people. This shift in the 1970s was led by Elihu Katz's research. This developed out of a "minimal effect" academic context that questioned whether people were as vulnerable to mass media as many social scientists working on media had previously supposed (Livingstone, 1997). Observations along these lines opened the door to enquiry into how people use and derive gratification from media content (Katz et al., 2003 [1974]). This complicated the proposition that media simply affect and influence them towards a predetermined activity (belief in brand, sales, change in outlook or ideological persuasion). Instead the media environment is seen as a matrix (or public sphere) of interaction, conversation, opinion, action and ripples (multi-steps of influence, not just of media>people, but media>person>person). This chain-like approach to influence is arguably best expressed in today's social media environment, despite being developed much earlier.

Katz underappreciated the ideological impact of media content on our values, goals and outlooks. After all, our long-term assumptions about gender, consumerism, race, nationhood and other worldly phenomena are connected with the media we are exposed to. However, the suggestion that 'people bend the media to their needs more readily than the media overpower them' is an agreeable one (Katz, 1973: 164–165). At the very least it requires that long-term effects proponents provide actual evidence of their argument about how content affects people. Katz's (1957) two- and multi-step modelling is of direct consequence to our own discussion of what is termed by advertisers and PR professionals as 'earned media', because Katz argues influence occurs through leaders of people's peer groups (and not simply directly on people). These groups in turn can be thought of as a network of communicating actors imbued with internally generated norms, beliefs and pressures to conform to the group outlook. This means that study of peer-shared advertising is productively examined by studying the nature of the peer group, as well as the advertising itself. Put otherwise, it is to study production (the advertising), reception (seeding of advertising and reaching influencers within the group), dissemination (viral circulation, what people are saying and what group norms are being appealed to) and life cycle (how long interest in the campaign lasts and what factors dictate this). This, then, is a shift from the suggestion that people are defenceless against manipulative advertisers to one of negotiation. The appeal to social context has practical lessons for online content creators who want their ads to be circulated. It means they should consider (if not study) the values and norms of the community networks they would like their ads circulated within, and how they can interact with and reward audiences (be this by incentive or creativity). Note that networks have less to do with cables and computers than how things and information are moved.

Interactive audiences

Closely related is the notion of interactivity and the somewhat obvious fact that today we do not just consume media content, but we produce it. As Henry Jenkins (2006) coined it, we live in a participatory culture. Media scholars see this principle in different ways. Some, such as Clay Shirky (2008), tend towards the celebratory, seeing participatory culture in terms of liberation and capacity to do wonderful things with interactive communication tools. Others, such as Maurizio Lazzarato (2004, 2014), equate participatory culture with a technique by which people produce media content that in turn generates revenue for people who did not produce it. Further, in this more critical view, we not only produce media content for others, but also a great deal of information about ourselves that generates revenue for others (more on this in later chapters). As to what interactivity actually is, it is less about clicking buttons and swiping screens than involving consideration of:

- The degree of control we have over interactions with people, objects and machines;
- Capacity to influence and modify content;
- Ability to do things when we want (a matter of temporality and time shifting, as opposed to mass experience when someone else says so);
- The nature of synchronization between two parties in real time (as with a telephone call) or time-shifted (as with email);
- How information moves (this might be between person and machine; machine and machine; or person to machine and on to person);
- Generation of heterogeneous media experience (where media companies are able to respond to individuals' interests and provide each user unique content);
- How machines simulate interpersonal communication (where machines might address us by name and/or know our preferences);
- A sense of immersion (for example in virtual environments, but also traditional stories);
- A sense of being elsewhere (telepresence);
- How machines are sensitive to bodies, behaviour, emotions/feelings, preferences, location, personal histories, what we see, what we say, how we say it;
- Contextual understanding (or how people and machines comprehend a person's motives, history and how a person's background contributes towards present behaviour).

From the point of view of creative advertising and agencies, traditional advertising involved beaming commercials *at* people. This was a low form of interactivity, not just because people did not have screens to swipe or buttons to press, but also because there was little opportunity to influence the message or collaborate with advertisers in co-creating the advertising experience. Indeed, this might also remind us of Bill Bernbach who urged ad-writers to make allies rather than targets out of consumers (or *with* rather than *at* people). Again, the value of interactivity is not about media but the quality of interaction. By quality I mean immersion, the nature of experience and the extent to which we are affected by that experience (how do we feel about that brand as a result of single or multiple exposures to communication from it?). The lesson from this is that although media have distinct properties that can contribute to novel experiences, the medium should not be fetishized.

Earning attention

Young people do not suffer from "attention deficit", but possess very good filters. Social media provides two opportunities for advertisers. The first is the use of behavioural targeting and retargeted advertising (ads for products a person may have browsed but did not buy), and the second is *pull*-based advertising. Rather than forcing advertising on people (as with traditional broadcast media), pull-based approaches are based on the idea of creating advertising that is either of creative or incentivized interest. This includes coupons, free access to a service or behind-the-scenes access of some sort. For example Burberry, the fashion company, was early to use Snapchat and Periscope by broadcasting its fashion shows. By means of Periscope, audiences were able to access all areas of Burberry's LA fashion show, see the arrival of celebrity models and virtually occupy a real-time front row seat for the entire show. Burberry used Snapchat to chart and share models' journeys from London to Los Angeles (Cara Delevingne, Naomi Campbell, Jourdan Dunn, Sam Rollinson, Charlotte Wiggins and George Barnett). The notion of push/pull is based on the principle of either pushing content at people, or the situation where people will seek out or share advertising of interest to them and their peers. These peers may be real friends, trends taking place within favoured apps, or trusted content curators. Following trends and curated content act as filtering mechanisms to make media and content options more manageable. For advertisers, this requires close attention and adaption to audience's wants, needs, patterns, friend networks and communities of interest. The upside of this situation for advertisers is that the pulling of advertising content and engagement reflects genuine interest in the brand. Willingness to share and repost also means that brands are receiving free exposure with the added bonus of being endorsed by the person doing the sharing.

The reader may have already detected some problems, because advertising has historically involved *paid-for* content in press, television, online display, search, radio, direct mail, outdoor or cinema; and public relations (PR) has sought to influence editors and gatekeepers, promote messages and gain recognition outside of traditional paid-for routes – such as shares on social media. Things get blurry at this stage because standard definitions of advertising as paid-for persuasive non-personal communication for named sponsors through media are shown to be inadequate. To understand the impact of earned media it is worth breaking down the possible media options and why they are used. These include the following:

Owned: this is where a company owns the channel of communication. This might be space on their building, retail space within a building or marketing materials such as leaflets developed by the company and sent direct to potential customers. However, the expression typically means a company's website, blogs, email communication and corporate social media accounts. This type of media is useful in building long-term relationships with customers and is able to host a large amount of well-written information about products and services. The chief problem with owned media is scale and that not many people will engage with it.

Rented: this refers to what used to be called above-the-line media in which space is rented for a limited period of time. It also refers to sponsorship, display ads, search ads and Facebook ads. The chief benefit of rented media is scale. It allows communicators to leverage existing channels that can reliably deliver content to a large audience. It allows control over the framing of the message, and where and when it is delivered. However, rented media frequently suffers from lack of credibility and low response rates, and may be seen as cluttering the wider media environment.

Earned: this involves a more organic form of message distribution. As it is not paid for, it relies on people to forward messages and content. This might be online, but it might be offline in the form of word of mouth and buzz marketing. Other examples of earned strategies include: ratings, reviews, forums and social media posts. Although this is difficult to stimulate, the rewards are high because they come with the credentials of the person who shared the content and the fact that it is not overtly advertising (to which even the most ardent supporters are often sceptical). In sum, earned media provides credibility and impressions of authenticity. The downside is that communicators have little control over the medium and the conversation that takes place around a brand. The power of earned media becomes clearer when one considers that:

▸ Ninety-two per cent of consumers around the world say they trust earned media, such as word of mouth and recommendations from friends and family, above all other forms of advertising.
▸ Online consumer reviews are the second most trusted form of advertising, with 70 per cent of global consumers surveyed online indicating they trust this platform.

▸ People's trust in television advertising has declined by 24 per cent; magazines by 20 per cent and newspapers by 25 per cent since 2009 (Nielsen, 2012).[27]

While few would be foolish or brazen enough to say that earned media will supersede owned and rented media, the figures from Nielsen are cause for interest in earned media. This more credible, authentic and peer-based approach to marketing begins by targeting influencers.

The influencers

Influencer marketing draws heavily on the two-step approach to audiences outlined above where influence occurs through leaders of people's peer groups. As is becoming clear, to engage with social media users, agencies and clients using social media are keen to use social media influencers to initiate multi-step communication (media channel>influencers>the rest of us). There is both a mass and niche character to this in that agencies recognize that many YouTube channels have an extraordinarily large reach across relatively large segments, but that niche content also generates large followings when taken across a global population. Online, this typically makes use of value-added influencers who may be leading channel owners, prolific Twitter users (with large followings) or have some other means of generating credibility with audiences (such as knowledge or celebrity status). We will outline some examples below, but people chosen as influencers do not only have large followings but they *fit the brand*, they are willing to *back the brand* and act as advocates for it, and their influence is quantifiable so to measurably *grow the brand*. Although there is a clear connection with longstanding use of celebrities in advertising, the objective of using influencers is different. Where the former is about glitz, attraction and endorsement, the use of influencers has more to do with credibility, authenticity and speaking the language of the target audience. This is less about aspiration than trust and respect.

Agencies are keen to learn from the social media natives and appropriate their authenticity. In the UK, perhaps the best example of this is Zoella (real name Zoe Sugg) who offers hair and make-up tutorials targeted at girls between 13 and 17 years old. She has 7,866,232 subscribers to her main channel (as of 13 April 2015) and is now endorsing Superdrug (having also worked with the high street clothing brand New Look). If we use the above bullet points as a checklist, we can see a perfect match between the online personality and the brand: both are youthful, outgoing, fun, oriented to the mass market (non-premium) and down to earth. The influencer is able to back the brand as she has a history of reviewing mass-market stores and brands, and is clearly interested in the products (posting videos such as 'What's In My Handbag 2015 Edition').[28] The success of the campaign can be judged by sales, hits on the Superdrug site, media coverage, social media posting/mentions, and sentiment analysis of social media (see Chapter 10 for more on this). Another example is the freerunner, parkour expert and gymnast Damien Walters, who also maintains a popular YouTube channel with 514,968 followers (as of 13 April 2015). He teamed with the brand Pepsi Max to success-fully run a vertical loop, or a loop-the-loop, meaning he was briefly upside down.[29] Titled #LiveForNow, this generated 11,172,938 views. Filmed in what appears to be an empty warehouse, the video showed the mathematics of what speed is required, the failed attempts, and Walters getting continually closer until it was time to take crash mats away. After a number of aborted attempts, the electronic dance music built to a crescendo as Walters successfully made it all the way around. However, the point already mentioned, that communicators have little control over the medium, is illustrated well by this example as com-ments directly below the video discuss Coca Cola (rather than Pepsi), refer to all sodas as 'cancer inducing shit', and describe aspartame as a 'deadly engineered sweetener'. Clearly not the result that Walters or Pepsi Max were seeking!

Similarly, PewDiePie (Felix Kjellberg) and his Let's Play game com-mentaries generate an annual income of $7 million by means of his 35,978,482 views (as of 13 April 2015). In addition to his game com-mentary (announced from a small box in the corner of the YouTube player window), he offers lifestyle commentary and amusing life hacks (for example taping a toothbrush to a vibrator to make an electronic toothbrush that looks amusing when used). His success is not just online, because in 2015 he published a satirical self-help book with lines such as 'You can never fail if you never try' and 'Don't be yourself. Be a pizza. Everyone loves pizza' (PewDiePie, 2015). What is remarka-ble is that it is just Kjellberg making the videos, with no extra filming/editing crew. He entertains by means of inane gestures, saying his own handle in a signature high-pitched voice, shrieking and yelling, cheer-fully "f-bombing" his way through gameplay. While he divides the gaming community (many hardcore gamers see his commentary as banal and more irritating than Justin Bieber), PewDiePie has the capacity to generate mass sales of games. This has led to games companies explicitly giving "shout outs" in attempts to feature on his channel. What is notable is the lack of professional high-end production that in turn generates a form of intimacy, personal contact, genuineness and credibility with many gamers. This directly echoes our earlier point about two-step flow communication as brands use influencers to get to a larger network of viewers and gamers.

While games, fashion and sporting endeavours are of interest to many, the unpacking of toys is on first consideration a more specialized interest. However, funtoyzcollector on YouTube has achieved 2,306,304 page views (as of 13 April 2015) and she is one of the five highest earners on YouTube, collecting over $5 million dollars in 2014. No one knows her real name. She unpacks toys so children can see what can be done with them and while unpacking toys may appear extraordinarily niche for a whole channel, the combination of scale (global) and focus (unpacking toys and displaying what they do) leads to high levels of advertiser interest (and thereafter revenue).

Earned media, social content and authenticity are not only for the young. For example the audio company Bose made use of Tumblr, Twitter, YouTube and Spotify. Authenticity was leveraged by means of offering a mini-documentary of Norman Cook, a musician well known to ravers and clubbers from the 1990s and 2000s. The documentary titled 'Behind the Sound' told the story of how the track 'The Rockafeller Skank' came together (a mixture of 7" records, samples, testing in clubs and speeded-up breaks).[30] Uploaded to YouTube, presented on Tumblr, tweeted by #listenforyourself and with shareable playlists via Spotify, this was a highly popular social media campaign.

The success came about not just because of the range of interacting social media platforms, but also for a number of other reasons: the respected nature of the Bose brand (never foregrounded in the campaign for a crass sell); absence of cheesy product shots; the fact that Norman Cook was an underground musician who took his artistry overground without compromising style; because what he does is fun; and because Cook's studio is not a sterile characterless space, but a room in his home stacked with samplers, keyboards, history, rave paraphernalia, a Technics deck and equipment that conveys authenticity. This was not simply a case of following the audience onto social media, but a credible means of engagement. The process is one of reaching audiences, nurturing them through interesting content and, ideally for brands, leaving consumers with a positive impression of the brand (which in the case of Bose emphasizes musicality and that its equipment is used and abused by musicians). Creatively #listenforyourself is easily digestible, enjoyable, not about the product but about the brand and its values. At an executional level, this is achieved by means of personalized narratives and journeys of key actors.

Going native: the case of BuzzFeed

Native advertising is sponsored content online. In the UK in 2014 it was worth around 45 per cent of the mobile display market (IAB, 2014a). In the grand scheme of digital advertising (that itself is only a portion of the total advertising market) this is not a large amount, but it is an interesting medium because of its non-interruptive qualities and branding potential. The word "native" refers to being part of a context. Context in turn is the user's experience. In practical terms this might be a sponsored tweet on Twitter, a suggested post on Facebook, a branded movie clip, a quiz, an interesting set of facts or a story. Another way of thinking about it is to liken native advertising to advertorials. These are not pure ads, but they are not journalistic content either. The purpose of both advertorials and native advertising is to be less intrusive or, seen otherwise, to get under a reader's suspicion radar. They are a non-interruptive approach to sponsored communication that fits with the context or content feed that a user is scrolling through, but stands out enough to be noticed. This is a different approach to advertising, because historically we have benefited from a clear demarcation between sponsored content and impartial editorial content. The Advertising Standards Authority, the UK regulator, insists that ads 'must be obviously identifiable as such' and that they 'must not materially mislead or be likely to do so' (ASA, 2014: 1). Advertisers have to tread a careful line because although they *can* make the content more similar to interesting editorial content, they should not fall foul of the regulator by camouflaging their advertisements. This was illustrated when Wayne Rooney tweeted, '"My resolution – to start the year as a champion, and finish it as a champion #makeitcount" gonike.me/makeitcount', because it was unclear that Nike's tweet via Wayne Rooney's account was sponsored communication.[31] Again, the ASA's point was that it was not clear that the tweet is in fact an ad. The guiding principle of advertising and media is there should be a clear separation in the reader's mind about what is sponsored communication and what is not.

There are three key problems with native advertising – each revolving around the central point of consumer awareness about what is sponsored and what is not:

1. It fractures the advertising/editorial contract, whereby much native content is by definition more difficult for consumers to understand what is sponsored content and what is authentic expression;
2. When dressed as news, native advertising arguably harms journalistic integrity and quality news, because sponsored content is by definition cheaper than paid-for journalism;
3. It may involve unwanted tampering with users' postings where advertisers use images and comments from users to further the interests of brands.

Each social media company offers capacity for native advertising. Until recently Facebook offered advertisers a service called Sponsored Stories. With these, a Facebook user was delivered an ad that reveals actions a friend has taken. For example if a user "liked" a product, his or her friends were later told about it in ad form. This content appeared in users' newsfeeds, seeming deceptively like status updates from friends. Promoted tweets are more clearly marketing material, but again appear in the home timeline of targeted users. Tumblr similarly offers sponsored opportunities native to the platform by means of putting sponsored blogs in the trending tab of its mobile apps, and listing them with recommended blogs on the dashboard. It is not just social media platforms that are offering these services, but news outlets too. *Forbes*, for example, is one of the most ardent proponents of native advertising in publishing. This embeds sponsored stories (from companies such as IBM and JP Morgan Chase) with its regular journalism. Similarly, at an IAB event in September 2015 I attended in Manchester, UK,[32] Mark Field, Director of Innovation for the Trinity Mirror newsgroup, highlighted the need for news vendors to 'editorialise brands'... and 'create content that matters to audiences'. The key for Field is to generate content that is shareable because mobile is increasingly the future for news. This means that brands may work with Trinity Mirror's editorial team and while editors still have freedom to publish news damaging to brands, they are being called upon work with brands to create engaging content.

However, native advertising is most commonly associated with BuzzFeed which has become successful by means of the 'listicle', or an article presented in the form of a list. BuzzFeed is an online news company that does not use online banners but instead relies on native advertising, or content that matches its editorial content. It also has a knack of producing content that is highly viral, shareable and that reflects and creates popular media culture. BuzzFeed is a good example as it works with brands to access its 200 million readers of whom 50 per cent are 18–30 years old. Content is largely accessed through mobile and social media sites. The content may be humorous or inspirational, and presented in a range of various formats including listicles, quizzes, infographics or cinemagraphs. BuzzFeed's creative teams work with agencies and brands to: produce content suitable for the audience the brand wishes to reach; seed the content so the right people find it; and track how the content is performing in real time. This content is written in such a way so as to capture a brand's voice and communicate the values it wishes to project. Virgin, for example, made use of BuzzFeed to create a 24/7 newsroom strategy based on conversations taking place on social media. This capitalized on unfolding popular news events about figures such as Miley Cyrus (resulting in articles such as '13 Celebrities Posing With The Old Versions Of Themselves').[33] The point is that the Virgin Mobile brand is positioned as the communications company that understands immediacy, trends and social dialogue. What is highly notable is that these are *not* ads with an explicit message, but humorous content that reflect the overall strategy of 'Always On'. The objective was to position Virgin as a brand that understands its users as individuals and reacts to them. Phrased otherwise, the objective was to build familiarity, trust and positive feeling towards the brand. While many of BuzzFeed's articles are humorous and quirky, others are based on lifestyle. A piece for the budget supermarket Lidl focuses on *12 Ways to be a Frugal Foodie*[34] that suggests readers buy: when food is in season; in bulk; frozen; own brands; at certain times of day (when shelf stackers cut prices), and that they ignore sell-by dates. While seemingly banal, this is a consumer insight executed in an engaging way. This is to reward and allow the discerning middle classes to congratulate themselves at being smart enough to shop at Lidl, find luxurious bargains and avoid wastage at other more expensive supermarkets. The difference between this and regular advertising is that the strategy is never blurted out and the reader is not told to 'Shop a Lidl Smarter' (or some other patronizing campaign line). Similarly, Buzzfeed also worked with the ice cream company Cornetto to develop *18 Stages of Developing a Crush*.[35] By means of humour, photos and gifs this charted the beginning of a crush (being oblivious) to awareness, denial, butterflies, playing it cool, failing to play it cool, regret at seeking advice from friends, courage, rejection and joy.

The article itself does not discuss ice cream, nor ever mention summer, refreshment, rewards or any theme that might usually be associated with a mid-market ice cream brand such as Cornetto. The piece presumably is about a slice of life undergone by all teenagers whom Cornetto wishes to reach. It is less about commodifying crushes than an attempt to ingratiate Cornetto with the BuzzFeed audience, and to position itself is as fun, authentic and capable of empathizing with highs and lows of teenage life. Google also made use of BuzzFeed's services to produce *11 Animals With Privacy Issues*.[36] Featuring a cute cat attempting to hide in a drawer and a little fat owl hiding under a woolly hat, this is a curious piece because Google is clearly aware that privacy is an important topic for its customers. Most obviously Google is associated with using a great deal of information about consumers to target advertising, but it was also involved with the Edward Snowden leaks of 2013 where it was found to have shared users' data with the US National Security Agency. An ongoing objective is thus to win consumers' trust regarding what happens with their data and to make consumers feel they are in control of their data. By using cute animals hiding in a variety of places in the home, this allowed them to promote the functionality of their My Account page that allows people greater control over what they share with others on the web.

Branded entertainment

This merges advertising and entertainment. Despite advertising and marketing being in large part about attracting people to products, branded entertainment does not overtly sell. Instead it presents images of lifestyles, values, themes and interests that reflect the brand. When done right, it can maintain audience interest far beyond the length of a television spot or the seconds given to press and magazine ads. Although much branded entertainment takes the form of cinematic mini-films, it is content that is funded by a brand so therefore might be an event, music, art, a game or anything else that can convey branding. In essence, branded entertainment creates intrigue, deepens experience of layering of brands, extends its value system, is emotionally resonant and self-referential, and potentially creates dialogue between the brand and its consumers. In a sense it is a way for advertisers to tell the story of what a brand represents without having to sell. Examples of branded entertainment include:

- Chanel teaming up with Martin Scorsese to make *BLEU DE CHANEL – The Film*, for their fragrance, Bleu de Chanel (a shorter section was screened as a television commercial);
- Archer's Mark producing *Next Goal Wins* for Nike *and* Adidas about Samoa being officially the worst football team in the world;
- For Hellmanns, OgilvyEntertainment producing *Truckers in the Wild*, an eight-episode series on Vice.com about New York City chefs, brothers and cookbook authors;
- TBWA\Chiat\Day creating a short film called *Lemon Drop* for Absolut Vodka that stars a martial arts heroine fighting to get her kittens back.

Formally, branded entertainment often runs for longer, has better storylines than ads, scope for character development, does not end with a packet shot or campaign line, and requires that we find the content rather than having it pushed at us. Although these types of campaigns do not have the same reach as traditional commercials or online display advertising (fewer people watch them), they grant the capacity to depict the core emotions and experiential truths behind the brand. This is what in Chapter 5 we referred to as *creativity as disclosing*, or understanding of products and brands in both physical dimensions (what they do) and immaterial dimensions (entailing quality, emotion, experience and the cultural significance of those products within the lives of a target market). Further, because they are not overtly ads, they may be picked up by press addressed at trades, interest groups, fan communities and enthusiasts – or even mainstream media.

Virality

The capacity to be likeable and shareable is key to "going viral". This does not happen by chance or even on the strength of the content alone. As discussed in relation to Elihu Katz and "two-step flow", campaigns are carefully seeded with influencers and thereafter tracked by means of likes, shares, retweets, re-posting and online conversation to understand reach, scale, performance and sentiment (whether liked or not). Recently, the not-for-profit sector has had huge wins with Cancer Research's #nomakeupselfie and the ALS Ice Bucket Challenge. The first in 2014 raised more than £8 million for Cancer Research UK in six days as women posted barefaced selfies online. This saw celebrities such as Beyoncé, Rihanna, Cara Delevingne and Cheryl Fernandez-Versini take part in the trend, which spread across Facebook, Instagram and Twitter. While the use of celebrities to highlight good causes is nothing new (somewhat cynically, it provides good PR for the celebrity too), the appeal to authenticity and to literally remove layers of artifice to reveal the real self was a compelling idea. The ALS Ice Bucket Challenge of 2014 encouraged nominated participants to be filmed having a bucket of ice water poured on their heads and then nominating others to do the same. This was to raise funds to research and fight Amyotrophic Lateral Sclerosis (ALS), a progressive neurode-generative disease that affects nerve cells in the brain and the spinal cord. Nominated participants had 24 hours to comply or forfeit by way of a donation to charity. In addition to regular people, the Ice Bucket Challenge saw politicians, celebrities and business leaders take up the challenge, and nominate other public figures. Videoed and shared on social media (and often reported on mainstream media), this provided a degree of intimacy, a reduction of distance between public figure and viewer and, most critically, a very novel and effective marketing tactic to raise revenue for non-profit organizations. In April 2015, the ALS website reported that the campaign generated $115 million. In addition to cash, it generated 17 million videos and 10 billion views by 440 million people. What this campaign helps highlight is the power of viral effects as those who took the challenge were keen to nominate others. This was the key to its success.

There is financial value in authenticity although there is a danger that consumers will see brands as manipulative and dishonest. #LikeAGirl (2014) and *Unstoppable* (2015)[37] by Leo Burnett for Always (that make feminine hygiene/menstrual products) is a good example of a campaign that taps into the zeitgeist, but risks being caught using empowerment as corporate strategy. Respectively, these capitalized on negative language used towards girls and women. The first illustrates the linguistically negative phrase 'like a girl' (such as 'You run like a girl!' or 'Don't cry like a girl!'). The second highlights limitations girls feel are forced on them by society (be these in terms of bravery, musculature, intellect, strength, experimentation, sassiness, speed or argumentation). Elsewhere in the for-profit sector, TMWLimited's *Turn Off To Turn On* for Durex was based on the finding that 60 per cent of people spend more time on their phones in bed than having sex. Durex said it 'couldn't stand aside and let relationships suffer, so we started a mission that fought for change'. The language is telling in that Durex is 'on our side', 'with us', and it is 'campaigning for positive change'.[38] It released a series of statements and videos on YouTube that subsequently captured mass media attention. This campaign also illustrates the utility of earned media by generating 6 million views on YouTube and topping Mashable's viral video chart. By the end of the two-week campaign it received 1.96 billion campaign impressions (when part of the campaign had been seen), 346 million engagements (when someone clicks on part of a campaign) and 85 million video views. It ran through 23 languages in 56 countries.

Metrics still matter

On first consideration viral may appear imprecise because, unlike commercials, it is difficult to pre-empt by whom, and how often, the sponsored communication will be seen. Numbers do matter though, not least because the most popular hosting sites (such as YouTube and Vimeo) count the number of views. Advertisers will also record numbers of shares, likes, retweets and all mentions recordable in the social media environment. More advanced analysis will make use of sentiment analysis to chart not just quantity, but also the quality of discussion taking place around the brand after the release of the commercial. We will discuss analytics in greater depth in Chapter 10, but suffice to say emotional reactions are tracked by means of key words (such as excellent, rubbish, ace, bad). Wieden + Kennedy's 2010 *Old Spice Guy* is arguably the exemplar of how to carry out a viral campaign. While admittedly a few years old, it is the best viral campaign ever. Consider the statistics: it generated 6.7 million views within 24 hours, and 23 million views after 36 hours. This was achieved by seeding the first commercial on sites such as Twitter, Facebook, Reddit, 4Chan[39] and blogs. This featured a parody of masculinity, Old Spice Guy (Isaiah Mustafa), asking women whether they would want their men to smell like him. He also invited questions from the online community. This is when the real work began as Wieden + Kennedy created a bathroom film set and had Old Spice Guy (Isaiah Mustafa) reply to 186 online comments.

The campaign ran for three days and included 87 short video responses (as well as tweets and other messages). While clearly hard work, the return was extraordinary and deserving of its Grand Prix at the Cannes International Advertising Festival. Questions came from

Fig 6.1

Old Spice Guy

celebrities (such as Alyssa Milano) and fans asking questions such as, 'If there was an epic battle between you and a rabid lion, who would end up looking better after?' Old Spice Guy even engaged in matrimonial duties when a fan named Johannes S. Beals tweeted, 'Can U Ask my girlfriend to marry me? Her name is Angela A. Hutt-Chamberlin' to Old Spice. In response a video appeared up on YouTube within an hour, and Old Spice tweeted it at Beals.[40] In return people tweeted, shared, posted and linked to the videos across their social networks. Old Spice Guy did not respond to everyone, but behind the scenes were social media specialists tracking who had written the comments and, perhaps more importantly, what their influence was and which comments had the most potential in helping create engaging content. Another dimension to this campaign is that Old Spice's marketing team allowed Wieden + Kennedy to literally write and share advertising in real time. Compare this with traditional advertising where advertisers (clients and agencies alike) seek to rigidly control all aspects of the advertising process. By means of trust in the agency, Wieden + Kennedy were able to begin repositioning the brand, maximize engagement, grow intimacy with users and enjoy authentic interaction with communities. While one might question whether this was manipulation of an online community, for the campaign to work real-time writers *had* to come from the same lived context of people who enjoy a juvenile but brilliantly surreal sense of humour.

Opportunities in virtual reality 2.0

A book about digital media should be allowed a little indulgence to peer a few years into the future. People spend time with non-interruptive advertising and branded content on the basis that it is engaging. New modes of virtual reality (VR) provide brands with a unique way of imparting their values, storytelling and product information. The mid-2010s has seen a renewed interest in virtual reality through much online conversation about headgear from Oculus Rift, Samsung's GearVR and Google's less expensive Cardboard that allowed people to insert their phones into a cardboard with optics to be able to view stereoscopic content on their Android phones. This provides a convincing sense of what virtual reality can deliver today. The most notable feature is a strong sense of telepresence, or the sense of being at a location other than where the physical body is located (Manovich, 2003). Usage of these technologies means users suspend engagement with real life and rather than sitting and watching a piece of entertainment, VR users need space to move around, turn, bend, crawl, look up and leap. Again, sense of presence is key to understanding VR and it is not hyperbole to suggest that in-world simulations (realistic and otherwise) may be more affective (emotionally engaging) than experiences in real space.

Critically for brands, the experience has potential to be deeply impactful because in-world storytelling quite literally moves the self and the body (if an in-world character approaches, a person's physical body will react). Although dependent on storytelling, narrative and the technical adeptness of the ad-makers, VR provides a level of spatial engagement, visceral closeness and emotional stimulation unrivalled by other media. Further, given that the business of advertising is largely about attention, a person is utterly committed to the VR experience. This is unlike other media where other environmental factors reduce screen and audio attention. Engagement with in-world actors is also of a highly different nature from other media, particularly if that avatar is programmed to interact with the user and the ad-experience allows in-world user input. One might also note that because attention is fully mediated, all in-world behaviour and points of interest can be captured for advertisers and media owners. This presents us with a novel take on behavioural advertising.

Creating advertising content for VR is different from both television and the web because of the sense of immersion within the environment. While presaged by cinema and gaming, the sense of being inside an environment is much more pronounced. Whereas branded content has allowed creatives to fashion self-referential films without logos, packet shots and hard sell messages, VR promises branded experiences within 3D/360-degree environments. There are some significant characteristics to note, not least that a sense of immediacy is generated by the following:

▸ 360-degree wrap-around imagery that feels like a Star Trek holodeck, whereby the user is transported to another world;
▸ Closer relationships with in-world objects (when things are heading towards the user it feels like an object is really approaching);
▸ The user can be up close and personal with characters in the narrative;
▸ VR content producers can convey a true sense of being at live events (such as gigs, sports events, or meetings with celebrities or influencers);
▸ Potential for suits and gloves that provide tactile feedback. This allows the body itself to be a controller and participant in virtual world (rather than just VR viewing). The end goal for haptic feedback suits is to have lifelike in-world sensations so, for example, stroking an in-world cat feels like stroking a real-world cat.

Although many brands are rushing to inhabit VR, Nike, Coca Cola and Budweiser were early to explore these opportunities. For example, in *The Neymar Jr. Effect*, Nike used a point-of-view perspective of the Brazilian football (soccer) ace as he unpicks the defence of a rival team. The ad benefits from a sense of immersion in that the viewer can turn, look at fellow players, see what the goalkeeper is doing, see the reactions of team mates and opponents, and look at the crowds in the stadium stands. Apparently the ad includes a number of inside jokes and even a streaker, but I did not find those! Coca Cola's is a Spanish language ad overlaid with Coca Cola's 'For the Very First Time' song (sung in English). Created to celebrate the 100th anniversary of its iconic bottle design this is based in what appears to be a warehouse with a diverse range of characters (cooks, dancers and film stars all happily dancing around the building and the viewer). It is early days yet for VR in advertising, but already there are lessons that can be discerned about the medium and how it may be best used. My thoughts include:

▸ Ideas still matter: how is the overall brand message being advanced?
▸ How can the affordances of VR be used to provide people compelling experiences they will engage with more than once?
▸ VR users are not viewers. How can they interact with the brand and the created environment?
▸ How can the emotional layers of a brand be rendered in-world? In-world experiences do not have to be literal images of brand icons (be these bottles or football boots). As with BuzzFeed's native advertising, existing brands can use the fact that people already understand the values of a brand so as to be freed to create less obvious representations. These will be more affective because they can stimulate emotions without being an obvious "sell".

Conclusion

The task for non-interruptive approaches is to generate attention (nothing new there), credibility, authenticity, meaningful engagement and willingness for people to share content within their own peer networks. Although search, display and classified digital advertising receive higher levels of expenditure, non-interruptive content is more imaginative. It reflects the premise that advertising does not always have to be launched *at* people. Clearly non-interruptive and branded entertainment tactics are not appropriate for all clients. They better suit those seeking to invest in their brands and reputations, and who want to enrich emotional connections consumers have with products and related brand attributes (such as logos, designs, characters). Beyond opportunities, advertisers and their agencies are aware that trust levels in traditional advertising are dwindling, and most people prefer product recommendations from respected others, friends and family. The suggestion that advertisers are all-powerful is not something that the industry believes, particularly as it works to capture dwindling attention time. Non-interruptive techniques are a key attempt to fly under the sceptic's radar to win perceptions of credibility and authenticity.

Think points and questions

▸ Where do you sit on the polar possibilities of participatory culture? Liberatory or exploitative?
▸ Using the list of interactivity types provided, how interactive is your favourite digital advertising?
▸ Provide three examples of earned media not discussed in this chapter.
▸ Do native advertisers overstep the mark regarding editorial and the ASA requirement that ads 'must be obviously identifiable'?

7   Media Hacking

Historically the tools of art directors and copywriters were very simple, often just involving pencils, marker pens and A3-sized pieces of paper. Teams would sit down to identify precisely what the proposition is (what does the product do and/or what is the benefit to consumers). The task was then to distil this insight into a clear identifiable message, and then communicate this in an attractive and influential way. This involved the principle of economy to communicate 'clearly, quickly, simply, relevantly' (Barry, 2008: 19). In this arrangement, media has a somewhat blank character. It is seen as a delivery mechanism through which suggestions are encoded, and subsequently decoded and acted upon by receivers. By ignoring the properties of media, campaigns have traditionally followed more or less the same pattern in terms of media choice, which media to privilege and which should act as ancillary vehicles. At a creative level, the fault does not lie with people working in creative departments because they receive creative briefs that prescribe what the objective of the advertising is, who it should speak to, what tone of voice is required and which media they should be designing for. In other words, media are typically a strategic decision that takes place elsewhere because the choice of media (which dictates the nature of engagement with the advertising) tends to be decided by either media planners and/or the client's marketing team. Budget, advertising goal, type of message, audience receptivity/location, minimization of waste on uninterested people and cost effectiveness inform this decision. This means the scope for creativity with media is limited and (as highlighted in Chapter 5) while creative teams may bend the strategic direction of the advertising, they are less likely to design for a totally different medium than that prescribed. In sum, historically: *creativity tends to be associated with the message rather than the means by which it is transmitted.*

This chapter examines what happens when media are re-imagined and creatively put to work. Put otherwise, how can digital media be leveraged, transformed and played with to create experiences that suit an advertiser's particular brand and the overall message that is to be communicated? I pay particular attention to the use of non-standard media (or media not intended for advertising) and how they can be hacked and repurposed. This has traces of what in Chapter 5 we discussed as transformational creativity. This is to switch from hooking, attention and delivery of messages to audiences, to engagement that includes innovative use of media. Importantly, this engagement surpasses the few seconds usually granted to traditional media so as to provide opportunity for deep branding (exploration and unpacking of values).

Requirements for media hacking

This involves what elsewhere I have referred to as the 'poetics of media' (McStay, 2013): knowledge and sensitivity to media, their properties and how they can artfully be used to stimulate particular experiences. If this appears vague, then consider that:

▸ Painters know their paints and canvases;
▸ Potters know their clays and glazes;
▸ Clothes designers know their fabrics and fasteners;
▸ Sculptors know their stones, metals, woods, carving tools, moulds and fires;
▸ Architects know space and materials, and will shape experiences for inhabitants;
▸ Computer hackers know hardware, software, code and that the internet is essentially a multi-pathway transmission of electrical signals.

Each of the creative practitioners above is able to use properties of their media to help them achieve their goals and communicate better. Following these examples, it makes sense that creatives in the business of communication should not only understand the content that is to be communicated, but that they have should have deep familiarity with how their own media affect and enhance messages. My point is that there is nothing especially new about media hacking, because the link between media, materiality and creativity is not new. After all, mastery of materials and processes is essential for any other trade or art. To add to this, my suggestion is not just that creatives should understand media, but that they should also be able to *hack* media. This is the same principle of bisociation we met in Chapter 5 where we discussed culture hacking (typographic styles, photography, film, art history, music, literature, or any cultural object that can be combined with other signs to generate novel effects for advertising). The same can be said of media technologies and the experiences they help create – all can be used in different contexts, and manipulated for goals that the medium in question was not intended for. In a digital context, non-interruptive approaches often involve repurposing media platforms, technologies and tools found elsewhere, and where appropriate even creation of non-standard media. This might include music platforms, maps, location sensitivity, installations, video players, web media, graphic design software and social media sites. These are not just used to *deliver* advertising messages (where media are seen as a channel or blank vehicle), but instead media are *instrumental to the message* itself. This is to think about media in less simplistic terms. The origin of media theory is synonymous with the work of Shannon and Weaver (1949). They were engineers and mathematicians working on telecommunications. They framed the nature of communication in terms of a sender (for instance, Sarah), an encoder (such as a telephone), a channel (telephone line), and noise (where voices converted into wave signals meet faults on the line that get in the way of fully effective communication), a decoder (telephone) and a receiver (Ali). This is a deceptively simplistic way of thinking about communication and while not incorrect at an interpersonal level, from the point of advertising it leads one to believe that advertising is about encoding the right message to be decoded at the other end. If only it were so easy! The reality is that people have different types of relationships with different media, media have different properties, and some communications work better through some media than others. Traditional media planners have always known this and their job is to select the best blend of media for an advertiser's goals. However, we can go a step further to involve the creative department in media decisions. This involves media hacking, or pushing formats beyond what they were built for; and coordinating them so media intermingle, interact and inform each other. While interesting, I suspect by now we are in need of some examples to put some flesh on the theory. Read on.

Case example of creative media hacking: B-Reel

Lauded by websites such as inc.com as the agency that is changing advertising and obliterating the line between selling and entertainment, B-Reel has produced a roster of work respected throughout the advertising industry. Neither a traditional advertising agency nor a media production company, it acts as a creative partner for companies such as Google, Volvo, Spotify, Virgin, Ford and more, but also works with traditional agencies such as BBH (on work for clients such as Barclays, Google and Mentos). The B-Reel homepage highlights it is 'a team of storytellers and technologists creating new ways to connect brands and audiences'. Its work exemplifies the blurring nature of advertising today because little of it is aimed *at* people, but rather it is seeded, shared and referred. As a company it is symptomatic of a shift in the advertising business. Rather than simply realizing the Pentel-enabled visions of agency creatives, B-Reel's combination of skills has granted it greater autonomy for media innovation than is typically the case with advertising. This opening up to new actors is as it should be because as the nature of paid-for communication alters in reaction to new media and new audience behaviour, it makes sense that new actors will come to the fore to redefine the nature of advertising, sponsored communication and commercial influence. Its clients are also less prescriptive. Anders Wahlquist, one of the five Swedish founders of the company, recounts that one client said: 'We want something that's never been done before and that is going to make our brand the coolest thing on Earth.'[41] If this is not an open brief, then what is? Note, too, companies the size of Google are opting to work directly with B-Reel, so there is no agency intermediary between client and production. B-Reel's most famous work to date is *The Wilderness Downtown*, an interactive film produced in 2010 by Google Creative Labs and B-Reel director Chris Milk.[42]

The purpose of the film was to promote Google's nascent Chrome browser, which people in the technology community were using, but which was failing to attract mass attention. By creating engaging content best viewed on Chrome, people would download it. The "film" opens by asking the user for the street address where they grew up. After loading, with Arcade Fire (an indie rock band) playing in the background, the first window opens depicting a young person running along a street. Utilizing both Google Street View and Maps, other windows on the user's computer open, and it becomes clear that the street the character is running down is the street of our youth. Use of Street View and Maps means both aerial and street-level images are obtained and as the camera zooms and rotates (synchronized with the camera in the other windows), we realize the youth is heading towards our former home. Not only are Google tools opened, but flying birds and rapidly growing trees also overlay them. The campaign's cachet was confirmed by the "film" not being pushed, but shared via Twitter, Facebook and influential blogs such as Gizmodo.

Discussing this campaign and more, I met with Alex Jenkins, Creative Director from the London Office of B-Reel. Despite B-Reel being an agency renowned for digital and technical creativity, Alex highlights that what is important in advertising (be this traditional, digital and earned media) is still narrative, character, stories, storytelling and capacity for affect, or to move people. Although the link between Google's brand and the campaign is not clear, the film is moving, engaging and evocative. Far from being a dinosaur of the *Mad Men* era, and clearly possessing expertise in digital media, he was keen to highlight that advertising remains less about media and still very much more about ideas. I was surprised at the adherence to Ogilvy's "Big Ideas" (discussed in Chapter 5), not least because of recent trends towards small reactive ideas, and quick tactics over bigger strategy. The interest in ideas is less about repetition of industry rhetoric than a sincere belief that media exist to enable myth making, storytelling, impression making and practice of branding, and that media alone should not be fetishized. The principle of media hacking is thus not a swing to media determinacy, but an extension and understanding of how digital tools can assist myth making and spinning branded narratives. More examples might help consolidate the effectiveness of media hacking and campaigns that rewire media at fundamental levels to work in their favour.

B-Reel's work for Microsoft, that promotes the Xbox One game, *Sunset Overdrive*, is based in a dystopian future where most of humanity has been transformed into mutants having drunk the tainted fizzy drink 'OverCharge Delirium XT'. The teaser campaign for the game entailed creation of a secretive alternate reality game beginning with a hidden glitch in a television commercial run in the UK and US. Working with McCann London, B-Reel created an online journey beginning with a broadcast from Floyd, a rogue scientist from FizzCo, pleading for players' help in exposing the sinister truth lurking within this seemingly innocent drink. Players became detectives as they sought clues that on being found led to even more clues. These were scattered over LinkedIn pages, blogs, inside Photoshop files and Soundcloud audio clips, on CCTV footage, and even required calling up the FizzCo offices. The search lasted for 5 days and 21 hours before the game was won and FizzCo's secrets were uncovered. As gamers are a notoriously hard (but potentially loyal) community to reach, commercials or standard linear advertising (where consumers are talked *at*) would not have worked. The campaign had to be social, it had to be non-linear and it had to have engagement baked in to the campaign.

The innovative use of media is further illustrated by B-Reel's campaign for Disney's film, *Guardians of the Galaxy*. This begins with a very generic online travel ad for 'Galaxy Getaways' depicting sunny beaches and clinking champagne glasses. Viewers are disturbed on being told that these 'look like shit compared to the rest of the galaxy'. On watching the rest of the ad depicting various fictional places across the universe, the user is encouraged to explore these fictional hotspots via Google Street View. Indeed, by means of entering your postcode into Google Maps, Galaxy Getaways even sends a spaceship to pick you up. While on holiday we pick up travel tips, local knowledge about worlds we visit, and play a mini-game and take quizzes on 'Which type of galactic traveller are you?'

Re-imagining stories with hacked media

Droga5 deftly used technology to assist in storytelling for headphone manufacturer Beats. Tallying with UK electronic band Rudimental's nomination for two Brit awards in 2014, the agency created a film to explain the process Rudimental went through to create its most popular track, Powerless. Importantly, this film had a strong storyline based on inception to resolution through depiction of how the song came together; characters, in the form of getting to know how Rudimental was formed; and background *mise-en-scène* in terms of cultural context (Hackney, raves, incidents, and the London Drum and Bass scene). Launched online, this video provided an intimate backstory to Rudimental and strong branding for Beats. Fans were rewarded because the storyline was told across six videos. Each of these contained elements that can be played and mixed simultaneously via a custom YouTube player. This allowed fans to control the YouTube page as if it was a sound-mixing desk.

A campaign by Google from 2012 (working with Johannes Leonardo and Grow Interactive) further illustrates the point about interconnection. The idea for this was to show the advertising industry the potential in online and mobile display advertising. To do this it re-imagined Alka Seltzer's famous commercial where the central actor, Ralph (Milt Moss), continuously groans, 'I can't believe I ate the whole thing.' Whereas the original commercial harnessed the properties of television (mass reach, audio-visual messaging and simultaneity of experience of the ad among its target audience), Google demonstrated affordances of newer forms of media. In the US, the 1970s version became a viral success of sorts around dinner tables in its own right because of the universal feeling of having overeaten and the experience of actually eating 'the whole thing'. The campaign went on to feature in the board game Trivial Pursuit and *The Simpsons*, and the line 'I can't believe I ate the whole thing' is listed as one of the ten best quotes of the 1970s by *Newsweek*. The commercial was also elected into the Clio Hall of Fame (a significant US award for outstanding advertising work). Its success was demonstrated by the fact that Alka Seltzer became synonymous with being the cure for indigestion and heartburn.

There are some key fundamental differences between the original and the 2012 version, not least that one has to download an app (iOS/Android) to experience 'the whole thing'. Framed as a 1970s sitcom, the new version shows a series of short episodes following Ralph's day over breakfast, lunch and dinner that leads up to the end of the day and Ralph's famous line. Each experience of the ad is tailored for the viewer by means of changing the video story according to location, time of the day, weather or the context of the user's app. For example, if the user is in New York, they might see Ralph drive through Time Square while those in Chicago would see landmarks there. The commercial contained content based on time of the day, visuals and words spoken which changed depending on the viewer's own weather at the time of viewing (or what was referred to in Chapter 6 as heterogeneous media experience). Elements of the ad also changed based on the viewer's interests so, for example, when Ralph receives a package from a delivery guy, the content of the package changes accordingly (for example board games or a cutlery set). Users could also interact directly with Ralph, so when Ralph and another character in the ad disagree about a song, the user could step in and select a song type. So, if a love song, the characters will go on to a share a tender-hearted moment. When Ralph needs waking up, iPhone users are able to shake their phone (and its accelerometer) so to rouse Ralph. During Ralph's birthday dinner, users can also affect the narrative of the commercial by knocking on their phones, which knocks on the window of Ralph's home. Each of the possible narratives leads up to Ralph groaning, 'I can't believe I ate the whole thing' – an experience most have been able to relate to.

Mixed reality and transmedia

Transmedia storytelling remains a key theme for sponsored communication in the social sphere. Alex Jenkins from B-Reel highlighted that transmedia approaches tend to be used by advertisers that know what they want, who are keen to work closely with their agencies and, at least in the case of B-Reel, are already media and technology companies (B-Reel has produced promotional work with Google for its browser, calendar, Glass, Maps and email services, and is also working with Tumblr and WhatsApp). In many ways transmedia storytelling shares formal similarities with integrated approaches to marketing where communication about brands is relayed across a broad array of media, including offline. Advertisers' usage of transmedia storytelling intends to facilitate brand involvement at a much deeper level. Important aspects of the advertising may be dispersed and fragmented across different media texts, or be experienced on different platforms (such as televisions, phones and tablets, and games, social media, forums and apps accessed through these devices). Key characteristics follow traditional storytelling in that worlds or settings should be immersive, characters should be engaging, the story should have an arc of some sort and should not date (as with the Alka Seltzer example). The strength of a strong emotional base, situations we can relate to, human truths, a story with a clear internal logic and identifiable actors allows scope for engaging non-linearity, audience interactivity and open-ended meaning. The key feature of much of this non-interruptive work using media hacking is that it does not allow the user to simply undergo a passive experience, but it requires that users become part of the story in interesting, personal and emotionally engaging ways.

So far we have discussed media hacking and interactivity in terms of screens, manipulation of content and experience. This is to miss a vital characteristic of networked life – it is increasingly embedded in everyday experience with its streets, bricks, people and breathable air. A small agency in Cardiff (Wales, UK) called Yellobrick created a self-initiated (not for a named brand) street game called *Reverie*.[43] This project was a showcase for the company to demonstrate to potential clients what is possible, to trial Yellobrick's work, and show what Yellobrick can do (it ended up winning significant business for the agency). The street game mixes digital technologies with theatre to create immersive events with character and open-ended narratives. This involves collaborative storytelling in that the nature of the event is dictated by people joining in and co-creating the event. Yellobrick's work is a bisociation of education, backgrounds and careers (one of the company founders has a theatrical background and the other was in graphic design and technology). This is fascinating because the removal of the fourth wall that divides audience from theatrical performance is also tantamount to removing the medium (the screen). Seen otherwise, *the brand itself becomes the medium* through which mixed-reality stories unfold. As technologies have properties and allow certain things to happen, a brand also has a make-up, logic and properties that influence narratives.

Yellobrick's mixed-reality game, *Reverie*, demonstrates a range of storytelling devices by which audiences could experience the narrative through digital *and* physical forms. It makes use of street-gaming (where events take place on real streets), online storytelling technology (including social media, blogs, RFID systems, telephones and text messages). Purposefully disorienting and unclear, the story begins:

> Beyond wake and sleep lies a place tangled with sweet reveries and twisted nightmares. A place where we find ourselves lost, victims of our vivid imaginations and memories. Reality is altered and dark-ness falls. Lost in reverie will you ever wake up? Only one man has the answer. Tom Watson.

> Get ready for an experience that will stretch you to your limits. Listen, play, explore and RUN... Run like your soul depended on it.

The *Reverie* website explains that to build excitement and expecta-tion, online content was published four weeks before the live event. This was communicated over Twitter and a website with an internal blog. Participants were asked to hack into the blog by deciphering a code displayed on all *Reverie* branding. The blog led to weekly video updates, which introduced two characters and extended the rules of the story world. By immersing oneself in the pre-event online narra-tive (where much of the story remained unclear), this led to a richer experience for the live event itself which took place across 12 locations in Cardiff Bay. This combined online multi-platform storytelling, mobile and RFID technologies. Yellobrick timed phone calls and text messages, and intertwined these with the RFID system, to allow for location-based instructions and storylines to be fed to players during the experience.

There are a number of creative principles and theories we can develop out of this theatrical marketing for Yellobrick's services, not least that the production itself is the marketing act. This is a deviation from standard modes of creating marketing/advertising material where the finished product appears to have arrived fully formed from nowhere, i.e. with no indication of the means by which it has been constructed. Whereas traditional above-the-line advertising is about control of messages and per thousands of populations reached, mixed-reality sponsored events mean that the commercial event is not a finished polished piece, but an occasion where the act of branding occurs as the event takes place. It is highly uncontrolled because the event depends on engagement by people, which in turn, invites unanticipated situations. While one might reasonably argue this requires brave clients, Yellobrick argues that statistics presented to clients hide lies (for example: did 150,000 passing people *really* engage with the bus shelter ad?).

Reverie has a postmodern character to it in that it emphasizes the construction of its own making. By this, there is no created artefact, but only the mixed-reality event, and subsequent chatter on social media and reporting by mass media. A key characteristic of mixed-reality events is expertise in digital methods, but also theatrical management. This entails tight integration of online (email/social media), offline, mobile, RFID, staged interventions, letter mail through the post (tactile experience), interruption, depiction of story-worlds, convergent cultures (multiple ways to enter the story), retention of physical experience (which tends to be lost in PC/console gaming), new social connections in real life and new ways to discover cities. Digital techniques have for some time blurred the distinction between advertising, public relations (PR) and marketing communications, but mixed-reality campaigns challenge the principle of communication itself as they collapse the distinction between medium and message, or even media and reality.

The role of play

Mixed-reality events and augmented storytelling whereby created narratives overlay the real world often entail play and gamification. This is the way that storytellers, advertisers and marketers can make use of the fact that people enjoy competing, achieving, being surprised, discovering, learning and being rewarded. Linking well with mixed-reality events, playing is also the suspension of normal life for another reality and set of conventions (Caillois, 2001 [1958]). This reality is pleasurable, but containing uncertain outcomes – often dictated by competition and attempts to outwit others (be they people or machines). Play is also something that is voluntary, cannot be forced, is not a task, is done at leisure, involves separation from everyday life, has a defined duration and is predicated on freedom (Huizinga, 1955 [1938]).

A more familiar example of this is from 2010 when Volkswagen and its agency, AlmapBBDO, based a campaign around the hashtag #FoxatPlanetaTerra to send players on a good old treasure hunt, albeit with a few media hacking and mixed-reality twists. To find festival tickets hidden in ten different places around the city, players had to use the hashtag #FoxatPlanetaTerra. The more they collectively tweeted about the VW Fox at the festival, the closer Google Maps would zoom in on the location of the tickets. Twitter users called on other Twitter uses to forward the hashtag so Google Maps would zoom towards the tickets. While the idea of a treasure hunt is not especially novel, although it is unusual in an advertising context, #FoxatPlanetaTerra became a trending topic on Twitter within two hours, remaining there for the duration of the four-day campaign. In addition to the playful, gaming and mixed-reality nature of the campaign, it is noteworthy that it employs media hacking and an interconnective/ecological approach.

Key theorization

As we progress towards the end of this chapter, it is useful to tease out core principles. Theorization is the formulation of principles that can be applied elsewhere, and while many creatives claim not to 'do' theory, they do, but they may not realize it. From the examples above we can deduce numerous take-away points for either academic study of campaigns, or campaign development itself:

▸ *Media hacking*: understanding of how media technology affects and enhances messages. This principle highlights that creatives are not only in the business of creating content, but also, today, of how media can be used (particularly non-standard media opportunities);

▶ *Non-interruption*: media hacking techniques frequently draw upon non-interruptive approaches. Rather than use media properties to grab attention, they aim for deep branding, and emotional connection between consumer and product/brand attributes;

▶ *Temporality* (or questions about time and experience): the emphasis on pull-based creativity in the creative digital sector can lead one to assume that agencies do not have to fight as hard for attention. The reverse is true. As agencies compete online with free content (professional and self-published), and sponsored communication (seeking to "go viral"), the attention time left for ads dwindles. While tactics may gain attention, compelling ideas are still required to sell;

▶ *Prosumerism*: one of the key features of much of this advertising is that it involves 'prosumerism' (Ritzer and Jurgenson, 2010). This word describes a situation where it is unclear who is the producer and who is the consumer. Applied to a creative advertising context, audiences become part of the story and assist in creation of the advertising;

▶ *Behavioural targeting* need not equate to banal and poor creative content (as is currently the case), but can be used to enhance storytelling (as with Ralph and Alka Seltzer). There is no necessary separation between technologists and traditional modes of mythmaking in advertising;

▶ *Homogenous experience over heterogeneous media experience*: this is the distinction between when each viewer receives the same content (homo) from one in which in creative content takes personalized forms by means of behavioural data and filters (hetero);

▶ *Transmediation*: this allows for greater audience involvement across different media texts and platforms (e.g. televisions, phones and tablets). The key point is that media are not used as channels to deliver the same message but that the range of media employed are used to seed different parts of the story to make a larger whole;

▶ *Non-interruptive approaches* may be ecological and interconnective in that elements of a campaign will mutually reinforce one another to become more than the sum of their parts;

▶ *Interactivity*: as highlighted in Chapter 6, this is not about fetishizing buttons and technology, but rather is the means by which interaction, engagement and immersion is enhanced. This includes the capacity to influence the narrative, what happens in ads and to have ongoing relationships with characters in ads (in the case of Ralph, oddly, by linking on Google+).

The essence, then, of media hacked digital advertising is less about technology than type and quality of engagement. This breaks old truisms. Traditionally advertising is an exercise in synthesis and the distillation of clear unique ideas so as to communicate with an audience using off-the-shelf media in an extremely short period of time. Although propositions and clear thinking are still required to identify a benefit, thought, value, emotion and impression ad-writers want to leave consumers with, *temporally* this has changed. The word "temporality" refers to time and experience, and this is a key difference in both non-interruptive and media hacked digital advertising. Rather than existing in a push-based environment where messages have to jostle for a few seconds of attention (in commercials, on billboards, on radio, in magazines and so on), a pull-based digital environment means attention time is theoretically limitless (particularly if a service is provided).

Conclusion

Although ideas, storytelling, character, personality, humour, subversion and strategy (and bucking strategy) remain longstanding interests for creative advertisers, the media environment *is* changing. This does not mean that we should obsess about new waves of media and technologies to the extent that we miss the communication itself, but that we should pay attention to the roles that technology plays. Media are *not* simply channels through which an idea is conveyed. Instead they are tools whose affordances can help tell a story and breathe life into products and companies to turn them into brands. The problem with seeing media as channels and as separate from ideas is that opportunities are missed. B-Reel's work exemplifies what can be achieved by seeing non-standard media as ingredients integral to the final creative output. As depicted, all other art forms require that artists know and manipulate their tools, and advertising is no different. Some of the most interesting agencies see this and are actively bisociating and hacking both culture and media to generate strategically sound but original work. This is also exemplified by work for Alka Seltzer by Google, Johannes Leonardo and Grow Interactive which harnesses a wide range of media opportunities, yet stays true to the story.

Think points and questions

Select a commercial that you remember from your childhood. How might you "re-imagine it", as was done with Alka Seltzer's *I Ate the Whole Thing*? Consider:

▸ What is media hacking?
▸ What media might you 'hack' to use in unexpected ways?
▸ How might behavioural targeting (opted into) be used to enhance your campaign?
▸ How will you balance the opportunities of heterogeneous behavioural targeting with the need for branding and rich storytelling?

8   Adblocking and Fraud: Threats to Advertising

Despite the fact that data-powered digital advertising promises accountability and clear returns on investment, there are two spectres in the digital closet: adblocking and click fraud. Adblocking is the use of software to remove ads. Click fraud is when a malicious actor uses software or manually repeatedly clicks on an ad they have no interest in to use up an advertiser's budget. Together, these challenges pose real threats to digital advertising increasingly reliant on third-party tracking and programmatic means. This chapter explores the scale of adblocking and click fraud, key actors, the ethical debate surrounding the use of adblockers, and the legal status of adblocking software.

Web adblocking

The reason why people use adblocking services such as AdBlock is that ads are often interruptive, poorly targeted and raise concerns about privacy. A report written by Adobe and PageFair, and published by PageFair (2014) illustrates the scale of adblocking. It highlights that in the second financial quarter of 2014[44] there were approximately 144 million monthly active AdBlock users globally. This equates to 4.9 per cent of all internet users – a number that represents an increase of 69 per cent between Q2 2013 and Q2 2014. Further, AdBlock adoption is global. For example Poland, Sweden, Denmark and Greece on average had 24 per cent of their online populations using adblocking software in Q2 2014. Countries such as Japan, Spain, China and Italy are catching up. The percentage of their online populations using AdBlock plugins grew as much as 134 per cent between Q2 2013 and Q2 2014.

It is useful to recognize who is adblocking. For example 54 per cent and 31 per cent of women between 18 and 29 years said they use adblocking software. Younger people surveyed were far more likely to use adblocking software. Thus, although the initial figure of 4.9 per cent of all internet users is not cause for alarm for Adland, the younger demographic is. Over half of people surveyed found out about adblocking from someone they knew. Motives for adblocking are mixed, with the majority (45 per cent) not wanting to view any advertising online. Others expressed privacy concerns (17 per cent) in regard to third-party tracking and a wish to remove 'ads that seem to know what websites I visit'. A key point for publishers is that 80 per cent of people surveyed are unwilling to pay for ad-free content. This is complicated by the finding that 61 per cent of the same respondents were 'completely unwilling' to see ads that support free content. However, notably, 30 per cent of users were open to non-intrusive advertising (text and still ads were preferred). Ads containing animations and sounds were disliked. Specific formats considered intrusive were popovers, interstitials and non-skippable video ads.

In the UK 15 per cent of British adults online currently use adblocking software, while 22 per cent have downloaded the software at some point. As with international statistics, there is a notable gender split because men are currently more than twice as likely to block ads as women (22 versus 9 per cent). At 34 per cent, 18–24 year olds are most likely to block ads. At 80 per cent, most are using adblocking software on laptops, 46 per cent on desktop PCs, and 19 per cent on tablets or mobiles. IAB (2015), who commissioned the UK research, found that 52 per cent of those who have used adblockers said their main motivation was to block all ads, while 12 per cent said it was to block certain types of ads and 11 per cent said it was only to block ads from certain websites. Ads are most likely to be blocked because: they are interruptive (73 per cent); the design can be annoying (55 per cent); ads slow down users' web browsing experience (54 per cent); ads aren't relevant (46 per cent); and there are privacy concerns (31 per cent). These findings point out that people do not reject advertising per se, but do reject intrusive advertising. The lesson from this for advertisers is a need to genuinely work with users to allow them control, to create non-intrusive advertising, to raise the game creatively and to make commercial communication that people want to engage with. This is possible because many people adblocking who were surveyed are not anti-advertising per se, but seek greater control over their online experience.

AdBlock Plus

The expression "adblocking" is slightly incorrect because what it actually does is to block online display advertising techniques that people find intrusive and do not like. The intention for adblocking companies is to allow users to experience the internet as they want it. The most popular is called Adblock Plus, made by a company called Eyeo GmbH. The idea of screening out ads is not new. After all, many us will make cups of tea or coffee, brush teeth, or go for a "comfort break" while a television ad break is on. Those born in the analogue era will remember fast-forwarding ads on video and those born digital may have skipped ads with TiVo. Dislike of display ads aside, there are some good reasons to block them. Ads and trackers loaded from multiple *third parties* require time and processing power that can dramatically slow load time of webpages (and use CPU power). The term "third parties" refers to when ads on phones, tablets or PCs are not placed there by the owner of the page a user is browsing, but by another organization – an advertising network that serves ads on behalf of web publishers (see Chapter 3 for more on ad networks). This means that when a user is a browsing a webpage with third-party ads, their device is actually communicating with more than one computer because the desired content of the webpage comes from one machine and the ads that are served on the page come from elsewhere. This costs battery power and internet bandwidth because of extra information travelling to and from machines. There is, of course, the privacy dimension of the data economy where trackers share data about readers to increase ad revenue. We will address the principle of privacy in Chapter 12, but it is worth considering the business dimension of ad revenues. An article for TechCrunch[45] points out that annual online media spend in the United States reached $51 billion in 2014. This represents the total amount of money spent by advertisers on online advertising. While this *is* a large amount of money, it equates to around $170 per person per annum (on the somewhat large assumption that all US citizens are online).[46] This is a significant amount, but this breaks down to $14.17 a month. Phrased otherwise, the entire infrastructure of online advertising and data mining that supports "free" media content could be replaced by a 10–20% increase in internet subscription fees or mobile phone bills. As the article continues, the increase may not need to be this high because our monthly fee only needs to replace the revenues received by publishers of websites and services, not the expenses of the online ad and data industry. In sum, the answer to how much our online privacy is worth (monthly) is less than $14.17 (USD), $18.55 (AUD) £9.27 (GBP), ¥1773.96 (Yen), €12.71 (Euro) or 0.0632 in Bitcoin.

Adblock Plus was released in 2006, although the digital advertising industry has been relatively quiet on this issue, possibly mindful that loud criticism of the plugin would raise people's awareness of it. In 2015 Adblock Plus was released for Android mobile phone browsers. The appeal for users is immediate because, as mentioned, ads are frequently slow to load and use up a phone's power. To this end Adblock claims its service will save up to 23 per cent of a smartphone's battery life. The ad industry has responded by highlighting that this will damage its bottom line (mobile represents £1 in every £6 spent on digital advertising). Although one can see obvious appeal in ridding our screens of unwanted display advertising, there are arguments to be made against it. The first is that adblockers hold the ad business to ransom. The second is that publishers that rely on behaviourally targeted advertising worry that adblocking undermines their revenue model. The third is the stifling of new sites and start-up services that are dependent on advertising as a means of generating revenue.

In theory, if advertising revenues are removed, all that is left are subscription-only services. This is something that only large corporations are good at building, rather than small start-ups that can use advertising to generate funds for new apps and services. While there is some truth in this, this argument assumes that start-ups (whether apps, a new social media service, mobile taxi service or an online newspaper) have access to a large user base with which to generate ad revenue. This tends to not be the case when firms are starting up so the actual revenue generated by ads is extremely small and not enough to sustain a company. Instead, start-ups require investment to help them grow as quickly as possible so as to be self-sustaining.

Further, Adblock Plus does not block all ads, but it keeps a "whitelist" of websites that are allowed to serve ads despite the presence of the Adblock Plus plugin. This is the revenue source for the business: if an advertiser meets the Acceptable Ads standard and pays, it is allowed past the blocker's filters. Evidence of concern about adblocking is confirmed by the fact that Google, Microsoft, Amazon and ad-serving company Taboola have deals with Adblock Plus. To make whitelisting possible, ads have to abide by the Adblock manifesto. This states:

▸ Acceptable Ads are not annoying.
▸ Acceptable Ads do not disrupt or distort the page content we're trying to read.
▸ Acceptable Ads are transparent with us about being an ad.
▸ Acceptable Ads are effective without shouting at us.
▸ Acceptable Ads are appropriate to the site that we are on.

For large companies, this also involves a fee which creates an inter-esting dynamic (for smaller websites, whitelisting is usually free as long as criteria are met as outlined in Adblock Plus's Acceptable Ads Initiative).[47] Today 10 per cent of the sites and entities whitelisted by Adblock Plus have paid spots on the whitelist.

Mobile adblocking

These principles also apply to mobile phones and tablets as users download adblocking apps such as Adblock and Crystal for Android and iOS platforms. However, there are additional characteristics and debates relevant to mobile media. In 2015 a company called Shine became the focus of the technology industry because it promised to remove ads from the mobile online experience. This is not just an app to be downloaded, but a piece of software that Shine would license to mobile carriers. This means that carriers would decide how they would provide an ad-free service to their customers. This could include a pre-mium service (where customers pay extra per month), it could be opt-in (where customers get their monthly rates dropped because with ads removed they are using less data), or it might be free and pre-loaded on smartphones. Like Adblock Plus, Shine can also unblock ads for a fee.

As with web advertising, the mobile ad industry has a reason-able argument to make in that content has to be paid for somehow. However, mobile provides an additional factor to this debate because each of us pays for a data plan. Shine estimates that, depending on where we live, ads use 10–50 per cent of a user's data plan. Moreover, because our phones are sending and receiving information, this also means that ads drain precious battery life as well as slowing the time it takes websites to load. On potential harm to the ad business and mobile publishers, the CEO of Shine, Roi Carthy, is unrepentant. At an event in Brussels in 2015 and in post-session conversation, Carthy said that ad-tech 'might as well be working with the NSA', that it is akin to 'tech developed by spy agencies', 'abusive to user experience and the network itself' and finally that 'consumers have an unalienable right to block ads'. Interviewed for a *Business Insider* article, Roi Carthy expands these points:

> 'We believe ad blocking is a right, full-stop. If the consumer decides to use it, we believe that it should be their right, and they should be able to do it with full integrity ... nobody [in business] has a

god-given right to exist. If you own a trucking business, and gas prices rise, and you can't afford to pay your bills because you were not able to manage your business, you go out of business,' he said. 'There will be causalities [sic], absolutely, but I know I'm not losing any sleep knowing remnant inventory ad networks will disappear.' (O'Reilly, 2015)

In the ad industry's favour is the fact that in the US and potentially Europe, use of Shine would mean discriminating between different sets of data flowing across their networks. This contravenes a principle called *net neutrality*, which means that a person or organization should not have their internet data discriminated against. This exists to make sure that the web is equally open to all and that players with the most influence are not able to prioritize their traffic over other traffic. Also, because it works at a network level, Shine is arguably not technologically compliant with European regulations, because it intercepts data traffic via a technique known as deep-packet inspection (DPI), reads the traffic, and identifies the ad-tech to be extracted. Shine says this is OK because it seeks to read and extract unwanted content, but the fact that it would gain insight to the pipes through which all data flows is a point of concern.

Anti-adblocking

Approaching all-out warfare, consumer use of adblockers has also given rise to anti-adblocking companies such as PageFair, Sourcepoint and Secret Media. These aim to detect and track use of adblocking, and then serve users with messages encouraging them not to use adblockers. Secret Media goes further and employs encryption technologies to smuggle ad content past adblockers. It argues this is acceptable practice on the basis that blocked ads cost publishers money and that advertising delivered by third parties helps keep the internet free. As will be developed in Chapter 12 on privacy and consent, this is a difficult argument to make in Europe because a user's browser is a means of opting in and opting out of *behavioural* advertising (the sort that tracks us across the web to work out what our interests are). This is a legal right under Article 5(3) of Europe's ePrivacy Directive. This means that browsers are a legal means of saying, 'yes I'm happy to accept third-party tracking so I can have relevant ads' or 'no, I prefer not to be tracked'. As adblockers are typically installed at a browser level this places anti-adblockers in a difficult legal situation in Europe.

This is reinforced by the fact that users have to actively go and find the add-on and install it, further highlighting that they do not consent to tracking and third-party behavioural advertising.

Notably, the use of browsers to indicate consent to third-party advertising and tracking was something that the advertising industry lobbied for (on the basis that browsers come with third-party tracking switched on and few people change settings). Another point to be made is that the idea that irritating advertising is a positive step for brands is a difficult one. It begs the question of which brand (large or small) would want to be associated with annoying their customers and intruding upon the user's experience. Although publishers are right that advertising helps to reduce costs, and consumers of content benefit from this, the use of automatically generated advertising that irritates is based on short-term interests. A better approach for companies and publishers that care about the image their advertising projects is contextual advertising. This is advertising that targets types of websites and content, rather than types of people.

Fraud

Lurking at the centre of data-driven advertising is another problem for the advertising industry: fraud. Foremost is the use of "bots". To put a value on this, White Ops (2014), a leading bot detection firm, reckons that in 2014 over $6 billion dollars were pocketed by fraudsters. This is a form of *ad fraud* that entails infecting people's computers with a "bot" (or a web robot). This is software designed to simulate a human being browsing the web. The reason why this is fraud is because bots (or non-human traffic) will never buy anything so the ad exposure is useless to an advertiser that is paying the ad network, who in turn is paying the publisher. How does it work? It happens when, for example, a user downloads clean-up software from the web, which in turn is a Trojan horse, which downloads a bot engine, and that connects to a bot centre. Once connected with the centre, the user's computer can be used to connect with the servers of websites without the user knowing. Effectively a criminal has taken over a person's computer and, although our focus is ad fraud, botnets can be used to execute bank robbery, identity theft, and distributed denial of service (DDOS) attacks. The ad fraud bot centre typically commands our computers to visit sites that mark out people as "high value". This means visiting sites such as *The Economist*, BMW and others that signify that the IP address represents someone wealthy (even though in reality the user may not be). Indeed, bots can be refined for different sectors so a bot can be made to look like someone interested in sports, possessing a large income, or a grandparent looking for holiday gifts for grandchildren (White Ops, 2014). The user's bot infected machine is then commanded to go to websites that sell bot traffic.

How do bots get into the ad ecology? This occurs because of *traffic sourcing*. This is when publishers acquire more visitors through third parties who provide the non-human traffic. Why do they do this? The answer is that when an advertiser wants to reach a given number of a certain type of people (such as grandparents looking for gifts), a publisher may not have enough ad spaces (inventory) to be able to fulfil this. Rather than turn away this business, publishers will instead try to buy more inventory from a third party that is capable of providing the right audience for the advertiser. This bot traffic is mixed with real traffic to be able to meet the demand for a certain type of audience of a given size. It is worth noting too that use of bots by disreputable publishers puts reputable players at a competitive disadvantage. The outcome is loss of revenue and pressure to give in and use non-human traffic. White Ops (2014), in a report co-published with the Association of National Advertisers (a US trade association), say that some links in the bot supply chain are unaware of the bots in their traffic and do not intend to profit illicitly. Others, however, actively encourage and concentrate bot traffic to increase profits. This traffic is often bought as "unknown quality", which for industry insiders will indicate this is bot traffic. One industry insider interviewed by Digiday (2014), who bought fake traffic, confesses that:

> When we told them we were looking for the cheapest traffic we could possibly buy there would be sort of a wink and a nod, and they'd make us aware that for that price the traffic would be of "unknown quality".

On being asked if publishers know when they're buying fake traffic, the former publishing executive says:

> Publishers know. They might say 'we had no idea' and blame it on their traffic acquisition vendor, but that's bullshit, and they know it. If you're buying visits for less than a penny, there's no way you don't understand what's going on.

The executive adds that ad networks are also culpable because they do not scrutinize where the extra traffic comes from. The suggestion is that ad networks have an incentive not to assess traffic too closely. This type of fraud sees numerous actors profiting: the organization/person who created the botnet, publishers and ad networks. It is always the advertiser that loses out. The scale of this problem is huge. In 2014 White Ops said that globally advertisers would lose $6.3 billion in advertising to bots in 2015 (remembering that bots do not buy), from what White Ops estimated as $40 billion spent globally on display ads and the estimated $8.3 billion spent globally on video ads.

There are other sorts of fraud too. *Click fraud* is where a competing advertiser repeatedly clicks the ads of a competitor when the original advertiser is paying on a pay-per-click (PPC) basis. This incurs costs for the original advertiser and consequently uses up the budget the advertiser has allocated to search/Adwords/pay-per-click campaigns. Although a few clicks may appear harmless, when one considers that computer programs can automate clicks, this presents a considerable problem for advertisers. Basic programs can be tracked to clicking from one particular source, but more sophisticated programs can have many computers from multiple geographic regions and unique IP addresses clicking on the ads. Clearly this is harder to diagnose. There is a second related version of click fraud that involves *affiliate* websites and publishers. For example, a blogger might allow Google ads to be displayed on their blog. The blogger can defraud the system by splitting the revenue with anyone who clicks on the ad being hosted on the blog. This does not just apply to blogs, but any form of website capable of carrying affiliate advertising. *Arguably* Google, and other search engines that run AdSense-type programs, benefit from click fraud because it burns up an advertiser's budget. There are other possible fraudsters, not least other publishers, who might seek to frame the publisher on whose site the AdSense program is running and make it appear that the original publisher is trying to illicitly boost their own clicks. This may not appear as significant. After all, do these clicks *really* matter? The answer becomes clearer when we consider that the essence of Adland is based on the premise that organizations that own media space sell potential and real audiences to advertisers and their agencies. It is paramount that the audience figures are correct, because if not this affects the very edifice of the contract between media owners and advertisers (who pay to put their messages in media spaces to be seen by known audiences).

Conclusion

For a business that increasingly relies upon numbers and metrics to provide clients information about how their investment in advertising is performing, adblocking and ad fraud are real problems. The rate of people using adblockers such as Adblock Plus is high, which leaves the online advertising industry two options: the first is to fight users and adblocking firms by lobbying for legal change but the second, more interesting, route is to create a model that works for everyone. Rather than fighting the tide, is there a way for the advertising and publishing industries to work with it? This requires creative solutions, giving people something that is useful and of value, and making people's lives easier. As will be developed later, there is potentiality for programmatic advertising to help rather than harass. The ad fraud problem is a matter of accountability, auditing and what the industry phrases as hygiene factors (where ads are verified to have been seen by humans). The use of bots makes it look as though there is more people viewing ads than there really are, which distorts the market and reduces advertisers' faith in digital advertising. It is worth comparing this with traditional media such as newspapers and television that have long had their ratings audited by outside organizations. The task is to remove fraud before it gets to the ad exchange where it becomes harder to trace. This requires a self-regulatory mechanism whereby publishers and exchanges would sign up to good practice principles, transparency regarding where inventory is bought, and deployment of monitoring tools to verify whether traffic is human or not. Advertisers can play a role here by insisting that all third-party traffic is verified.

Think points and questions

- Explain what is meant by ad fraud and click fraud.
- What are the key features of the debate about the ethics of adblocking? Where do you stand on these?
- Is there a tacit contract between online publishers and users that we should abide by?
- What remedies for adblocking do you suggest?

9   Advertising to Children: Regulations and Ethics for Digital Media

Ethics is a staple topic for books on advertising, but the specifics of the digital sector have received far less attention. Ethics in advertising are moral guidelines that govern the industry's behaviour, and articulate what is right and wrong. Although one might think that ethics and regulations act to hinder the advertising business, this is only partially correct. The ad industry is aware that many citizens do not trust advertising. From an agency and advertiser point of view, it is important for advertising to appear credible because if not, consumers will switch off altogether. The industry thus has a vested interest in protecting its reputation so as to have standing with advertisers who make use of advertising, and potential customers. A breakdown of trust helps no one. To explore the ethics of advertising in relation to digital media, we will focus on advertising to children. These are persons under 16 who are deemed not to have the analytical abilities and judgement of adults. I will outline how the industry is regulated, the balance between laws and self-regulation, changes in recent years, and how regulators are dealing with new media and native advertising. I use the UK regulatory situation for my case examples, but non-UK readers should compare and contrast with their own countries.

Studying ethics in advertising

To study ethics, regulations and advertising there are many resources at your disposal, and many of these are only a few web clicks away. The first port of call is your country's regulator. Read what it does and identify both classic and recent case examples of ads that have contravened regulations. Also, have a close look at the codes of advertising practice it enforces. As will be developed, the regulation of what advertisers can and cannot do involves a balance between codes generated by those in advertising and laws generated by governments. It is important to understand these too. Further, a key task is to understand the political balance between legislation and self-regulation. In countries such as the UK laws are light touch, which means the government prefers to leave the industry to regulate itself, but elsewhere they are more prescriptive. As we will see, many of the regulations and laws exist to protect children. Also see your media regulator because it will have a great deal of information about how advertising affects children. In the UK this is Ofcom, but non-UK readers should use the search term 'media regulator [insert your country here]'. After all, evidence about effects is important to generate informed insight ('The available evidence points to X so I argue that...') rather than uninformed opinion ('I think it's wrong/ right'). Lastly, students of ethics in advertising should of course make use of academic books and journals that will address advertising history, questions of ethics, the significance of laws and new media developments in much greater depth than regulatory or industry reports.

Legislation and self-regulation

The regulation of advertising involves a balance between self-regulation versus legislation. The first reflects the initially strange idea that people might be best served if the advertising business regulates itself. The second involves the types of laws that guide what can legally take place. Most countries employ a balance of laws and self-regulation to regulate advertising. Legislation refers to laws of countries and wider jurisdictions (the UK for example has European Directives and Regulations that it abides by). Laws are characterized by *not* being specific about what can and cannot happen in advertising, rather offering general guidance. In the UK, laws say that advertising should be an accurate description of the product or service, and that it should be legal, decent, truthful, honest and socially responsible. This means that it should not encourage illegal, unsafe or anti-social behaviour. The key UK law is The Consumer Protection from Unfair Trading Regulations (2008).[48] In general, this means advertising to consumers should not mislead or harass consumers by: including false or deceptive messages; leaving out important information; or using aggressive sales techniques.[49]

Self-regulation in the UK

The majority of complaints about advertising involve puffery, taste, decency and product placement. Puffery involves praising products without specific facts, making the advertising overblown and exaggerated. Weight-loss ads, for example, are often found to make claims about their effectiveness that are untrue. In the UK, if people are unhappy with advertising they complain to the Advertising Standards Authority (ASA) which enforces codes developed by the Committee of Advertising Practice (CAP) – a detailed set of prescriptions that go beyond what is required by laws to deal with the fast-moving realities of advertising and media. In the UK self-regulation addresses two area of advertising: that which is broadcast and that which is not.[50] Broadcast advertising regulations primarily address television and radio; whereas codes for non-broadcast advertising cover non-broadcast advertisements, sales promotions and direct marketing communications. Among other formats, the non-broadcast regulations cover digital advertising.

In relation to children, key sections and recommendations of the non-broadcast codes say: ads should not result in physical, mental or moral harm (see §5.1); ads must not exploit their credulity, loyalty, vulnerability or lack of experience (§5.2); ads must not exaggerate what is attainable by an ordinary child using the product being marketed and must not exploit children's susceptibility to charitable appeals (§5.3); ads must not actively encourage children to make a nuisance of themselves or include a direct exhortation to children to buy an advertised product (§5.4). The latter point is about what is often referred to as pester power. As often found online, appeals to buy products through direct-response mechanisms must not be directly targeted at children (§5.5); promotions should not cause conflict between a child's desire and a parent's (§5.6); promotions that require a purchase to participate and include a direct exhortation to make a purchase must not be addressed to or targeted at children (§5.7).

Although stipulating that a child is someone under 16, the regulations are sensible and recognize that strict applications of regulations appropriate for a 4 year old might be excessive for a 15 year old. The same applies in reverse, as marketing communications acceptable for young teenagers will not necessarily be acceptable for younger children.

Are children growing up too quickly? The Bailey Review

A recurring criticism of advertising and our broader media culture is that children at a young age are exposed to content intended for adults. Further, on occasion, children are treated like adults. In the

UK the Bailey Review of 2011 addressed this situation. Reg Bailey was the Chief Executive of the Mothers' Union, and was asked by the UK government to carry out an independent review of the proposition that children are pressured to grow up too quickly. This came about because parents were feeling overwhelmed by the increasing levels of sexual imagery and commercial messages reaching their children. This proposition was echoed by study findings that supported the review (TNS Omnibus, 2012). These found that on being asked if 'These days children are under pressure to grow up too quickly', 61 per cent of parents in 2011 strongly agreed with this, followed by 27 per cent who somewhat agreed. The intention of the review was to provide clear and straightforward suggestions for all involved stakeholders to address these issues, and to ensure that businesses did not take advantage of gaps in advertising and marketing regulation, especially regarding new media.

Although the outcomes are somewhat UK specific, the questions the review asked are relevant to all countries with a developed media culture where children are under increasing pressure to become consumers, and where the world in which children live contains more graphical and suggestive media content than when their parents were growing up. The full report, *Letting Children Be Children: the Report of an Independent Review of the Commercialisation and Sexualisation of Childhood* was published on 6 June 2011.[51] The recommendations sought to find a middle path between the *maintenance of innocence* view that sees the world as a 'nasty place and children should be unsullied by it until they are mature enough to deal with it' and an *adultification of children* view that argues 'we should accept the world for what it is and simply give children the tools to understand it' (Bailey, 2011: §18–19, 10). Instead the recommendations promoted a family-friendly society that recognizes that parents have a primary role to play, but so do business, media and regulators. For lecturers covering ethics and advertising in seminars, I recommend making this report a key reading for the week. For students writing essays on the topic, you will find this a useful source to identify key ethical questions for the UK and your own country.

The key recommendations of the report are:

1. Ensuring that magazines and newspapers with sexualized images on their covers are not in easy sight of children;
2. Reduction of the amount of on-street advertising containing sexualized imagery in locations where children are likely to see it;

3. Ensuring the content of pre-watershed television programming better meets parents' expectations;
4. Introducing age ratings for music videos;
5. Making it easier for parents to block adult and age-restricted material from the internet;
6. Developing a retail code of good practice on retailing to children;
7. Ensuring that the regulation of advertising reflects more closely parents' and children's views;
8. Prohibiting the employment of children as brand ambassadors and in peer-to-peer marketing;
9. Defining a child as under the age of 16 in all types of advertising regulation;
10. Raising parental awareness of marketing and advertising techniques;
11. Quality assurance for media and commercial literacy resources and education for children;
12. Ensuring greater transparency in the regulatory framework by creating a single website for regulators;
13. Making it easier for parents to express their views to businesses about goods and services.

To tease out the *digital dimensions* of these recommendations about how advertising and marketing should be improved, the study behind the review (TNS Omnibus, 2012) found that in 2011 there were numerous concerns about digital media:

▸ 42 per cent of parents thought that what their children saw on the internet encouraged children to act older than they are;
▸ 52 per cent of parents thought that social networking sites (such as Bebo or Facebook) encouraged children to act older than they are;
▸ 36 per cent also expressed concern that online imagery put too much pressure on children to conform to a particular body shape and size;
▸ 38 per cent thought that social networks put too much pressure on children to conform to a particular body shape and size (although the prime concern about body image was celebrity culture at 65 per cent).

The study also found that in 2011 parents thought the following digital media should not be used to promote products to children:

▸ Adverts sent to mobile phones (35 per cent);
▸ Companies encouraging children to click the "like" button on social networking sites (34 per cent);

- Peer-to-peer marketing – where children are paid to promote goods and services to other children they know (27 per cent);
- Adverts on the internet (27 per cent);
- Advergames (17 per cent).

Notably, a 2012 follow up to the 2011 survey found increases in responses to each of the digital questions (TNS Omnibus, 2012). In 2013 the outcomes of the Bailey Review were reviewed to see if, and what, progress was being made in implementing the findings. Titled *Letting Children Be Children: Progress Report*,[52] the UK government reported the following changes in the 18-month period since the original Bailey Review:

- There were fewer advertisements which use highly sexualized images in public places;
- Pre-watershed television programming is suitable for family viewing;
- Parents faced an unavoidable choice on setting up parental internet controls if they sign up for broadband from one of the five main internet service providers (ISPs);
- Parents were more likely to find clothes for their children which are age-appropriate in style and design;
- Parents found it easier to complain about advertising, television programmes and video games that they think are inappropriate for their children to see.

The review of progress highlights that these changes were made through self-regulatory means and without recourse to further legislation. It also points to:

- Ongoing need for *vigilance from parents* and that they make responsible choices to ensure their children have a healthy childhood by means of factors such as age ratings for films, DVDs and video games, the television watershed, and parental controls on the internet.
- *Businesses should not exploit children's gullibility and vulnerability*, or encourage peer pressure. This involves both written and unwritten rules (matters of principle) that should apply as 'technology and business models change'. The emphasis is on children's integrity and personal development.

To paraphrase the report, this means *not*: treating children solely as consumers; confronting them with a limited range of gender roles;

promoting highly idealized stereotypes of body sizes and shapes; and pushing them towards an adult sexuality at a pace they find bewildering. It urges business leaders to not promote things for other people's children that they would not accept for their own.

The magic age of understanding in the online context

Historically, for advertising researchers, a key question has been: when can children comprehend that they are being sold to and when can they distinguish between sponsored communication (advertising) and regular non-sponsored media content? These were reasonable questions to ask when ads were those things that typically broke up television shows and appeared in magazines. The nature of this advertising allowed academics and industry researchers to seek out a "magic age" when children could understand the persuasive intent of commercial messages and differentiate it from television programming (Marshall, 2010). To use the language of audience studies, this sees children as more active in both engagement and negotiation of ad messages and media content (Morley, 1980; McQuail, 2000; Ross and Nightingale, 2003).

For example Oates et al. (2003) explored children's understanding of advertising through the use of focus groups concluding that: their perceptions of advertising on television are not well developed; and that this raises implications for the regulation of television and advertising. They found that: 'Children's understanding of advertising is less developed than previously thought and by no means all of the children at age 10 years expressed understanding of its persuasive intent. None of the 6 year olds demonstrated this understanding' (2003: 69). Having studied whether younger children (from 2 years onwards) are more vulnerable to advertising than older children (up to 16 years), Livingstone and Helsper (2006) conclude that younger children are *not* more easily influenced. Instead, children are influenced in different ways and 'different processes of persuasion operate at different ages, precisely because literacy levels vary by age'.

A problem today on seeking a magic age when children can understand the differences between persuasion and entertainment is that advertising and marketing techniques are increasingly sophisticated. For example in most cases it is clear to older children and adults that we know an ad when we see one – whether on television, a poster on a bus shelter, in a magazine or newspaper, or a display ad online. This is because we are able to separate advertising out from its background. However, as we have read in this book, the division between content and advertising is often unclear. Older children, for example, studied in the research for the Bailey Review, found it hard to say whether advergames are designed to entertain or to persuade (Bailey, 2011). Similarly, as discussed in relation to native advertising in Chapter 6, much sponsored content today works hard *not* to appear like advertising because advertising sales pitches are believed by agencies not to be credible with young audiences. The upshot of this is that when ads are no longer ads, it is increasingly difficult for adults and children alike to distinguish between the two. Whereas historically we have benefited from a clear demarcation between sponsored content and regular content, areas of the advertising industry increasingly employ more covert techniques. In combating this the ASA, the UK regulator, insists that ads 'must be obviously identifiable as such' and that they 'must not materially mislead or be likely to do so' (ASA, 2014: 1).

Advergames

The ASA has not always been as comprehensive in its coverage, because the old version from 2003 of the non-broadcast CAP codes did not cover editorial or web content, but only sales promotions and advertisements in paid-for space. This means that the ASA was able to regulate digital ads appearing in emails and in paid-for spaces such as display ads and paid-for search listings on Google, but not marketing messages on companies' own websites or on social networking sites such as Facebook and Twitter. Although the specifics of UK regulations may be of little to no interest for non-UK readers, this provided a big loophole. This allowed owners of brands to blur the distinction between editorial and media. McDonald's, for example, maintained a site featuring a Kids Zone section that invited children to play a range of shoot 'em up games where McDonald's logos were shot at. Today's advergames are accessible on social media sites, downloadable apps, social media under the advertiser's control (such as a Facebook page), companies' own websites and as downloadable content for mobile devices, but crucially the regulations changed from 1 March 2011 so that the ASA would now regulate marketing communications on companies' own websites and on social media sites.

YouTube channels: the case of AmazingPhil

As discussed in Chapter 6, some video bloggers (vloggers) are incredibly popular with millions of followers. Their success is built on authenticity, so there is a clear reason why advertisers and marketers want to use them. This is because they appear more credible than regular media and the vloggers seem more like us. They are less removed and we can more easily interact with them – if only just to "like" their channel and post comments. Their credibility makes them a perfect conduit for commercial messages and for brand association. This is legal if vloggers are clear that their content includes branded content, but problems arise if they do not indicate that payment has taken place. Oreo (made by Kraft and Cadbury trading by the name Mondelez UK), for example, paid a number of YouTubers (Dan Howell & Phil Lester (Figure 9.1), Emma Blackery, P.J. Ligouri and Thomas Ridgewell) to promote their biscuits. The problem is that they did not make it clear that the videos in question were ads for the Oreo brand and that they were rewarded to promote it.

The promotion revolved around the concept of the Oreo 'lick race' and YouTubers licking Oreos and then eating them on video. Although the video contained spoken lines such as 'Thanks to Oreo for making this video possible', the ASA said it remained unclear that

Fig 9.1

Dan Howell & Phil Lester (AmazingPhil) promoting Oreos

the YouTubers had been paid. The presentation was also problematic because each Oreo ad was very much in keeping with the editorial content of the respective YouTube channels, so the difference between advertising content and regular content was unclear. This is the difficulty for advertisers: they want their sponsored content to be as indistinguishable as possible from editorial, but the regulators want a clear distinction between ads and content. This point is made by Chyaz, a lifestyle and beauty vlogger, who told the UK's BBC[53] that companies sponsoring her videos had told her: 'Please don't make it very obvious.' Instead, regulators recommend that vloggers paid to promote a product put 'ad', 'ad feature' or 'advertorial' (or something comparable) in the title of their video. Similarly, they might use a symbol in the thumbnail telling viewers what they're about to click on is an ad. Importantly this should happen before people are exposed to the content.

This was formalized in 2015 as the CAP published codes for vlogging. The codes now state that the Oreos situation is clearly an advertorial. This is where 'the whole video is in the usual style of the vlogger but the content is controlled by the brand and the vlogger has been paid (not necessarily with money)' (CAP, 2015). Although not stated, the CAP seems to be reacting to the Oreo case because they urge vloggers and marketers not to use 'Thanks to X for making this possible', nor use other vague terms such as 'Supported by' or 'Funded by'. In the case of product placements within vlogs, the commercial nature of this should also be made explicit. The CAP says that the vlogger has some flexibility regarding how this done because each video will have a different style, but it will involve 'onscreen text stating "ad", "product placement", holding up a sign, or the vlogger explaining that they've been paid to talk about the product' (CAP, 2015). As with the case of Zoella, a beauty vlogger discussed in Chapter 6, she might say 'In this tutorial I'm using brushes from Brand X, who paid for me to feature them and want you to know about...'. As with traditional journalism and reviewing, public relations firms and agencies will send products and items to vloggers. The vlogger is under no pressure from the CAP to disclose this as long as the brand is not influencing the review.

Conclusion

This chapter has explored how advertising to children in the digital environment is regulated. Understanding that the regulation of advertising practices requires a balance of laws and self-regulation, we considered the Bailey Review of 2011 and the principle that children are being forced to grow up too quickly. The review rightly points out that advertising is part of a much broader promotional culture. However, parents had a number of concerns about the digital sector, not least that what children saw on the internet and social networking sites encouraged them to act older than their age. Other parents pointed to concern about online imagery, social media sites and pressure on children to conform to a particular body shape and size. In the past academics and regulators debated the question of the age at which children might be aware they are being advertised to. This focused on television and media where ads featured in breaks of content. Today it is far less clear what an "ad" actually is. Although we can still be sure that it is content that aims to influence towards a given strategic goal (such as changing attitudes or encouraging purchasing, voting, donating or some other action), ads are no longer what they once were. This makes a magic age of understanding less tenable and increases need for regulatory oversight. On vlogging, one might question whether it matters that content is sponsored or not. Is it really important whether we know if a YouTuber licking biscuits is getting paid to do so? The answer is a definite yes. As citizens and viewers of media content, we should know when someone is being paid to sell to us. If we know we are being sold to, we can make informed decisions and possibly enjoy the sales pitch for what it is (clearly many ads are entertaining!). Without being upfront, there is deceit and lack of transparency about motives for the communication.

Think points and questions

- ▸ Non-UK readers: what is the situation in your own country? What stance has been taken on the sexualization of your media environment?
- ▸ Trace a typical day from start to end (waking, watching television, ambling through the streets, shopping, browsing magazines, internet surfing, more television, more online content, etc.): to what extent do you agree that advertisers promote an excessively sexualized media environment?
- ▸ How are regulators dealing with ads that are not ads (such as native advertising, advergaming and advertising through vloggers)?
- ▸ To what extent should we be concerned about digital advertising and marketing to children: does it represent the commercialization of childhood, or should children be exposed to commercial realities of the world from an early age?

10   Ad-tech: Analytics, Big Data, Profiling and Identity

The aim of this chapter is to develop understanding about how information collected about our online lives is processed and put to work to better target advertising. This is achieved by "analytics", or the process of transforming large amounts of unstructured information into a usable set of data that can be analysed to target the right advertising to appropriate people at a time when they will be most receptive. This is optimization, or the act of executing advertising by the most efficient means possible with view to generating maximum gains. As the chapter will highlight, the use of computers to do this is not new, but the variety of sources from which information is drawn is increasing. While one would expect online data to contribute to digital advertising processes, this is only a small part of a big story. Information about us is collected from all domains of everyday life. This chapter examines the history and nature of analytics, the role of "big data", correlational logic, consumer profiling, social media, application to advertising, and lastly the rise of virtual personal assistants.

Yesterday: origins of analytics in advertising

The desire of marketers and advertisers to know more about existing and potential customers is not new. The origination of professional audience analysis goes back to the early 1900s, when the Audit Bureau of Circulation (ABC) was established in the US in 1914. The significant point is that this period generated realization in advertising of the need for *data collection*, *processing* and *feedback*. The notion of feedback is important because it provides organizations information by which they can make short- and long-term decisions. Feedback provides data on who people are, where they are, what they do and what they like. In his excellent book *The Control Revolution*, James Beniger (1986) highlights that between 1905 and 1935 there arose an armoury of techniques that improved the targeting process. These included testing effectiveness of ads, closer attention to retail data, audience questionnaire surveys, direct mailing by means of post/zip codes, audits of publishers' circulations, greater attention to market research, house-to-house interviewing about dwellers' preferences, closer attention to economic cycles of product demand and saturation, innovation in research methodologies for large-scale surveys, growth of national opinion surveys, and audimeter monitoring of broadcast audiences (developed by AC Nielsen, this records and transmits whether a television is turned on and measures popularity of channels). These methodological innovations in consumer preferences and behaviour reflected the modern belief that advertising, marketing and consumer research should be treated as a science through the use of feedback as a means of understanding what techniques work and what do not. This approach was exemplified by figures such as Daniel Starch (1914) and Claude Hopkins (1998 [1923]) who were insistent that advertising should be treated as a science. This entails collecting information, analysing it, using insights to improve campaigns, gaining feedback about campaign performance and measuring effectiveness. Through use of feedback, Hopkins sought to understand what techniques work and what do not, remarking that 'we test everything pertaining to advertising' (ibid: 216). Starch (1914) similarly sought to establish the scientific foundations of advertising. He argued that propositions and plans for campaign execution could be assessed *with certainty*, along with any other relevant aspect of audience research and marketing that may be subject to laws of cause and effect. The wish for certainty is understandable because what all businesses seek is stability and predictability (as well as opportunity to grow). If guided by logic, the theory was that advertising process could be predictable. This is the search for perfect efficiency, or capacity for *control* and ability to dictate future outcomes. The notion of control is an important one as it reflects broader societal, industrial, technical and organizational change in the late 1800s and the 1900s, particularly in terms of speed, movement, communication, precision, logistics, management, feedback and effective use of resources (also known as the Industrial Revolution). Innovation in audience research and advertising should be seen against this historical context where clear and understandable industrial processes could be applied to generate predictable results.

Today this is largely done by means of computers and algorithms. Although the latter are receiving an increased level of critical attention from surveillance and technology scholars (Pasquale, 2015), the use of algorithms to process audience behaviour and profiles is decades old. Although potentially complex, the principle behind algorithms is simple because they are merely step-by-step sets of procedures to achieve a goal. In the case of audience behaviour, this involves creating a series of steps to match information about groups of people (audiences) with ad campaign and marketing efforts. For example, by 1970 geodemographics, or the technique of pinpointing direct mail campaigns, was computerized and by the mid-1970s audience research firms CACI and Claritas had created the first geodemographic targeting systems by combining mapped postal code data and census-generated socio-economic information (McStay, 2011a). However, the application of computer algorithms, data mining and warehousing came to greater prominence in the 1980s and the 1990s as a digital way of *extracting meaning* from large data sets. As computing power became less expensive, by the 1980s all major organizations had built infrastructural databases about their clients, competitors, products and customers. On what they analysed, computers were useful for market segmentation analysis, new product development, attitude measurement and predictive patterns. By the 1990s, companies' systems had proliferated to use a range of publicly held information sources (Phillips and Curry, 2003). Importantly, they were also using information provided by consumers, such as product registration cards. Again, note the point about feedback in that these cards told companies who was buying these products. As expertise and methods improved, profilers were also able to refine geodemographic searches into much smaller units.

The key point is that use of large amounts of information to classify and find relationships, clusters, correlations, commonalities, co-occurrences, affinities, variances, patterns, associations, and reactions to products, prices and advertising content is not new. Nevertheless as mathematical, statistical, computational and marketing techniques advanced (along with the internet as a means of capturing data) this resulted in greater success in profiling, categorizing and using purchase patterns to promote other goods and services. There are two key developments that characterize analytics today and separate it from what has gone before: the first is granularity of profiling and intimacy; and the second is that this takes place in *real time*. The possibility of being able to do this is solely associated with the internet and web. The fact that advertising can react to events as they unfold is a point to be emphasized. However, although more recent, this practice is not a new trend, because behavioural advertising has been around on the web since the mid-1990s.

The big data context

Historically, advertising has been targeted on the basis of the content a user is looking at (such as celebrities in magazines or a politics discussion on a website), but behavioural advertising is targeted by *who* is looking at a particular web page. This means that a person with an interest in *Game of Thrones* may receive ads for fantasy films while searching a rail company's website for the next train to London. It is not the rail company that puts the ads on their page, but third parties that track our movements around the internet and then serve us advertising on the basis of what we have been doing. To be able to effectively target people by their behaviour in real time as life unfolds requires a high level of information about them from multiple sources, capacity to process this information and ability to use it in a meaningful way.

Big data is not a specific form of data. Coined by tech industry analyst Doug Laney (2001) big data refers to three Vs: volume, velocity and variety. It refers to an increase in *volume* of data, the *velocity* by which it moves and needs to be reacted to, and the *variety* of forms it comes in. Phrased otherwise, this means the amount of data circulating through digital networks; the speed with which it can be processed so people and systems can receive feedback that is meaningful in some way (such as advertising that is relevant to time, place, interests and what we are doing); and the different sorts of data in circulation. The upshot of this is that big data refers to more than just size and amount, but also the speed by which data is collected and processed so to provide meaningful feedback in real time. One example of big data applications is programmatic advertising[54] that uses data from multiple sources to generate advertising relevant to what people are doing, on whatever screen they are looking at and wherever they happen to be. This requires a lot of information about time, place, history, preferences and hardware. As will be unpacked, although big data involves a great deal of information, big is a relative term. What passed for big in 2001 is different from big today. Where volume certainly plays a role, speed and range of data types should not be overlooked, nor should the sorts of insights that big data generates. Although our focus is advertising, big data processing is affecting the business and study of governance, education, healthcare, engineering, weather patterns, disease, financial services, creditworthiness, insurance, identity authentication and situations where it is useful to generate insights derived from a variety of information sources in real time. It is less about size than aggregation, correlation, cross-referencing and finding non-obvious valuable relationships to assist in planning and decision making. For marketers big data and analytics assist in overcoming John Wanamaker's truism that 'I know half the money I spend on advertising is wasted. The trouble is I don't know which half', because advertisers increasingly know whether they are targeting the right person in the right place at the right time.

The twenty-first century: data and correlation

Big data is the tracing of multiple and often strange behavioural correlations. For advertising and marketing, this helps understand audience and consumer behaviour. The term "correlation" literally means "*co*" (together) and "*relation*". Some of these correlations are valuable and some are not. To generate them, data analysts put machines to work to accumulate data and identify trends, patterns and links. For example if a health data miner has access to population records on diet, disease, geography, family history, exercise, work and poverty, valuable results will be generated that can be used to improve individual and societal health. On the other hand, one could trawl the history of UK elections in relation to results of sporting fixtures. There *will* be correlations, but the value of these is highly suspect. There are correlative gems on the web. For example, there is a very tight fit (99.79 per cent) between patterns of US spending on science, space and technology and suicides achieved by hanging, strangulation and suffocation. Other correlations involve divorce rates and margarine consumption, and death by getting tangled in bed sheets and cheese consumption.[55]

During a UK summer, supermarket marketers will see correlations between a rise in temperature and rise in the sales of charcoal for barbecues (along with ice cream, shorts and other goods typically bought in the summer). A correlational approach to knowledge *doggedly avoids causal explanations* and while a rise in temperature may cause people to have more barbecues, one would not say that a rise in barbecues causes people to wear shorts, although there are strong correlations between these. Although correlations are interesting, they are not always meaningful. For example, ZestFinance, a US finance company, found that taller people are better at repaying loans. Should ZestFinance increase the lending rates because of the risk posed by short people? (They didn't!) The core suggestion is that greater amounts and analysis of data will open up truths about the self, health, economics, policy making, disaster management and processes where expertise in information management is desirable. This is true to an extent as information can provide insights missed by people because the data sets are too large. Conversely, reliance on automated data processing leads to comedic (and dumb) outcomes.

On big data and advertising

Big data is big business for advertisers. Firms who use big data to target advertising include Adobe, Beckon, ComScore, Datalogix, eXelate, Krux, Marketshare, Mediamath, Merkle, Neustar, Teradata and Unified. Between them they measure the effectiveness of advertising campaigns in real time (through clicks, ad impressions, audience reach, engagement with ads and whether people click through to websites). They also make inferences about our intentions to purchase and what parts of our online experience are more influential than others (or what in Chapter 3 we referred to as attribution). Advertising is a good example of big data processes because advertising works better when it is relevant to where we are and what we are doing. The task for digital advertisers is to reach the right people with the right message at the right time. Although we are fairly familiar with the practice of having our web histories used to serve behaviourally targeted advertising, big data processing goes further to make use of what are called *data management platforms* (or DMPs). We briefly discussed these earlier in relation to programmatic advertising and third-party data in Chapter 3. DMPs are central hubs for collecting, integrating, managing and putting to work large volumes of data that marketers gather from any online or offline source. They make use of data generated from our web travels and communications, but combine it with offline data about our interactions with a company. A company that sells holidays, for example, will have data about its sales to me, phone calls, interactions I have had with them (such as mail), past targeted communications (such as brochures), loyalty schemes for repeat customers, and how well these schemes have performed. DMPs also make use of third-party data such as demographic information, social media data, monitoring of online conversations (such as Twitter), analysis of images we have posted, and information bought from other data brokers. The task of DMPs is to establish who we are and then track us through as many means as possible to serve advertising across the devices we use. For another example consider in-store experiences.

The potential here is based on our mobile devices because they say a great deal about us. In-store beacons may gather data from mobile devices and transmit offers to us. This involves practices of *geo-marketing* (inclusion of geographical awareness into marketing efforts), *geo-targeting* (targeting by where a person's device is) and *geo-fencing* (a virtual radius around a store or device). Each of these assists brands in sending real-time ads and offers to a consumer's location. We can begin to see big data processing in operation as we have a lot of data moving throughout the networks, coming from different sources, that needs to be employed in real time as we move through streets, shops and commercial spaces. Further, these will not just react to give us offers for the present moment, but they will also *predict* what we will do next. This may involve products we might be interested in, where we will visit next, or whether it is time to take the weight off our feet and enjoy an iced coffee nearby. (And then once we have settled and feel renewed, provide suggestions on what to do next.) The character of big data-mediated environments (where our behaviour and actions are digitized and mediated through networks) is notable because of real-time reactivity. This gives a sense of *liquidity* in that we have a tailored information layer that overlays physical reality (buildings, street signs and items in-store). As we saw in discussion of programmatic advertising and as will be developed below in regard to big data techniques, the data is *dynamic*. By this I mean that data changes consistency in real time as fresh incoming data affects the original data set. This augmented informational layer alters depending on the behavioural history of the person, their devices and connections with others in the vicinity, store loyalty memberships, location patterns and purchasing history. These increasingly provide opportunity for targeted ads, in-store promotions and collection of data about our devices. This subsequently enhances customer relationship management programmes (such as later emails, display ads, telephone calls, recommendations on related products, social media targeting and so on).

Profiling and identity

Profiling simply means generating information about individuals and groups, and turning that information into knowledge that is useful in some way. Although this book is primarily interested in digital profiling it can be done directly by people, as in the case of focus groups, vox pops, in-person surveys, interviews, other qualitative tools, and what we can summarize as *person>person profiling*. It may also be carried out by *machinic profiling*. There are two sorts of this: the first is *machine>person* when we are directly assessed (such as when moving through retail environments, airports or through streets; and the second is *machine>machine* profiling where our devices (such as phones and wearable gadgets) are assessed.

Machinic profiling is suited to generating information about large amounts of people because machines are better at identifying trends, patterns and correlations in large data sets (such as Amazon's 'because you bought X, you might be interested in Y'). The machinic approach entails 'a set of technologies, which share at least one common characteristic: the use of algorithms or other techniques to create, discover or construct knowledge from huge sets of data' (Hildebrandt, 2008: 17). The word *construct* is an important one in that machinic data does not reflect truths about people, but by means of patterns and behavioural tracing it creates simulations of target groups. These profiles may then be used to make decisions. In advertising these decisions are not incredibly important to people because they simply affect the sort of advertising and marketing we receive (although differential pricing remains a concern). In other industries, such as insurance, for example, the construction of our virtual identities is more important because it affects premiums and whether we are deemed to be a good risk. In surveillance and crime prevention the stakes are even higher. Decisions about people may be reached by automated machines alone, or with some sort of human intervention. In an advertising context, this involves knowing where potential recipients of advertising live, what they do, where they go, who they associate with, what they say to each other, their income, their interests, their political dispositions, how they are feeling, what motivates them to action, and what they buy. When advertisers and marketers know what type of people they are communicating with, and who is buying their goods, this allows them to refine and personalize their advertising, to offer more relevant products, to reward loyalty (and therefore encourage more purchasing) and potentially offer pricing strategies based on what is known about a person.

We typically think about identity as who we are and our similarities to and differences from other people. Profilers agree with us, but would also add that identity is a valuable business. Nielsen, a leading consumer trends firm, proclaims on its homepage that 'Nielsen Knows

People'. This presents an impressive paradox in that the data industry is keen to be intimate with consumers at a global scale. This is not just global localism, but aggressive global intimacy where the digital data industry understands consumers through 'expressed, observed and inferred data points' (Bluekai, 2014: 3). The task for the data industry is the 'pursuit of consumer identities' to understand likely wants, needs and behaviours of people. The phase in quotation marks is not mine, but the title of a report published by eXelate, a company that owns one of the world's most successful DMPs. Elsewhere eXelate's website promises to 'connect customer identities across all formats – including display, video, audio, offline, mobile and smart TVs – enabling marketers to engage individuals and households with personalized messages to drive performance, at scale' (eXelate, 2015). To put this into context, eXelate tracks 5 billion unique users and devices worldwide (PCs, tablets and mobile data) and makes use of over 200 online data providers (different companies tracking online). To simplify this for advertisers who want to advertise across multiple devices, it categorizes this massive data into the following categories: demographic information that comes from online and offline publishers. This is collected from social networking sites and aggregated into demographic, psychographic and lifestyle segments. It also collects information about *interests* from online consumer interactions that indicate a proclivity towards certain topics, including memberships of specific interest clusters or enthusiast groups such as mountain biking or science fiction movies. The most valuable segment is *intent*, because people are actively searching for products or services and are ready to become customers. This data is sourced from e-commerce sites, shopping comparison portals and lead generation lists (where advertising has generated expressed interest in a product). Its *brand* data is a direct challenge to traditional media buying agencies. eXelate says:

> Offline advertisers used to rely on big names in data to help them raise brand awareness and sell products. You can now do the same with digital advertising. Our smart data includes top-tier data owners and publishers who sell their segments directly and transparently to you. (eXelate, 2015)

This allows brand advertisers to bypass media agencies and buy space direct from eXelate. Lastly, it also offers *business-to-business* (B2B) services that target business professionals, budget holders and influential decision makers. While all of this sounds very impressive and (with a privacy hat on) potentially sinister, it is worth keeping in mind comments in *Advertising Age* from Bob Ray who runs DWA, a media-planning and communications agency for tech companies. He tells that for one of its clients DWA employed three ad-tech platforms: Affectv, Bizo and Quantcast. What he found is that despite rhetoric of pinpoint targeting, advanced consumer insight and claims to being almost psychic when it comes to reading behaviour, the final reports about the client's audience contradicted each other (Ray, 2014). We might also keep in mind lessons from Chapter 8 on fraud, bots and lack of clarity about whether portions of audiences are even real.

Social analytics

Sentiment analysis is the use of digital means to extract understanding and meaning from group behaviour, people's preferences and what we say on social media. Consider how familiar some of the following posts, tweets and check-ins are:

▸ LOVE the Old Spice Guy. Marry meeeeeeee!!!
▸ I'm looking for a new set of golf clubs. Any recommendations?
▸ The new Apple OS sucks big tiiiime
▸ Tim S. @Starbucks
▸ Just got tweeted on X-Factor. Full of win! Lol ;)
▸ Ed Miliband. Liked his ideas but couldn't have voted for him. His brother though...
▸ In London tonight. Meet at All Bar One Covent Garden?
▸ I crushed a 9.3km run with Nike+ and pace of 6'14
▸ Zoella, please help me (if you can). Love the Ted Baker handbag, but no cash. What should I buy?
▸ Keanu Reeves in new #StarTrek. Hunky!

While individually these posts mean very little, when mentions are traced and combined from the various social networks this *social data* provides a useful picture for marketers. There are many companies working in this area, but the aim is the same: to monitor online conversations and understand what people are saying, where they are saying it and how they feel about it; to understand the impact of campaigns; to recognize who is influencing conversations; and to be able to ascertain how campaigns, brands and messages are performing in relation to the competition. From *billions* of posts, check-ins, tweets, snaps and so on, information first has to be collected before it is mined. Clients of analytics companies will have questions they want answering. For example Volkswagen might ask, 'How is our new model, the Golf 5.0, being received?' Analytics companies will then search social media sites and provide historical data (what has been said within a given timeframe) and real-time data (as the conversations unfold across social media). Datasift, for example, is a company that describes itself as a provider of Human Data Intelligence and analyses posts and communication on social media sites such as Sina Weibo, Facebook, Instagram, Tumblr, Google+, Reddit, YouTube, WordPress and Disqus (among many others).[56] It also examines online news sites to see how products, brands and services are performing. This is done through massive providers such as DailyMotion, blogs and the LexisNexis database that covers over 20,000 media outlets globally. It analyses social media sites to: gather market insights (for example, by understanding interests this allows more targeted marketing/advertising); build audience profiles; measure results and effectiveness of marketing activities; and optimize marketing efforts and campaigns (such as perfecting the emotional tone of the content to resonate with the people that it is aimed at). This is another good example of a big data company in that it has vast amounts of incoming data from what Datasift claims to be thousands of sources. This is filtered by means of questions asked of that information. Answers are fed to a company's own database so it can use insights derived from social networks in real time.

Notably social media companies such as Twitter are seeking to do this kind of big data analysis themselves. They ended agreements with third parties (such as Datasift) for reselling firehose data (the unfiltered full stream of all tweets). Instead, Twitter will use its own analytics team (helped by its acquisition of Gnip in 2014),[57] to build direct relationships with organizations interested in consumer sentiment, market trends and tracking online conversations. Twitter is a particularly good example because it is often lauded as the 'thermometer of public opinion'. Likewise, sentiment analysis is the examination of language (and images) by marketers, political strategists, and anyone interested in understanding feelings towards their brands, services, products, political organizations, individual politicians or policies. For example, American Airlines uses MutualMind Command Center.[58] MutualMind provides real-time analysis of social media (again, especially Twitter), and positive and negative brand mentions. In the case of American Airlines, this allows the company to understand what travellers, employees and other stakeholders are saying. In addition to understanding people's feelings towards the brand, this also flags up specific problems, for example inadequate legroom, complaints about food or compliments on in-flight staff. As a consequence, this allows American Airways to improve its long-term planning and procurement, but also its real-time public relations, responses to crises and the introduction of brand/product initiatives. (Somewhat ironically I wrote this section while enjoying a six-hour delay waiting for an American Airways flight in San Francisco!)

Text

Most sentiment miners assess text in social media environments because it is more easily identified, clustered and categorized than images. The process works by 'scraping' (collecting) data from social networks to generate 'insights' into what people think, feel and do. As mentioned, brands typically use sentiment analysis to chart and categorize brand mentions and relevant discussion to generate a picture of what people think and feel about a topic. Companies such as Cluep promise to target people based on their social media conversations, feelings, topics, demographic and location, and serve ads on their mobile. Sentiment miners also identify the sources of these conversations and influences on people (by means of profiling individuals, connections and environments). Insights include profile matching and capacity to create identifiable groups of people on the basis of pre-specified criteria (e.g. behaviour, personality, likes, purchases, brand mentions or demographic criteria) and identifying communities of interest; and personal dimensions (leisure, what people do in their spare time, what they do for a living, educational background, purchasing history and brand interests). Beyond the interests of a given organization (such as brands or political parties), sentiment analysis is also used for assessment of social sentiment surrounding competitors' products and brands. Scraping also generates insight into "customer journeys", customers' interactions with a company's "touchpoints", advertising, marketing and social media activities so as to map positive and negative engagement, and improve sales and marketing. Improvement of marketing not only includes a company's own marketing; sentiment analysis also grants opportunities for working with other companies. This is because sentiment analysis can identify other brands audiences are interested in. This allows opportunity for alliances of brands, communities of brand interests, and cross-branding and editorial content, i.e. where marketing efforts of two separate companies are combined. There are, however, methodological problems with text-based approaches to sentiment because words do not always reflect intention. For example, 'that worked out well' can be said sincerely or sarcastically, which hinders the categorization and reliability of text-based analysis. Greater contextual understanding is required to situate meaning and intention. Much work within computer sciences and linguistics is going into understanding the *context* of language use so as to better understand intentions.

Images

Instagram, Snapchat, Meerkat, Periscope and Super indicate that social media are increasingly visual. Indeed, on social media sites such as Tumblr, the overwhelming majority of posts are images. For the next wave of sentiment analysts, images provide a great deal of insight into what people are doing with their products, what they are doing with those of their competitors, and in general they provide a great deal of insight into how brands are used and what people feel about them. There is a wide range of companies working in the visual sentiment analysis field. For example the UK-based company, Aurora Creative, has biometric facial recognition tools able to tag gender, age (young/old), ethnicity, expressions (emotions) and how long someone has spent looking at an ad. Its clients currently include the UK government, for whom it creates bespoke hardware and software, Heathrow airport, brands such as Barclays bank and advertising agencies including RAPP. To quote its website: 'Aurora Creative was set up to meet the demand from brands and advertising agencies to use our technology to create cutting edge biometric experiences for their customers' (Aurora Creative, 2014).

Some of our favourite social media sites such as Instagram and Pinterest allow images to be scanned in bulk or downloaded for marketing purposes (although photos marked as private by users, or not to be shared, are not available to marketers). Visual data is important for analytics companies because they recognize that images are more impactful than text and engage emotions to a greater extent (text is more cognitive). As with text-based sentiment analysis, individually our posts mean little but when aggregated they generate useful intelligence for advertising and marketing companies. This market awareness allows companies to see the context in which their products are being used (how, where and with whom). It also allows them to do the same analysis of the competition to help strategically outflank them. Indeed, one US analytics firm called Ditto searches photos posted on social media. It discovers, collects and tags products, clothing, logos, scenes and emotional expressions on faces. This allows Ditto's users to analyse trends in content, understand competitors, and use this to target advertising and cross-promote brands (particularly if there is more than one brand in the image).

Images may often contain a great deal of useful information. Consider Instagram, Flickr or Pinterest, for example: we post photos of ourselves and our friends where facial expressions indicate emotional states; clothing and apparel brands we like to wear are visible; we might be holding a branded beer can or soft drink; and we might also disclose either the precise location, type of location or where we are using the products and brands contained in the photos. These insights are useful for brands, particularly if we consider that in 2014 Instagram had around 20 billion photos shared on its service, and now users are adding around 60 million a day. Firms such as Piqora[59] store images for months on their servers to be able to conduct longitudinal analysis. This is done to illustrate market trends and product usage, and thereafter advise companies on their visual social media strategies.

Another analytics firm, Crimson Hexagon, also makes use of Tumblr. As a "Preferred Analytics Partner"[60] it has access to Tumblr's firehose which allows it to retrieve all brand mentions (words) and logos (images), the capacity to assess how much conversation is taking place about a brand (volume), and whether this is favourable or not (sentiment). It does this to track text-based conversations that, on Tumblr, can develop rapidly so as to understand both *share of voice* and the *voice of the consumer*. The first refers to the popularity of a brand among an audience, and the second is the practice of understanding what people actually think. The principle of the voice of the consumer is an old one derived from when agencies used qualitative research and focus groups to attempt to understand what people *really* think. Analysis can be within a day, a week or over months to provide both short-term and longitudinal analysis about whether people are positive, neutral or negative about brands. It also allows companies to know where, when and in what conversational contexts their brands are appearing. Notably, it also allows them to identify who the influencers are within networks (for instance, are people being re-tweeted, liked and so on).

Crimson Hexagon's work with Tumblr also allows it to conduct image analysis on behalf of brands to understand *share of eyes*, and how images are being disseminated and distributed with a company's logo. Given the increasing tendency of social media towards visuality, this is important. There are consequences: (1) this image analysis does not require associated words to "anchor" the image; (2) and it allows brands to protect themselves and ensure their logos are being seen in a favourable light. For example, Monster, the caffeine-based drink and brand, is happy to be seen held by a young man with tattoos holding a guitar, but would be less happy to be seen held by a member of the Ku Klux Klan (to give a hypothetical example). The point is that image analysis allows brands the capacity to *see* how their brands are being used, to react if a PR/brand crisis emerges, to take advantage of immediate opportunities, and to use these insights to plan long-term strategy (such as sponsoring a music festival to get closer to young people interested in rock music).

Notably, because images are often posted for anyone to see and download, there are no regulations forbidding publicly available photos from being analysed in bulk. Although image-hosting websites are required in their terms and conditions of use to inform people of what may happen with their images, and who may use them, the language is vague and refers to 'third-party organizations' rather than clearly stating which companies will be using a person's self-image.

Marketing to our virtual personal assistants (VPAs)

As we look to "what next" in the identity and market intelligence field, there are a few things becoming clear. The first is that our smart devices will play a more pronounced role in managing our own online lives and our virtual identities. In addition to helping manage mundane parts of our lives (such as grocery shopping and entering calendar details), they will also mediate what advertising and marketing communications we personally receive. As Clabiorne et al. (2015), writing for PHD (a media and communications agency), highlight, the direction of travel for personal assistants is towards *sentient* artificial minds that manage our lives. This takes the principles of relevance, profiling and identity to a new level. As VPAs work on our behalf, they will filter and whittle down content to only that which we need to see, know or have expressed interest in. Working across all our screens, wearables, in-car systems, diaries, email and interactions with others, the VPA's sorting capacities will transcend each of these. The scope for relevant behavioural and predictive recommendations includes bookings and tickets for events, restaurants, holidays, services and consumer objects. This will be established by means of calendar space, planned activities, types of friends, moods and sentiment, exercise levels and purchase histories. Users of Google Calendar will be familiar with some of this as items such as details of flights and hotels purchased online are automatically inserted. The bigger picture is a mapping of the entire context of our lives. This sees the programmatic logic discussed earlier taken to another level because this would be a biddable ad-model in which only "ads" (really better seen as native pieces of content embedded in the VPA's communication) that pass a quality/relevance threshold established in relation to personal life context will reach us.

The programmatic, biddable and automated part of this is key as deep learning processes (the ability for machines to define important trends in large data sets) and algorithms (the step-by-step process used by a computer to achieve a goal) establish the ad content that is right for us at that given place and time. As the reader might recollect, programmatic logic today is about extracting information about us from multiple sources to target us with relevant advertising. VPAs promise to push the predictive dimension of this to the next level by having reliable access to our life contexts. For some years now, Apple's Siri, Google Now and Cortana from Microsoft have helped us schedule appointments into our calendars, find pudding recipes and get us to our hotels. As intelligent assistants increasingly act on our behalf, make purchasing decisions, advise on what to do over the weekend and sort reservations, they will become a target for marketing. How might this work? What techniques are required to convince artificial intelligence (AI) entities they should choose brand X over Y on our behalf? The answer is the same as with people: by understanding behaviour and decision-making processes. In the case of personal assistants, brands will have to market to algorithms. Just as companies have differentiated themselves by values, ingredients and associations with like-minded brands, algorithms will need to be addressed by a greater set of values than price. This is optimization, not unlike the discussion of search advertising in Chapter 3 whereby crawlers search the content of webpages to find relevant attributes to the user and search query.

Who would want these assistants? It is instructive to look to social media where we make a choice to share a great deal of information about ourselves. Although it is questionable whether people are happy to do this, whether they feel in control of their choices (see survey discussion in Chapter 12), and whether social media companies are being clear on the nature of data for service contracts, each of us do see a *value exchange* – despite it being built on questionable terms (also see Chapter 12 on consent). This is the service/ data transaction. The questions for our discussion are: (1) whether VPAs represent good value in terms of the data/privacy and service exchange; (2) whether we are able to live without them. Particularly for people who work in offices and maintain diaries, will we be coerced as a condition of employment into a VPA? Another outcome is multi-tiered VPAs, where some will be heavily based on ad models and need to give feedback about our experiences of products/events; others will be paid for, thus reducing need for an advertising and privacy-invasive model.

Conclusion

This chapter has focused on the specifics of big data in advertising. Big data analytics involves Laney's (2001) three Vs: volume, velocity and variety. In advertising terms, big data approaches are employed by data management platforms (DMPs) that collect data from all possible sources (offline and online) to assist in creating identity clusters and targeting advertising across all possible screens. Other smaller analytics firms focus on sentiment and social media. They provide insight to organizations about how brands, products, ad campaigns, politicians, policies and charities are performing. The point is that these processes analyse a great deal of information coming in from many sources so their clients can act on this information in real-time. However, to understand the significance of big data it is useful not just to understand the practicalities, but the character of big data. The term expresses clinical accuracy and access to truths that were otherwise impossible to access. This gives it a somewhat mythical, magical, and what in Chapter 13 we will refer to as sublime, status.

Think points and questions

▸ What are "analytics"?

▸ What is the difference between big data and lots of information?

▸ Look up some of the big data targeting firms: what do they do, how do they work, what clients so they serve and what data do they collect?

▸ This chapter's discussion of virtual personal assistants (VPAs) is an educated peer into the future. On the basis of what you understand about profiling and academic reading beyond this book, what does the future hold for advertising to mobiles and personal assistants? What opportunities are there for advertisers, companies that process VPA data and adblockers?

11 Empathic Media: Emotiveillance and the Future of Out of Home Advertising

Out of home advertising is, unsurprisingly, advertising that reaches people while they are outside of the home. The definition of out of home is broad because so much happens out of home. We have streets, squares, shopping centres, travel hubs, cash point screens and transportation that all make use of advertising, but also the little things that can be occupied (ranging from beer mats, tickets, lampposts and stairways to whole buildings wrapped in branded content). Out of home advertising possesses unique characteristics in that: we cannot turn it off; ads can be served at scale (such as cross-track advertising while waiting for a Tube train); and it can be linked with nearby retailers (whether through a poster, a QR code, or a message sent to our phone while out of home). It is an intrinsically *public* medium in that whereas television, print and most online media are consumed privately, out of home is targeted at people as they move through public spaces. Increasingly out of home is digitally displayed and networked, but 2015 saw the introduction of sensors employed to understand intimate information about what we are feeling. To explore this phenomenon we will examine M&C Saatchi's 2015 landmark artificially intelligent poster campaign, which *evolves* unique ads based on people's facial reactions. This was a test for a fictional coffee brand named Bahio and to gauge public reaction to this form of advertising. Secondly we will consider Mindshare's 2015 work at the Wimbledon tennis championship. This made of use of a wider range of emotional sensing technologies placed around the venue. Whereas other chapters have comprehensively accounted for other aspects of digital media (such as analytics, display, native advertising), this chapter focuses on specific developments in out of home media – these are: a) the ways in which digital outdoor advertising is using sensors and cameras to get closer to people by means of reading our emotions and behaviour; and b) advertising that improves itself on the basis of biometric and behavioural information.

Although advertising has always sought to get closer to us and be more intimate, this is the first time (that I am aware of) that advertising outdoors has *optimized itself* to be more effective on the basis of viewers' emotional reactions. This is a significant development because machines working for commercial companies are now watching what we do in the real world, and not just online. Although this is an extremely notable development in itself, this chapter uses this example as a departure point to consider what emotionally aware advertising portends. To do this, I advance two concepts: *emotiveillance* and *empathic media*. The first is the practice of monitoring of emotions, usually for the purpose of influencing and managing people. The second refers to technologies used to assess our emotions. This includes online techniques such as sentiment analysis, but also assessment of voices, faces and bodies to infer feelings and emotional states. Importantly, the cases examined here do not rely on personal data, but what I account for as intimate data.

Emotionally aware billboards

M&C Saatchi's homepage positions the agency as one that spans art and science. In the UK M&C Saatchi tested bus shelter ads with hidden Microsoft Kinect cameras that read viewers' emotions and react according to whether a person's facial expression is happy, sad or neutral. The test ads appeared on London's Oxford Street and Clapham Common in 2015. The ads did not feature a real brand, but a fictional coffee brand named Bahio. The objective was to test in public whether ads can read the reactions of audiences and adapt accordingly. I will also wager that they did not use a real brand because the agency and its partners, Clear Channel and Posterscope, wanted to gauge the public's reaction first. As explored below, one would be forgiven for thinking that advertising that reads people's emotions is a bit creepy.

Not only do the ads assess people's reactions but also, on the basis of people's reactions, improve themselves until they get positive reactions from their audience. This means the ad has purpose, it evolves, it improves and it kills off elements of itself that fail to trigger engagement, so only the strongest creative executions survive. This is an evolutionary form of intelligence in that it makes use of feedback from its environment to improve itself. This is exactly the same principle as when students receive essay grades and comments. The student acts on the feedback, amends, corrects, removes mistakes, optimizes for next time and (in theory) improves the standard of essay writing. When this happens more than once a *feedback cycle* is introduced because as students submit more than one essay they will get feedback on the already improved work, yet again go through the process of correction and optimization, and so on. On feedback loops and self-correction, M&C Saatchi's David Cox, Chief Innovation Officer, commented:

> This innovation is breaking new ground in the industry because it's the first time a poster has been let loose to entirely write itself, based on what works, rather than just what a person thinks may work... We are not suggesting a diminished role for creative but we know technology will be playing a greater part in what we do.

What are we to make of these out of home developments? There are four key factors to keep in mind: (1) we now have ads that read our behaviour in public; (2) this information is not just about what type of websites we click on, but about our emotions; (3) ads use this information to improve themselves; and (4) a new opportunity to industrialize emotional life emerges.

Artificial intelligence

The real genius of M&C Saatchi's ad is in using our facial expressions to learn and alter the design of the ad (by means of the feedback loops we mentioned). By changing according to our expressions, the ads have purpose. The logic behind this is an evolutionary one in that they improve and, with little human intervention beyond initial programming, become more effective. This was urged and foreseen around 100 years ago by luminaries in advertising such as such as Daniel Starch (1914) and Claude Hopkins (1998 [1923]). As described in Chapter 10, they insisted that advertising should be treated as a science based on collecting information, analysing it and using these insights to improve campaigns. Feedback is key, and little has changed today as Hopkins sought to understand what techniques work, what do not, and how to make the business of advertising subject to laws of cause and effect. The grandfathers of advertising would be very pleased with today's progeny.

Although the logic is old, the capacity to process feedback and self-correct in real time *is* new. This is an advertising landmark because although Google has for years masterfully led the way in how ads are automatically served based on our interests, ads in real space that improve themselves is another step. Much of the media coverage surrounding the M&C Saatchi ad lauds it as an artificially intelligent campaign. To an extent this is true, in that it makes use of feedback from its environment to improve itself. But, seen otherwise, the ad is actually quite mechanical, because it has no understanding of *why* we are smiling, grimacing or straight-faced. It is simply reacting to stimuli from its environment. Although the ads may appear intelligent they are actually quite dumb. This begs the question: what would intelligent advertising look like? The answer is that it should be able to engage with our life contexts in real time. What are these "contexts"? This is a somewhat philosophical question, but in the case of people they encompass our individual histories, and the bigger picture of natural spoken language, human values, politics, current affairs, popular culture, and art, aesthetic and typographic trends. M&C Saatchi's campaign clearly does not engage with these life contexts. As discussed in relation to the principle of feedback, the ad is better conceived in relation to *cybernetics*. The history of this is also involved (see McStay, 2011a), but the key principle behind it is the conversion of all domains of life into information. This is what happens in the ad campaign because the ad does not understand emotion in the usual sense of what it means to understand that a person is happy or sad. Instead it tracks the facial shape of emotion (smiles and grimaces) and accepts this information as "input". It then processes this information, internally alters the ad, and then publicly presents the "output" and awaits "feedback" from people (further input) so as to progress towards an ad that only generates smiles from its environment. Once rendered into information, which in the case of networked technologies is electrical signals, this can be treated like any other quantity. The M&C Saatchi ad used facial coding techniques. This maps faces by means of 3D mesh grids across points of the face used for expression such as eyes and the mouth. Software then analyses each pixel in the region to describe the relationship of different points of the face to each other. If this seems difficult to understand, try smiling. The corners of your mouth will rise in relation to the eyes. Similarly, try a shocked expression. Again, the geometry of your face will alter. These shapes and relationships can be mapped and coded which means, in turn, that public displays of emotion can be converted into information.

Cybernetic logic entails systems that: process incoming information from their environments (such as viewers smiling or grimacing);

self-regulate (to categorize incoming information); and thereafter allocate resources to achieve a pre-determined goal (that in the case of the ad means more smiles and less grimaces from the environment). Cybernetics is most certainly the road to artificial intelligence, but they are not the same thing. Real artificial intelligence (AI) in advertising involves two key factors: (1) the capacity to learn and grow; (2) the capacity to have an appreciation of the context or environment in which the intelligent agent is placed. We only need consider people to get a sense of what this means. We are not born fully formed, but as we mature our brains and thereafter our minds grow, make links, learn, understand languages, make connections, comprehend relationships between things, and we begin to understand the historical significance of our environments and life context. Large technology companies such as Google are creating machines that, like people, learn by means of neural networking. This refers to the way the infant human brain learns and grows in reference to events it undergoes (such as fire hurts, silk feels nice, or smiling at people means people are more likely to smile back at us). Similarly, when a machine gets a desired response back from a person or thing within its environment, the neural pathways are strengthened so the next time it undergoes a similar event, the machine is likely to respond correctly. We can see an aspect of this in the M&C Saatchi ad, but the range of inputs (facial arrangements that equate to happy, sad or neutral) is limited. Still, the capacity to process and self-correct *is* very notable. The path forward for this sort of advertising is a greater range of environmental inputs to generate greater machinic awareness. Google is working extensively in this area and its acquisition of DeepMind, an AI company, in 2014 reflects its intentions for and belief in technologies that learn. The emulation of biological systems means that machines will continue to be adaptive, to improve natural language capacities (understanding how people speak), get better at prediction, and be able to deal with more complex questions.

The tendency towards the capacity for adaption and *deep learning* is reflected in the following two situations. If we wanted to teach a neural network to learn we could provide it with images containing apples and oranges. If we labelled the oranges and apples, the machine would eventually be able to recognize apples and oranges in other images. Where deep learning differs is that it allows us to give the AI machine a massive amount of images and the machine will be able to categorize the apples and oranges by itself. The machine is not asked to identify specific trends, but rather it identifies similarities and categories.

If images each containing apples and oranges are scaled up to the entire history of Facebook (for example), we can see that machines can identify categories and answers to questions that people did not even know how to ask. The same applies for marketers too in that by applying deep learning techniques to databases on audiences (first and third party), this opens up interests, patterns, correlations, groupings, clusters, categories and opportunities that marketers would otherwise be unaware of. Further, as we provide these intelligent deep learning machines ever-diversifying data types, a very rich picture of people is generated. This might include a range of factors, including histories such as location and personal information held on our phones; facial tagging so as to compare a scan and our faces with a database; data derived from wearables such as breath and heart rates/responses; friends lists; social media postings; purchasing histories and banking data; tracking data from ads/retail environments equipped with cameras and other sensing technologies; opt-in check-in technologies as with Facebook and Foursquare; and more. From our current vantage point, this seems unlikely and spooky, but we only have to look at social media to see that people are very willing to share intimate information with real people and machines.

And over at Wimbledon

What these types of technologies do is use *biometric* information. This refers to the analysis of human body characteristics. In the case of M&C Saatchi, this was a person's facial expression. There are other opportunities that marketers and advertisers will take advantage of in coming years. We saw a taster of this at the Wimbledon tennis championship in 2015. In partnership with Wimbledon, creative tech partner Maido and wearables and human data specialist Lightwave, Mindshare launched a campaign called *Feel Wimbledon* that captured the mood and emotions of the Wimbledon crowd by means of heart rate variability, localized audio, motion and skin temperature of 20 fans in the crowd, via sensor-equipped wristbands. This allowed Jaguar to create 'living ads' by means of visualizing fluctuating emotions.

Other sensors were installed around the tennis courts and viewing areas. Analysts used emotional analytics to collect live sounds from courts as fans roared, heart rates of "super fans" that wore the devices on their wrists, and output on social media. Through this, they were able to read Wimbledon's emotions over the course of the matches, visualize emotion by means of readouts from people's bodies, assess noise within the event and track social media activity (biometric, atmospheric and sociometrics). When one considers the variety of emotions experienced at a tennis match (admiration, tension, elation, nerves, joy, frustration, exhilaration, relief and disappointment), the technologies provide interesting insights. Scaled up, this has implications for advertisers because increasingly they are able to access data on when we are most responsive to ads, environments and specific brands.

Theorizing emotive approaches

This is best understood in terms of what I call "experience architecture". To understand what takes place at events today, I suggest three informational layers that may be considered in campaigns making use of out of home empathic media:

1. *Physical reality*: this includes buildings, street signs and things we can touch and see without devices;
2. *Augmented reality*: by this I mean the informational, communicative and representational layers of information that overlay physical reality. This is typically accessed with smartphones, but also smart-glasses and other wearable technologies such as watches. These grant access to apps and services. Some of these will require users to turn away from physical reality to focus on the information (as with a phone screen), but others such as smart-glasses grant more interplay between the virtual information that one sees and physical reality;
3. *Emotional augmentation*: what is more novel for marketers and advertisers is the capacity to think in terms of emotional layers of reality. This has less to do with what people are doing, where they are, or what they are saying than how they are feeling. This is of consequence for retail, urban design and placement of advertising because data about emotions facilitates emotion mapping.

Emotiveillance

The emotional dimension of these informational layers is best understood by what we can phrase as *emotiveillance*, or the monitoring of emotions so to influence and manage people. In the case of analytics for advertising, there are three key categories:

▸ *Ambient and environmental*: as indicated by M&C Saatchi's work, this can be done with cameras embedded in advertising, but it can also be done with floor sensors, temperature, movement, voice analytics and activity (cameras not just in ads, but elsewhere too). Voice analytics can record both what people are saying, but perhaps more importantly from the point of emotion, *how* people are saying it.

▸ *Intimate*: increasingly we wear technologies that monitor our bodies. This potentially provides a rich data set for marketers and advertisers. These technologies measure heart rate, sweat, activity, respiration, thirst and ways in which the body is stimulated (which in turn is a good indicator of emotion). Moods and emotions are indivisible from the body, so emotiveillant data captured by wearables allow some inference into what and how we are feeling.

▸ *Communicative*: this reflects emotions expressed on social media (Twitter data being the most obvious real-time way of accessing this). Also, our mobile devices say a great deal in that they process data from our wearables and may have voice analytics that understand not only what we ask, but the mood we are in when we communicate to, and through, our phones. They also contain communication histories and the images we have snapped throughout the period of a given event.

Together these can be mapped onto a real-time chart that depicts incoming information from sensors, wearables, and mobile and social data. The real-time dimension of this is important because although we are used to the commercialization of online spaces to understand people's reactions (as done through analytics and social media), the capacity to directly chart emotion in real time allows for granular analysis in regard to: location; what people are feeling when they are engaged in an activity (be this purchasing or wandering through a gallery); what they are saying; what they have bought and done; and their interactions with objects (such as goods and ads). In essence this is to make people emotionally transparent. There are two dimensions of potential for advertising in that this information can be used for *subsequent campaign planning*, understanding of brands, demographic understanding and general post-event development. This information can also be used for *real-time campaign development* and marketing efforts. Although the M&C Saatchi work is based on traditional advertising, there is also opportunity to borrow strategies found in native advertising, which employs more oblique approaches to advertising. These focus on values, feeling, quality and sensation, as opposed to hard sell and the obvious display of logos and corporate icons. This is a more immersive approach suited to brands with well-established reputations that seek to intensify the connection rather than make people aware of their existence. Similarly, in contrast to standard ad formats, people may be encouraged to overtly interact with environments.

Empathic media

What I term *empathic media* refers to the capacity for emergent media technologies to sense, interpret and understand what is significant for people, act on their emotional states, pre-empt behaviour, and make use of their intentions and expressions (McStay, 2014). Whereas emotiveillance refers to monitoring of emotions, empathic media are the technologies themselves. Although the 2015 M&C Saatchi experiments in London made use of facial coding, the principle of emotional analytics and inferring emotions from bodily behaviour (rather than solely what we click online) is much broader. Cues perceived by empathic media include physiological change (for example pupil dilation, pulse, heart rate, blood pressure, body temperature or respiration), electrodermal responses, pheromones, galvanic skin responses such as sweat, facial/body expressions, sound and voice inflection, and speech and language selection. In each case, empathic media involve systems that directly monitor behaviour by means of our bodily movement and outputs. Empathic media are thus *media systems able to read people, animals and their environments by means of their speech, behaviour, bodily movement and responses to sensory and affective stimuli, and to act appropriately on their reactions.* We can even go a step further than this to say that machines can do a very good impression of knowing what it means to "be in the shoes of others" and to understand their emotional state. We know this to be true because they are getting better at being able to make predictions about a person's perspective and disposition. This has less to do with authenticity than what elsewhere I have termed *machinic verisimilitude* that involves the semblance of intimate knowledge of people (McStay, 2014). In more straightforward language this means that our devices and technologies *appear* to understand what we feel and think, but they do not – or at least not in same way that people think and feel.

The creepy factor: unrequited intimacy

Sir Martin Sorrell, CEO of WPP, was asked 'whether they [his company] would want to reach people with a marketing message knowing their emotive state' by the presenter for BBC's new media programme, *Click*.[61] He responded: 'Yes, one would like to do that but within the grounds of people knowing exactly what they're getting into so demystifying the process, simplifying the process, making people understand what they're letting themselves in for... that's really important'. As emotionally aware as out of home stands today, it is in the curious situation of not using personal data. There most certainly is scope to link with mobile devices and personalized wearables, and thereafter data management platforms (such as eXelate's, as discussed in Chapter 10), but we are not there yet. In the case of M&C Saatchi's work (that was conducted in public), all these ads are doing is reacting to facial shapes. As will be discussed in Chapter 12, societal and legal concern about privacy tends to be based on identification, or how information collected can be linked with individuals and/or single them out in some way for unique treatment. Today, automated emotion detection in advertising is intimate, but not personal. This is because analysis of smiles and grimaces, and potentially other biometric factors, is less about access to personally identifiable information than *aggregate* data about emotions. There is scope for legal and technical debate, but the key questions are whether a person is identifiable from the data collected and if a person is singled out in some way to be treated differently. This is important because if data is collected about a face that allows it to be singled out, this requires a viewer's consent.

A key task for scholars of advertising is to understand the implications of not just data privacy, but data intimacy. This may be achieved by use of personally identifiable information, but it is not vital. However, there is very good reason to believe that this information *can* be used to identify people. The reason for this is because of overlapping pieces of information. For example ZIP/postal codes, birth dates, and sex cannot in themselves give the identity of a person away, but when combined they will tell an interested party with access to this information the identity of a person. If companies begin collecting biometric information from devices, identification becomes difficult to guard against. As it stands today, although M&C Saatchi's campaign may seem to be a little more intimate than we might like, it is less invasive than the really spooky stuff online – particularly those "free" apps that have 100s of unknown trackers sucking at our devices. As privacy theory has little to offer, where else should we look to diagnose the creepy factor? If this advertising feels excessively intimate rather than excessively personal, on what basis can we complain? What is the nature of the problem?

A key question we have to ask is this: *is advertising in the business of persuasion or influence?* There is an important difference because the first, persuasion, is based on rationality, making a case, argumentation, and putting one's best foot forward to bring people around to a preferred point of view. It means that people are aware of what is taking place and that they understand that an act of selling is taking place. If advertising is in the business of influence, this is different because influence can be subtle and covert, but powerful. In the case of our emotiveillant discussion it equates to altering environments and making people predisposed to messages without their awareness. Another way of understanding the difference between influence and persuasion is that emotions are inseparably involved in cognitive and decision-making processes. Although we sometimes mistakenly separate the two, emotions help us make judgements and decisions, but they can also be swayed to lead to judgements we might not otherwise make. We need only reflect on our own lives to understand that when we are feeling low we behave differently and are more disposed to certain products than when we are elated. The advertising business is very much aware that people are not as rational as we like to think. The capacity to understand, harness and modulate emotions in people has less to do with suggestion or persuasion than the capacity to directly affect emotions so to steer decision making. Phrased otherwise, emotiveillance and use of empathic media entail innovations in making us predisposed to particular views. In addition to the question about persuasion versus influence, we also have to answer this: do emotional and biometric analytics in advertising represent an unhealthy level of control over society? The word "control" has alarmist connotations, but if we simply recognize that it means steering towards a predetermined goal, we see that this is what the business of advertising has always been interested in: steering people towards sales, and towards positive feelings and thoughts about products.

To date, our laws and regulations are not ready for emotiveillance, empathic media and emotional analytics. Data protection laws are currently based on privacy (unwanted identification), rather than consideration of intimacy. This is a challenge to be overcome in future years. One of the problems faced is that data protection regulators require evidence of clear and demonstrable harms, such as lack of care over what happens with people's personal data. This is reasonable, but emotion detection opens up questions about societal health, the role of advertising in society, the extent to which businesses should be using data about our bodies, and the *environmental* considerations of industrial use of human emotion.

By environmental I do not mean rising sea levels, but human-made technologies and practices that significantly contribute to our lives. Advertising, marketing, industrial activity and commerce have for the last 120 years deeply shaped personal and social life. This occurred first by means of exponential growth in production techniques and factory systems (manufacturing, organization, distribution, retailing and management techniques), and, in parallel, the mass advertising industry. As the latter cohered into a discrete and globally powerful enterprise, the twentieth century gave rise to a new form of economy: one based on attention and emotion. This occurred because the range of products on the market required different identities and branding. This subsequently gave rise to competition for our attention. To win this, advertising companies need to know as much as possible about what stimulates our emotions so as to influence thought. Although we should be wary of dividing social history into convenient neat century-long blocks, the twenty-first century increasingly involves not only twentieth-century human manipulation of attention, aspiration and public sentiment (in advertising agencies and political campaign strategy meetings), but also *machinic* engagement with publicly mediated emotion. Emotionally aware out of home advertising in "smart cities" is thus an environmental question.

To date, we can discern four modes of intimacy employed by advertising and marketers:

▸ *Cultural*: social-semiosis and construction of cultural codes, signs, meaning and broadly shared understanding about what brands stand for;
▸ *Informational*: identity, location, purchase histories, interests, communication;
▸ *Biological*: information about our bodies (heart rate, respiration, voice modulation, fitness and galvanic skin responses);
▸ *Emotional*: use of biological and informational insights to understand our emotional states. This will feed back into the cultural level to create more impactful advertising.

Thus, from an advertising point of view, the twenty-first century is so far looking like one based on electronic information, feedback, understanding patterns of behaviour, increased use of artificial intelligence, the partial automation of the advertising industry, and increased use of biological and emotional information to generate culturally salient content. We are still some way off from this, but given rapid progress being made in automated advertising and AI, it seems inevitable.

Conclusion

As an enterprise that profits from expertise in communication, advertising has always been in the business of emotion. The key difference today is that increasingly the advertising business can see and act on emotions, and programme machines to do this on their behalf. It would be easy to point to M&C Saatchi's ads and say 'that's creepy', 'it's a step too far' or 'what about privacy?'. On the creepy factor, there is an element of this because it represents the intentions of an industry that does not just want to infer our emotions, but that wants certainty about our emotional states. What the campaign represents is an attempt to *get closer* to us. This is a defining characteristic of the advertising and audience research industries: they want to know us more intimately to be able to craft messages that will affect and resonate with us. The act of monitoring emotions with a view to subsequently influencing and managing people is what I designate emotiveillance. The campaigns discussed in this chapter are examples of what I term empathic media because through reading facial expressions they make use of technologies able to bypass the guesswork and make direct use of our emotions (also see McStay, 2014). Although not *yet* based on personally identifiable information, the practice makes use of intimate information. If the industry is to avoid a backlash, it should consider both opt-in approaches and raising the creative quality of the work. This means there has to be a value exchange. This proposition is best seen in gaming where game makers are experimenting with biometrics and emotion and the use of these to enhance gameplay. The reward here is clear (better gaming for data), but in advertising it is unclear how the consumer will benefit.

Think points and questions

▶ Is this a world we want? Do we want businesses to have intimate insight into: a) our bodies; and b) our emotional lives?

▶ Do emotional and biometric analytics in advertising represent an unhealthy level of control over society?

▶ Consider case scenarios for empathic media and advertising. How might they be ethically employed?

▶ Consider creative opportunities: how can empathic media be used in interesting, engaging and ethically sound ways?

12 Privacy: The Case of Mobile Apps for Android

The advertising and data industry is keenly sensitive to concerns about privacy, use of personal and intimate data, and further legislation that would curtail what they can do. It is also caught in something of a bind because as it seeks to allay peoples' concern about behavioural techniques and ad networks, data management platforms and programmatic firms are simultaneously showing off how much data they collect about people and how precise their targeting is. This predicament is reflected in survey statistics from the advertising industry, academia and government-sponsored surveys, which continually show that people have negative views about online advertising and use of personal data. With some irony, Adland has an image problem. We will progress to criticisms of the industry but, before we get going, readers should ask themselves this: 'Do I really want to start paying with cash for my favourite news social media apps sitting on the front page of my smartphone?' Clearly these services need to be paid for somehow, and most of us are willing to participate in a value exchange. The problem is that the terms of the trade are utterly unclear. This raises questions about the nature of consent, privacy and the degree of control we have over information about us. In this chapter we will explore these issues in relation to the Google Android app ecology.

A practical test

One problem with discussion of data tracking is that although it *feels* like it should be an important topic, it is difficult to get excited about without having a sense of *who* is tracking or *what* is being tracked. This is one of the problems about the whole online privacy debate – what is actually going on? Before we go further I recommend the reader install at least one of the programs below. Options are:

For desktop/laptop:

Lightbeam (formerly known as Collusion): this Firefox add-on enables you to see who is tracking your activities on the web without being seen. It does this by means of lists and visualization that links trackers and sites together. If you keep this on throughout the day, you will be surprised at how many organizations are interested in the most banal of your web surfing habits!

Ghostery: this counts how many trackers there are on websites you visit. In class I have had my students compete to find who can find the site with the most trackers. The Perez Hilton homepage is the winner so far (with 146 trackers!).

Adblock Plus: discussed in depth in Chapter 8 and bane of the digital advertising environment, this enables blocking of ads and tracking, and allows users to see who is tracking them online.

Mobile/tablet:

Disconnect: this application tracks the trackers, identifies who they are, and tells the user what happens to the data that is being tracked. Importantly, this works with phones and tablets, and not just desktop computers.

Each of these services works differently, but all of them highlight the separate companies tracking our devices. Lightbeam is perhaps the most interesting because it can be left open during the day to see how different websites, analytics companies and ad servers all link together. See Figure 12.1.

This image in Figure 12.1 represents sites that I actually visited and third-party trackers collecting data from my computer. Usefully it also depicts how they interconnect. Having visited 13 different sites, I also connected with 127 third-party sites (many of which are ad servers or others employed to track a person's behaviour across the web). Roughly speaking, this means that although I may be fine with sharing some information about myself with the sites I visited, I had ten times this number collecting information about me and my online activities. The list in Figure 12.2 details more clearly the sites that are in the graphic in Figure 12.1.

Although we may be happy to share information with the site we are visiting, it is a different proposition to share information histories with people and companies you do not know, cannot see or contact. You will not find Ggpht.com, gstatic.com, dartsearch. net, nr-data.net, adnxs.com or pro-market.net in a telephone directory. My intention is not to spook the reader (scare stories do not lead to thoughtful discussion), but to highlight that underpinning

Fig 12.1

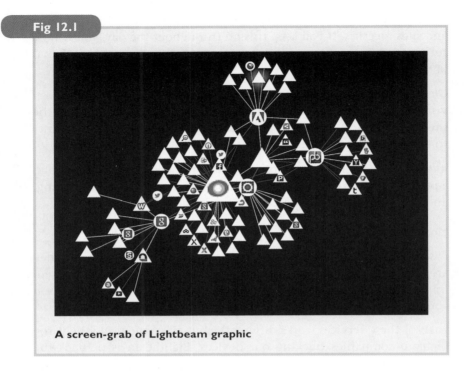

A screen-grab of Lightbeam graphic

the web that most people see is a vast hidden network of third parties, website/software performance enhancers, companies gathering
information and companies using people's data to provide personalized advertising. Very few are aware of this. Seen this way, the web
looks quite different from how we normally conceive it. Try this
for yourself by installing one of the apps I suggest and clicking on
sites you regularly use and visit. Also, click through and, if need be,
search for the homepages of the data mining sites listed. In studying
them, ask: who are they, what do they do, what types of data do they
collect and why is this done?

What is tracked?

Privacy concerns about behavioural advertising and tracking of
users relates to personal data. In Europe personal data includes any
information about an individual, 'whether it relates to his or her
private, professional or public life. It can be anything from a name,

Fig 12.2

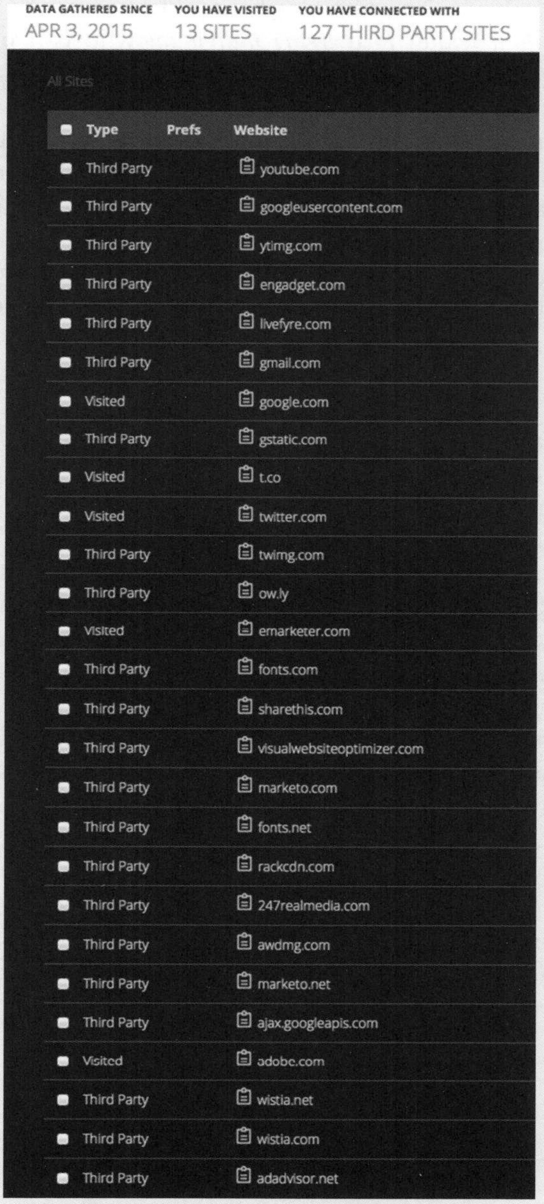

DATA GATHERED SINCE	YOU HAVE VISITED	YOU HAVE CONNECTED WITH
APR 3, 2015	13 SITES	127 THIRD PARTY SITES

All Sites

Type	Prefs	Website
Third Party		youtube.com
Third Party		googleusercontent.com
Third Party		ytimg.com
Third Party		engadget.com
Third Party		livefyre.com
Third Party		gmail.com
Visited		google.com
Third Party		gstatic.com
Visited		t.co
Visited		twitter.com
Third Party		twimg.com
Third Party		ow.ly
Visited		emarketer.com
Third Party		fonts.com
Third Party		sharethis.com
Third Party		visualwebsiteoptimizer.com
Third Party		marketo.com
Third Party		fonts.net
Third Party		rackcdn.com
Third Party		247realmedia.com
Third Party		awdmg.com
Third Party		marketo.net
Third Party		ajax.googleapis.com
Visited		adobe.com
Third Party		wistia.net
Third Party		wistia.com
Third Party		adadvisor.net

A screen-grab of Lightbeam list

a photo, an email address, bank details, posts on social networking websites, medical information, or a computer's IP address' (European Commission, 2012). The key to whether data is personal or not is *whether the data relates to a living individual* who can be identified either: (1) from the original data, or (2) from other data which is in the possession of, or is likely to come into the possession of, the data controller. In other words, if information either by itself or in combination with other information can uniquely single out or identify an individual, it is personal. The nub of the matter is the likelihood of being identified. If you are not a reader from the UK, by means of a search engine have a look for whether personal data means exactly the same thing in your own country (search 'definition personal data [insert your country here]').

A key question is this: does behavioural advertising use personal information? Although this is a straightforward question, it is difficult to give a straightforward answer because third-party behavioural advertising companies collect different types of information. Some such as DoubleClick, owned by Google, claim that they do not mix their behavioural advertising operations with parts of the Google business that deal with personally identifiable information. Others such as Adobe (explored below) are upfront about using personal data. Trade associations for the industry, such as the Network Advertising Initiative in the US, urge member companies to take measures to keep personally identifiable information separate from online browsing activities, but recognize that some companies will use personal data to assist with targeted advertising. Notably, too, we are asked to trust that companies to whom we give personal details will 'take measures to keep personally identifiable information separate from online browsing activities' (NAI, 2015). In Europe, our rules now say that because cookies often contain unique identifiers that allow for the tracking of user behaviour over time and across websites, and the possible combination of these identifiers with other identifying or identifiable data, we treat these as personal data.

Cookies

For the web to work, cookies are essential. They provide the web with memory because cookies allow our favourite websites to remember us. They also help with online shopping (such as the 'add to basket' button) and automatic form filling so making online activities easier and more pleasurable. These are *first-party* cookies because they are placed on our computers by the website we are visiting (the first party). The critical questions are reserved for *third-party* cookies.

As to precisely what cookies are, they are small text files stored on a user's computer by a web browser (such as Chrome in the case of the example presented in Figure 12.3). These store IDs that identify each session between the browser on our computers that we use to navigate the web and servers across the internet that provide information to our computers/browsers. A server hosts the website we are visiting and this is the computer that a browser "talks" with to receive the information we request. The third-party aspect to this is when our computers receive and share information with other computers/servers on the internet that we are not aware of.

Third-party cookies involve interaction with an unknown web actor (as listed in Figure 12.2). For example, if a user visits digitaladvertising.com and the domain of the cookie placed on your computer

Fig 12.3

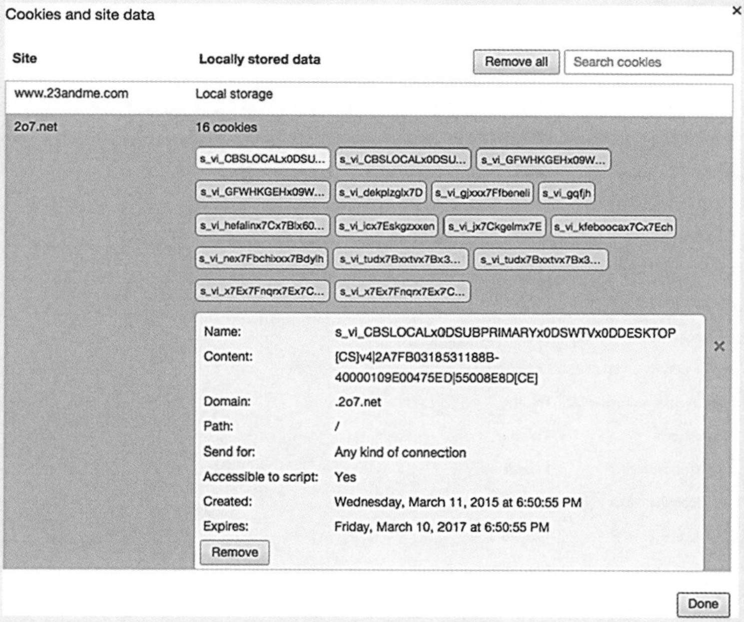

A screen-grab of cookie code

is digitaladvertising.com, then this is a first-party cookie. If, however, the user visits digitaladvertising.com and the cookie placed on your computer says adnetworks.com, then this is a third-party cookie. Further, they may either be *session* or *persistent* cookies. The first lasts as long as a person's browser is connected with a website and is deleted when the user closes their browser; the second (used by behavioural advertising) remembers users' preferences, choices, interests and web history. See, for example, the cookies I have on my own machine in Figure 12.4.

The critical concern is not with cookies themselves, but the fact that those placed by unknown third parties can track our web activities. For example, the Haymarket cookie halfway down Figure 12.4 remembers my password so I do not have to. Clearly this is a useful service. However, the non-descript cookie 207.net is actually owned by Adobe and maintained by the Adobe Digital Marketing Suite. This type of *tracking cookie* allows Adobe's clients to access information about my activities. By doing a web search for '207.net', this takes me

Fig 12.4

Cookies and site data   ×

Site	Locally stored data		
www.23andme.com	Local storage	Remove all	Search cookies
2o7.net	16 cookies		
msnportal.112.2o7.net	1 cookie		
thecooperativebank.112.2o7...	1 cookie		
tsleducation.112.2o7.net	1 cookie		
atlanticmedia.122.2o7.net	1 cookie		
experianinteractive.122.2o7....	1 cookie		
experianservicescorp.122.2o...	1 cookie		
haymarketbusinesspublicati...	1 cookie		
33across.com	1 cookie		
1.sic.33across.com	1 cookie		
you.38degrees.org.uk	Local storage		
5min.com	1 cookie		
cfiles.5min.com	Flash data		
www.abc.net.au	Local storage		

Sources of cookies

to the Adobe Privacy Center that says that its analytics services collects data (including personal data) on:

▸ The URLs of the web pages you visit and the time spent on them;
▸ The URL of the page that showed the link you clicked on that brought you to that company's website;
▸ The searches you have performed, including searches that led you to that company's website;
▸ Information about your browser and device, such as device type, operating system, connection speed, and display settings;
▸ Your IP address, which Adobe may use to approximate your general location;
▸ Information you may provide on that company's website, including information on registration forms;
▸ Whether you clicked on an ad;
▸ Items you've either purchased or placed within the shopping cart feature on that company's website;
▸ Social network profile information, including photos, fan and like status, user IDs, age, and gender.[62]

Adobe continues by saying that some companies using Adobe services may send them information that allows them to identify users personally. Further, some companies may also buy additional information about users and then add that additional information to the information collected by Adobe's products on their websites. This additional information may include things like email addresses, account information, or Facebook profile information, including photos and usernames (Adobe, 2015). Further (and particularly relevant from the point of view of consent), when Adobe either collects or receives personal information about its users, it asks companies to describe within their privacy policies their information collection and use practices, and gives users the opportunity to opt out. Hands up how many of you knew you could opt out?

Another cookie on the list in Figure 12.4 is from 33across.com. This is a *third-party advertiser* and if we recollect from Chapter 3, third-party advertising is where the ads on our webpages come from another server or website. For example, the *Guardian* news website is hosted (unsurprisingly) by *The Guardian*, but the ads on the webpage come from elsewhere. Our web browsers assemble incoming information from multiple sources across the internet so all items appear on the same page. For this to work, and for the browser to assemble the page and ads correctly, the website directs browsers to collect information from a different site's ad server. The third-party website creates a cookie in a user's browser folder as a result. Because so many websites use third-party ad servers, this allows third parties to deposit cookies and track a large amount of people. This scale of operation can be highly profitable. To provide a sense of the services that 33across. com offers clients, it says it provides information about 'how people consume and share' along with 'the full picture of what content is performing and what's shared privately' and 'insight into how people view, consume and share content across devices' (33across.com, 2016). In essence, this is behavioural tracking across devices to develop a holistic picture of what people are doing on websites signed into the 33across.com network.

Defining privacy: be positive

Despite what some might say, privacy is not dead. In a LinkedIn post[63] the privacy and law scholar, Daniel Solove, illustrated this with a range of book and magazine titles each saying 'Is Privacy Dead?', 'The Death of Privacy', 'The End of Privacy' or a close variant. What is eye opening is that these go back to 1969 – a long time before the web! Accordingly, we should be deeply sceptical when anyone tells us that privacy is dead. When it comes from heads of technology companies, they say this because they are either excessively pessimistic or want our data. Further, because privacy is demonstrably an ongoing concern, it should be taken seriously by any organization interested in goodwill and trust from citizens and customers.

However, when asked directly 'What is privacy?' we struggle to explain it. It is important we can do this because privacy is the number one concern facing the digital advertising industry and arguably also citizens of media culture. The connection of advertising with privacy goes back to the mid-1990s and the rise of online profiling and behavioural advertising discussed in Chapters 3 and 10. Today, it is not hyperbole to say that consumer and regulatory concerns about privacy threaten the existence of the digital advertising industry. Indeed, a recurring topic for representatives of the industry such as the Internet Advertising Bureau is how to develop mechanisms to protect the industry from further regulation. One might even go further and say that in addition to developing common standards for publishers, advertisers, agencies, networks and platforms to serve advertising, the Internet Advertising Bureau exists to stave off further regulation.

Now, we know that privacy is important and has been for some time, but what actually is it, how does it apply today and do we care about it? Privacy is not an easy word to define because when we think we have it pinned down, a new meaning can be provided that allows it to slip between our fingers. You might reasonably think that a dictionary definition would be a good place to start. The online *Oxford Dictionary* defines it as: a state in which one is not observed or disturbed by other people; or the state of being free from public attention. To expand slightly, this means shutting others out. Let us define this account of privacy as the *argument by seclusion*. In a moment we will see that this is a flawed perspective. Think about it. On considering the question, 'How does privacy apply today?' I expect that social media would have made an appearance in your thinking (it does with my students). The dictionary definition is flawed because few people set up social media accounts to be free from public attention. The argument concerning seclusion, while popular, is a simplistic, isolationist and *negative* account of privacy. It fails to take into account a basic observation: privacy does not just involve being alone, but how we connect and interact with others, and how we control and manage access to ourselves and those we are close to. Phrased otherwise: *privacy involves being open to others as well as closed*. Being open as well as reserved does not just apply to social media and what we do online, but everyday life too. Our relationships and interactions differ person by person and organization by organization in terms of what we are happy to share. This applies to the so-called 'nothing to hide, nothing to fear' slogan used by those who wish to increase levels of surveillance. The argument is an exceptionally stupid one in that no sane person on this planet wants every thought and action broadcast. (I also like the argument that we should all have some exciting misdemeanour to hide!) Instead, we are happy to share parts of ourselves with some people and organizations, in some situations and under certain circumstances. Again, it is about control over openness.

By recognizing that privacy is a fundamental principle that informs how we interact with others, how we like others to interact with us, and the courtesy and *respect* imbued within daily negotiations with others, we see there is no question of privacy disappearing. This is a fundamental point. Despite what some people say, we will not surpass privacy, it will not disappear, it will not go out of fashion and it will always matter. Yes, how we interact with each other changes, but the idea that privacy might be lost is an utter fallacy. This makes more sense if we switch from thinking about digital devices, social media and online activities to how we are intimate with others (that involves being very open with some but more closed to others); conversations, confidences and secrets (again both open and closed); things of value such as mementos, photos and diaries; and even how our homes are organized (such as doors, corridors and curtains). Another point about privacy is that we are continually told we have less of it than we used to. To an extent there is some truth in this. For many of us today, our phones and online environment is surveilled by both our own governments and others. However, if we put aside digital devices, we are less familiar with our neighbours, many of us had our own bedrooms when growing up, family sizes are smaller than they used to be, more people drive their own cars rather than use public transport, and religion (and thereby confession) plays less of a role than it used to. To re-emphasize, technology is only a small part of the privacy story, and it is always best understood by thinking in terms of interactions with other people and organizations.

Privacy: interaction, expectations and protocol

The suggestion that privacy simply equates to seclusion does not make sense. Instead, privacy is better understood in terms of how we interact with others. Possibly oddly, this involves how we interact with both other people *and* machines. This ranges from how comfortable we are being naked with other people to being tagged in photos posted to Facebook, and the extent to which we are fine with Google scanning our emails for keywords with which to target us with advertising. The first involves person>person privacy; the second person>person/machine privacy (as both other people and machines see us in the Facebook photo); and the third is person>machine privacy (because only machines read the emails).

We may be perfectly fine with each of the situations above, but they are still privacy matters because privacy is not about hiding or seclusion, but selectivity regarding whom we engage with. The principle behind this is self-determination, and the extent to which we are in control of what happens to our bodies, information and reputation. In this control-based account of privacy something is private if a person is able to control access to the 'something' (be this our body, images of our body, a smartphone, or how one is portrayed in public – such as how one appears in a news article). This is also a managerial view of privacy, or the capacity to manage how one appears to others, to have a say over information flow, and to be able to be open with whom we choose and reserved with others. Although the notion of control described above should be underlined, we should also recognize that life is complex. We interact with a variety of people and machines in a multitude of contexts (Altman, 1975; Nissenbaum, 2010). For example in our daily life we move between different domains, including home, school, work, bars, banks, hairdressers and the hospital, to interact with parents, sexual partners, friends, teachers, bosses, doctors, bank managers and hair stylists. Of course, often from waking, we interact with phones, computers, apps, email, websites, third-party trackers and wearable technologies. Indeed, some of these are collecting and sharing data as we sleep (actually, some wearables collect data when we do other things in bed!). The point of this account is that because we have so many different relationships with people and machines that we try to manage, privacy is dynamic. Elsewhere I have argued that privacy is a code, an agreement or a *protocol* (McStay, 2014). For example, if a housemate unexpectedly walks in to the bathroom while you are sitting in the tub they have broken a tacit agreement and protocol (hopefully unwittingly) that regulates how we live together. We rarely stipulate these agreements, but they are there. The same goes for when we tell a friend a secret or share intimate photos of ourselves with others – we expect them to abide by unspoken rules. Although privacy protocol is rarely written down, few would argue that it is not real. By seeing privacy as protocol (or a set of guidelines about how someone or a machine should behave) we can begin to talk about how privacy should be embedded into how we interact with others (such as prying parents or housemates) and machines (in terms of what information we are happy to share). Further, by thinking of privacy in terms of protocol, codes of behaviour and expectations, this allows us to question actors who take more information from us than we expected (a protocol breach). Mobile apps are a very good example of this situation.

The case of tracking and advertising in mobile apps for Android

Rather than thinking about privacy as seclusion and what is hidden, we now know that privacy is better seen connected with words such as control, dignity, management, context and protocol. As we know from everyday life, we choose to be very open with some people but not others. These "others" might be people, but in a digital context these are often the computers that our devices connect with and the businesses behind them. We have expectations of other people and we are right to demand good behaviour from machines and companies too. The point about devices is an important one because often we do not know who or what we are connecting with, what information is being extracted from us, or for what ends this data is used. Telephones are a good example of this. The traditional fixed landline is connected to an exchange whereby our calls are routed to the number (which is really an address) of the telephone we want to reach. Usually nobody else but the person on the other end of the call listens to our conversation. Today our mobile phones collect and share all sorts of data with a multitude of different actors. This is not wrong per se because clearly smartphones serve more purposes than a landline, but the comparison is illustrative. From an advertising point of view, the apps on our phones are very interesting. The "free" apps environment is an important one for advertisers and users. I use the scare quotes, because the truism 'If you're not paying, you're the product' applies very well here. This expresses a principle from media studies that recognizes that although we tend to think of media content as the main product of the media, it is often audiences – or, specifically, their data and attention time. The *audience-as-commodity* thesis (Smythe, 1977; McStay, 2011a, 2011b) sees "you" as the commodity because audiences' attention time, ears and eyeballs are sold to advertisers. In the digital context this principle is amplified because: it happens in real time; every member of the audience is tracked and has their data aggregated into larger databases (unless they use blockers); much digital advertising is provided by third parties; and finally because the audience data-tracking industry is such a huge business. Although the origins of advertising involve buying attention, today this process is intensified because of the amount of data in circulation, the speed at which it is acted on, and the fact that this process is able to deliver personalized advertising experiences (as opposed to more general types found with non-digital media).

Tracking mobile phones is a source of revenue for app developers, but it is also a point of concern for users because it is very unclear who the applications are talking to, to what extent, and what information is being shared. It is worth lingering on this example. As mentioned in Chapter 3, when mobile advertising began to prosper both Apple and Google originally used IDs. These were serial numbers used to identify phones and tablets. The numbers were visible to the applications on phones and tablets. IDs look like this: 7f6c8d-c83d77134b5a3a1c53f1202b395b04482b. Hold in mind that the ID is inextricably linked to the device. These IDs used by Apple and Google enabled mobile ad networks to track and compile information related to a particular device's location, demographic information and user activity, ranging from app use to mobile commerce transactions. The consequence is that browsing patterns, app usage and physical location of the device (and user) could be collected and sold to unintended recipients such as advertisers, data trackers, and even spouses, divorce lawyers, debt collectors or industrial spies (Smith, 2010). Users were unable to prevent their phones from leaking this information. IDs were not intended to be used this way, but the net effect was that mobile user tracking could easily be linked to personally identifiable information. Revealed by US research, apps that also collected personal information along with the Unique Device Identifier (UDID) included those from Amazon, CBS, Chase Bank, Target, and Sam's Club (ibid.). This research also revealed sneaky cookie usage. For example, the ABC News app did not store tracking cookies in Apple's Safari folder, but in the applications directory where it is much more difficult to find. It was also set to track for 20 years. In 2013 the link between the ID used for advertising and the handset was broken so users can reset the code. This in effect depersonalized the ID code so advertisers were targeting a changeable code rather than a handset which is directly linkable with a person.

To put apps into context, a study by Vigneri et al. (2015) found that a selection of 2,000 free Google Play apps connected to 250,000 sites spread over 2,000 domains. Although the majority of these share information with only a handful of sites (Google's ad services dominate the top 10), 10 per cent of the sites sampled connect to 500 or more. One site, Music Volume EQ from K&K Design, linked to nearly 2,000 sites/URLs. However, multiple URLs can correspond to the same domain. An app for the blog of Jean Marc Morandini (a French journalist)[64] has links with 113 separate top-level domains (with six separate ad networks within these). Google, or one of the companies it owns, does a large portion of the ad-tracking activity. DoubleClick is the most popular and the next two ad-related domains also belong to Google. It is worth noting too that although Google created Android, it does not sell or charge for licensing. Instead, revenue comes from the ad business that permeates the Android ecosystem. In other words, Android is an advertising platform. On the surface is the operating system, and apps tempt us to share data, but what we cannot see are the thousands of connections with other computers collecting information about us.

This tracking is widespread and completely unclear to users (Vigneri et al., 2015). The app with the highest amount of trackers is Eurosport Player[65] with 810. On the trackers themselves, although Google Analytics ranks the highest, trackers from other players such as xiti.com[66] also rank high. As with all examples provided in this book, they will be much more meaningful if the reader has a look around the site to obtain a sense of the data they track. In xiti's case, this is the user's operating system, screen size, resolution, smartphone model, manufacturer, navigation (where a person visits online), behaviour, visit times, visitor actions and geolocation (where a person is located in real space). Notably, initiatives such as Do Not Track do not address mobile app tracking, but only that which is done via web browsers. In other words, whereas the unwary might assume we only interact with the owners of the app, the reality is that we are sharing information with exponentially more organizations. This problem is less about danger (although links to malware sites exist, particularly through sex apps) than data exploitation and lack of control over whom we share our information with. Apps that talk with many other sites/URLs also use up a phone's resources (processing capacity and battery). Lack of control comes from not knowing who is tracking us and there being no way for the average user to block the connections they do not want. Further, unless individuals read specialist publications (such as this), it is unlikely they would ever be aware of the vast ecology of information that sits behind mobile phone screens. The problem is not that data is exchanged for services, but that more information is collected about us than we can be expected to comprehend. This is corporate misbehaviour and a clear privacy protocol breach.

Trust

A key problem for both digital businesses and users of digital media is that there has been a breakdown of trust. This is readily acknowledged by the behavioural advertising business as it seeks to simultaneously stave off stricter regulation and make its advertising techniques more appealing to web users. Nick Stringer (2015), for example, head of the Internet Advertising Bureau UK, highlights that privacy remains one of the most significant challenges in the digital era and that businesses need to develop ways to be more transparent with the data they collect and use. This urging for industrial reform can be seen against the lack of consumer trust in online advertising. The background context is grim. For example, in the UK, Ipsos MORI conducted research on behalf of TRUSTe (2013) with over 2,000 British consumers, finding that online privacy concerns are high and that consumers do not trust businesses. Specifically: 88 per cent of internet users are concerned about privacy online; 43 per cent do not trust companies with their personal information; 91 per cent said that they avoid doing business with companies where they have privacy concerns; and 96 per cent want the ability to control who can collect their personal information and who can track their activities online. Adland's own research conducted by the IAB (2012) finds:

▸ About half of internet users are happy to see advertising on all media;
▸ Happiness with advertising varies by age group;
▸ Internet users understand that content is dependent on advertising;
▸ Most internet users think that online advertising can be helpful;
▸ Just under half of internet users are happy to see relevant advertising based on their browsing behaviour;
▸ Four out of five would like to use one of the tools to control their privacy online.

The problem for Adland is that it alienates people by using techniques that are, ironically, designed to get closer to people. This presents us with a paradox in that people are unhappy with the status quo of data practices, but continue to use the services that make use of data, albeit without understanding what is collected and how the data is used. One might suggest that people do not really care, and that actions speak louder than words. A more intelligent view examines the control dimension of the privacy equation. To extrapolate from Adland's own findings, people find themselves in a condition of *learned helplessness*.[67] Applied to questions of data privacy, this is when a person has undergone an unpleasant and unwanted situation that they were unable to escape or avoid. The key part is that on having undergone this multiple times, a person fails to learn to escape or avoid the issue in new situations, even when there is opportunity to do so. This entails resignation rather than affirmation.

However, what the TRUSTe and IAB surveys also suggest is that people are willing to share information if they have control over it and know with whom it is being shared. This echoes the argument about privacy protocol being made throughout this chapter. No one is suggesting that the exchange of data for services is wrong, but that: clarity on the nature of the exchange is required; digital companies should not collect information surreptitiously; and people should be asked in the clearest possible terms whether they are fine with having data collected about them before collection starts.

Consent

Privacy concerns about third-party advertising raises questions about consent, not least: how should consent be obtained from people to use their data; and when should this be obtained? These may appear as technicalities, and to an extent they are, but for the digital advertising industry they challenge its existence. There are two hurdles for the industry:

1. How to stave off stricter regulation on how the industry uses people's data;
2. How to allay consumer concerns about privacy and a generalized lack of trust in advertising processes that target people according to their online behaviour.

What the industry desperately seeks to avoid is a situation where explicit consent (or opt-in) is required to use personal information. In effect this would make programmatic, behavioural targeting and third-party tracking unworkable because it would require people to change their settings on their devices to say, 'Yes, please track me so I can have advertising that targets me by my behaviour and interests.' Would you do this?

Opt-in/opt-out

Legally and financially speaking, much hinges on whether we "opt-in" or "opt-out" of advertising technologies that track our behaviour.

When one considers the size and economic value of both advertising and the online media industry it supports, we can begin to recognize the implications of opt-in/opt-out. To be clear:

▸ *Opt-in* means that people have to be asked if they are fine with having information about them collected, and they then have to give affirmative consent by means of clicking something;
▸ *Opt-out* means that consent has been tacitly assumed upfront, data tracking is the norm and if people are unhappy with this they have to turn off tracking – if it is possible.

These technicalities will become much clearer if the reader opens up their web browser and visits the website for their geographic region that allows you to opt out of behavioural targeting. I'll happily wager you have not seen this before! If your geographic region is not listed below, use a search engine with the term 'opt out of behavioural targeting'.

▸ Europe: www.youronlinechoices.com/uk/your-ad-choices
▸ USA: www.networkadvertising.org/choices/
▸ Canada: http://youradchoices.ca/
▸ Australia: www.youronlinechoices.com.au/opt-out

Figure 12.5 lists the companies that track online data, although because there are so many the screen-grab only contains companies beginning with letter A. The second column allows the user to switch trackers on or off.

Try switching all of them off and return back to the site 24 hours later after having used your machine for web surfing. Are they all still turned off? The answer to this will give you insight into the difficulties of opting out of having data tracked.

Legal context

In this section I focus on the European and British situation around consent to third-party tracking cookies, but very similar debates are taking place in different legal jurisdictions around the world about how to deal with this. Until 2011 the e-Privacy directive (officially known as the European Directive on Privacy and Electronic Communications 2002/58/EC) stated that organizations should ensure

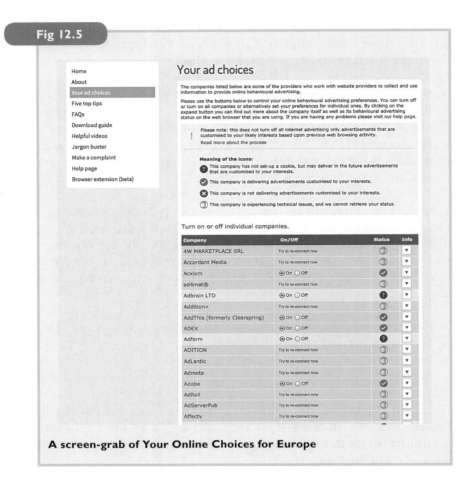

Fig 12.5

A screen-grab of Your Online Choices for Europe

people are provided with clear and comprehensive information about how internet cookies are used, and how to opt out. The revised version, implemented May 2011, required consent of the users. The difference is that the first means we should be able to access information about how to opt out, whereas the other *implies* that we should opt in. This is because when we consent to something most people would agree that what we are consenting to starts after we have said, 'Yes, I'm OK with that and I opt to allow that.'

The concern for the ad industry was that a true "opt-in" regime would make third-party advertising unworkable because it would require people to affirmatively click or say 'Yes I'm OK with this' *before* third parties can start collecting data about us. Their solution is in clause 5(3) that was added to the amended e-Privacy Directive. This says: 'users' consent to processing may be expressed by using the appropriate settings of a browser or other application'. This means that the state of a person's browser can be taken as a means of saying whether or not a person is happy to accept third-party tracking cookies. Most people, of course, are not aware of how to manage cookie settings on their browsers so this leaves us in a situation where a browser may indicate consent, but the user remains unaware of what is taking place. This does not equate to most people's idea of informed consent. As Kosta (2013) highlights, both the Article 29 Working Party and the European Data Protection Supervisor criticized this clause on the basis that consent gained this way runs counter to a proper understanding of consent. The UK's Information Commissioner's Office (ICO) is the UK's data protection regulator. Curiously it suggests tweaking consent from that which is 'expressed' to 'implied' on the basis that is more practical (ICO, 2012). In effect this staves off the EU Directive's recommendation of an opt-in approach.

The question for us is this: can consent really be gained after data collection has started and if we are not aware that information about us is being collected? There is a twist to this detailed and taxing story because the push by the ad industry to allow browser settings to be indicative of users' consent opened the door to adblockers (such as Eyeo's AdBlock Plus). Given that at the time of writing in 2015 Eyeo is being sued by the ad industry, this is an important line of defence for them. That is: adblocking is *not* an unfair attack on the ad industry and publishers, but instead a positive choice by people to assert their desire not to be tracked by third-party ad-servers and trackers. The irony is that this argument is made possible because the ad industry argued hard for browsers to be the consent mechanism.

US government surveillance enlists the ad industry... without *its* consent

Although we are reaching the end of this chapter, I should also highlight how tracking cookies employed for advertising are helping the US National Security Agency's (NSA) data collection efforts. This certainly does not help the industry's efforts to make behavioural targeting more palatable to consumers. What is happening is that the NSA is taking advantage of the fact that one of the wealthiest industries on the web already has tracking systems in place, so it is logical that state surveillance organizations would take advantage of this. This was a widely reported story in 2015, most notably covered by The Intercept (2015b) (managed by Glenn Greenwald who was instrumental in the 2013 Edward Snowden leaks that revealed the extent of global state surveillance), but also by advertising publications such as *Advertising Age*.

The NSA surveils through its XKeyscore program. This collects and analyses global Internet traffic.[68] Essentially, the program hitches a lift on private companies' tracking of users' browsers. To be clear, I am not suggesting collusion between the advertising industry and the NSA. Despite questionable approaches to consent and tracking, the advertising industry is a victim in this situation. This is a privacy issue for citizens, consumers and businesses alike. If we recollect, cookies are small pieces of code assigned by a web server to a person's computer so to recognize individual visitors to a website. Despite their reputation, cookies in themselves are *not* spooky or malevolent. Nevertheless, advertisers' tracking cookies allowed the NSA to trace information such as names, dates of birth, where people live, occupation, what sites they have visited, what they have searched for, and their interests. The latter includes harmless preferences, such as liking *Game of Thrones*, but also information people would probably prefer not to be shared – such as pornography preferences.

Other programs make explicit use of tablets, mobile phone data and apps. The UK's Government Communications Headquarters (GCHQ) and the Canadian Communications Security Establishment (CSE) acquired sensitive smartphone user data from the servers of a number of advertising and analytics companies. For example a presentation slide, published by The Intercept (2015a) from the Snowden leaks of 2013, shows that the UK and Canadian surveillance agencies used Google's advertising network AdMob to intercept users' data. This reveals information about how often a particular user opens the app and at what time of day; where the user lives; where the user works; where the user currently is; the phone's unique identifier; what version of Android or iOS the device is running; and the user's IP address. From Google's and app developers' point of view, this information is not sinister because it helps guide app upgrades and targeting of ads. However, when all of this data is combined together it does not just identify devices, but individuals too. Although the data industry has little interest in doing this, state surveillance organizations do.

Sadly the industry stayed silent on the matter and offered no advice to consumers about how to opt out of this surveillance (I also asked the IAB in both the US and the UK for comment, to no avail). Indeed, a smart approach would have been to be proactive and upfront about what is taking place so to firmly distinguish between ad cookies and state surveillance activities (although the industry may well have been prevented from publicizing this by state secrecy laws) which would have helped build trust in the sector. This puts the ad industry at odds with tech companies who, following the Snowden revelations, have worked to embed encryption into their businesses to win consumer trust. The workaround to the surveillance of ad cookies are: (1) if someone has opted not to have third-party cookies installed, they should stay opted-out; (2) for those who are happy to accept interest-based advertising, this cookie data should be encrypted. This is not as improbable as it sounds because use of https protocol (protected) rather than http (not protected) would go some way to mitigating surveillance efforts. Data should also be protected where it is stored and analysed, because unencrypted, or improperly protected data, is an easy target for surveillance agencies.

Conclusion

The question is not whether people consent to advertising. Most people understand that ads placed by first parties (the publisher) in magazines, on television, on radio, in newspapers and online reduce the costs we have to pay for media content. Most reasonable people are happy to accept ads for content. Our interest is ads placed by third parties and the nature of the tracking processes that collect information about us to serve ads. This raises questions about privacy. An aspect of privacy theory that too often gets lost is that it is a positive and *dignifying principle*. This means respect for others and what they wish to share, allow access to, or reveal. Consent is an active part of this because it involves affirmative decisions and clear expressions of our preferences. In the case of advertising, the argument is not about whether we should or should not accept ads in exchange for content. Rather, it is about whether the nature of extracting data is fair, appropriate, reasonable, privacy-friendly and subject to proper consent mechanisms. As we have read, people are willing to share information, but they like to feel in control regarding what is happening with their information and what is being disclosed. This echoes the argument of this chapter that privacy involves being open as well as reserved, and that privacy is really about protocol, agreements, meeting expectations and not being deceitful. Few could agree that app vendors in the Android app environment discussed in this chapter are upfront about where data goes.

One outcome of a truly opt-in approach is that networks brave enough to be upfront about their activities will be able to charge advertisers higher fees because they will have a superior user base interested in having advertising tailored to their interests. Further, a sincere, less deceptive, and trust-generating approach would encourage audiences to disclose more information than the minimum and to correct inaccuracies (wrongly targeted ads). In 2015 Apple managed to use privacy to re-invigorate its brand and move into new sectors; I wonder if Adland is daring, creative and imaginative enough to do it too? Finally we discussed the connection between the US XKeyscore program, and the UK and Canadian BADASS surveillance activities as revealed by Edward Snowden. The industry has remained silent on this and, while understandable for an industry with a behavioural image problem, it has shown weakness in not stating that using advertising cookies for state surveillance is wrong. Others in the technology industry have stepped up – the ad industry should too.

Think points and questions

- What is privacy?
- Non-European readers: how does the discussion of laws and regulations compare to your own legal frameworks? Are they akin to Europe, or do you have different provision altogether?
- All readers: consider the principles discussed in this chapter (privacy, consent, opt-in/out) and assess the terms and conditions of your favourite website. Are they acceptable to you?
- Devise an appropriate list of social/demographic categories, select a suitable sample size and find out how many of them know how to opt out of behavioural advertising.

13 Conclusions: Reconciling Art and Science in Advertising

As this book nears the end, we might see that it has danced on the border of two cultures: the creatives and the technologists. The fault-line is evident on a seemingly weekly basis in the ad industry press through feature articles such as 'Don't sack your copywriter yet, but are machines set to take over?',[69] 'Is tech going to kill the creative agencies?'[70] and 'Does too much data stifle creativity?'.[71] Adland is split on its reaction to digital technologies and analytics, and excitable voices that suggest 'algorithms that will take complete control of the creative process' have not helped its cause.[72] Tensions are exemplified by titans of modern advertising such as John Hegarty who, at the 2014 Cannes Lions creative advertising festival, likened the 'digital messiahs' to the Taliban – a colourful way of characterizing fanaticism surrounding analytics. Indeed, many attendees at Cannes Lions 2015 grumbled that Facebook and Google stood out as the biggest brands on the French beach.

In making sense of this, or even choosing sides, we should not fall into the trap of thinking that the technical and scientific approach to advertising is new. It is actually older than the creative camp. Consider, for example, the psychologist Walter Dill Scott, who in 1903 published *The Psychology of Advertising in Theory and Practice*.[73] Speaking about advertising as a 'serious thing with the business man of to-day [sic]', Scott says:

> In this day and generation we are not afraid of theories, systems, ideals, and imagination. What we do avoid is chance, luck, haphazard undertakings, parrot or rule-of-thumb action, and the like. We may be willing to decide on unimportant things by instinct or by the flipping of a coin, but when it comes to the serious things of life we want to know that we are trusting to something more than mere chance. (2007 [1903]: 1–2).

Echoing the need for systematization, rigour and method, 20 years later Claude Hopkins wrote that:

> The time has come when advertising has in some hands reached the status of a science. It is based on fixed principles and is reasonably exact. The causes and effects have been well analyzed until they are well understood. The correct method of procedure has been proved and established. We know what is most effective, and we act on basic laws (Hopkins, 1998 [1923]: 213).

Although 100 years of media and technological development have had a significant impact on advertising practice, the emphasis on data and feedback is clear in the early professionalization of the advertising industry that sought to understand what techniques and ads work, and what do not. As with today, this involved analysis of headlines, settings, sizes, pictures and the disallowance of guesswork. Although this concluding chapter progresses to consider digital data and artificial intelligence, what is clear is that the empiricism that Claude Hopkins envisaged is alive and well within advertising and consumer research. The difference is that in today's programmatic environment, machines test these variables and more in a tiny fraction of the time that it took Hopkins' employees to conduct the same tests. Similarly, companies such as Millward Brown (2010) make use of neuroscientific techniques to gauge thoughts and feelings about ads and brands. One might wonder what the titans of old would have made of facial coding, eye-tracking and assessing electroencephalography (EEG) signals from the brain. Although they might not have understood the technology, they would recognize the principle of deducing attention, reactions and what elements of ads we are drawn to, cutting extraneous content, removing distractions from the brand, optimization and redrafting ads.

The data sublime

Presumably invited in order to champion the role of analytics and science in advertising, Brian Cox, a UK celebrity physicist and scientist, spoke at Cannes Lions festival in 2015 arguing that the acquisition of knowledge is always better than not acquiring it. He argued:

> In advertising, whether the aim is to enhance the reputation of your client or sell more products, you know what it is you are trying to do, therefore gathering data seems to me to be always good. I cannot

conceive of any reason of knowing more about something makes it worse [sic]. (Campaign, 2015b)

Speaking to the point about the value of data, Cox argued that 'the more our civilisation as a whole respects data, respects measurements, respects the modelling of that data, then the more likely we are to prosper' and that, 'The opposite means we're trying to argue that the less knowledge we have then the better we'd be, and I can't really support that argument'. The audience fired questions back at Cox pointing out that clients and agencies complain they have too much data, and that it is difficult to manage and work out what is valuable so becoming a strain on time and resources. Cox replied, 'If you just throw mud at the wall is that a more effective strategy because you will get it right occasionally?' adding that although one might not be able to interpret a data set, 'I don't see how a dataset can be a negative'. Similarly, in an essay for *Wired* magazine, Chris Anderson (2008) exemplifies the belief in the power of machines to sort through massive data sets and provide insights of value for advertisers. He argues that a data-first approach is less interested in theory, meaning, causation, psychology, philosophy, or any question involving *why*. Instead:

> Petabytes allow us to say: 'Correlation is enough.' We can stop looking for models. We can analyze the data without hypotheses about what it might show. We can throw the numbers into the biggest computing clusters the world has ever seen and let statistical algorithms find patterns where science cannot.

This fervour, passion and belief points to what we will phrase in this concluding chapter as the *data sublime*. Also try for size this quote from Heinrich Hertz, a mathematician, who once said:

> One cannot escape the feeling that these mathematical formulae have an independent existence and an intelligence of their own, that they are wiser than we are, wiser even than their discoverers, that we get more out of them than we originally put into them. (Cited in Langville and Mayer, 2006: 30)

Although Hertz is suggesting a mathematical sublime, the passage perfectly expresses what we are calling the data sublime. Analytics that responds to incoming audience data in real time is not just useful, but alluring. The attraction of information, automation and algorithmic sorting is in large part down to scale and the fact these processes independent of ourselves can do things that we cannot. This is the definition of sublime – greatness beyond what is graspable and calculable. This does not mean mysticism or that which is beyond science (despite the last sentence of the Chris Anderson quote above). In fact it is precisely the opposite, as Enlightenment philosopher Immanuel Kant (an authority on the sublime) points out that the sublime is inextricably connected with Reason. For Kant, the sublime was an intuition of rational knowing and appreciation that underlies nature and thought. Bizarrely this is again echoed by Claude Hopkins who says: 'where they long exist, advertising and merchandising become exact sciences. Every course is charted. The compass of accurate knowledge directs the shortest, safest, cheapest course to any destination' (1998 [2003]: 215). What conjoins Kant and digital parts of Adland is a deep belief in the role of rationality that in turn has its foundations in the Enlightenment (or what is commonly referred to as the Age of Reason). Rationality involves three key principles in that: all genuine questions can be clearly answered; all answers are knowable and may be learnt and taught to others; and all answers must be compatible with one another as one truth cannot contradict another. These principles delivered Newton, Einstein and Stephen Hawking who have solved intractable puzzles in physics, cosmology and astrophysics. What this passion for the data sublime represents is a deep belief in rationality. This begs a question about the opposite: irrationality. Now why would anyone label himself or herself as irrational?

The creatives' riposte

The emphasis on reason and knowledge creates a set of binary oppositions, with creativity stereotypically being associated with unreason, knack, ignorance, fantasy and superstition. An Adland favourite, the creative director Tham Khai Meng (2015), brilliantly retorts at the data evangelists: 'The ancient Egyptians had no respect for the brain at all. When you died, they scooped it out through your nostrils and threw it away. The heart on the other hand was considered sacred'. A campaign from Diesel in 2010 takes the point further and builds an entire ad campaign around the values of vitality, heart and 'being stupid', including headlines such as 'Smart may have the brains, but stupid has the balls' and 'Smart critiques. Stupid creates'. It should not be missed, though, that the campaign is clever, deeply strategic and well considered.[74]

In Adland's war, this point about passion is being made in multiple ways. For example, on being asked whether the data deluge causes problems for creatives or all information is beautiful, Andy Jex (Executive Creative Director, Saatchi & Saatchi London) remarks:

> In music, if you try to predict hits just using data, you end up with *I Should Be So Lucky*. If you use talent, instinct and the heart too, you get *Good Vibrations*. The stuff that works best is the stuff people never knew they wanted (Campaign, 2015a).

Answering the same question, Mark Roalfe, Chairman and Executive Creative Director, RKCR/Y&R, says, 'The world's greatest ideas and innovations did not come about as a result of a collection of pure statistics. And let's not forget that a focus group never invented anything new. Intuition and instinct can be our most powerful tools' (ibid.).

These are arguments of the heart that champion irrationality over cool and clinical rationalism. To expand the topic, the tension between the humanities (that are interested in culture and history) and the sciences is a long-running debate in philosophy. The Italian philosopher Giambattista Vico (2001 [1725]), writing three centuries ago, points out that he has no problem at all with the effectiveness of science and mathematics in establishing facts, ordering events and arranging timelines. Vico's challenge is that this is not enough to understand the *lived world*. This foretells creative folk of Adland who turn away from analytics and data-based insights because, as Vico urges, we should not just understand the world in an abstract fashion (through numbers, graphs and charts) but through the eyes of those who lived and are living it. This involves intuition, empathy and understanding the motivations of others and their wants, needs, desires and aspirations.

Binary delusion

The heart/mind and empathy/quantitative knowledge dichotomy is appealing and, like all binaries (such as good versus evil), makes for an excellent story with easily identifiable characters. It is of course a fallacy. The two cultures (art versus science) is a misconception for a number of reasons, not least because much science is extraordinarily creative. One might even argue that science is by definition creative. After all, what is science if not the generation of new knowledge, understanding and insights? The ad man James Webb Young in his legendary advertising book, *A Technique for Producing Ideas*, first published in 1940, argues ideas for advertising are 'nothing more nor less than a new combination of old elements' (2003 [1940]: 15). This is also the basis of scientific experimentation, so both art and science are based on combinations and seeing the world in a new way. Science absorbs from the humanities too. Artificial intelligence research, for example, has learned painful but significant lessons from philosophy, and theories about mind and intelligence. Whereas once it saw intelligence in terms of being programmed with the right facts, with assistance from the humanities it saw that intelligence is achieved through learning, growing, exploring new contexts and making connections anew.

Both the science and creative camps in advertising are caricatures, or a pastiche. They are an imitation and manifestation of much old conversation about quality versus quantity, heart and mind, and long-standing philosophical tensions between the humanities and sciences (the "two cultures"). Accounts of creativity in advertising tend to be derived from a sense of being individual, maverick, intuitive, passionate, emotional, unstable, provocative, subjective and authentic. By contrast, the data camp in advertising is analytical, nerdy, enlightened, rational, purposeful, objective and devoid of emotion. To believe in this schism is to wilfully ignore a great deal of history. Leonardo de Vinci, for example, was a key figure of the Renaissance[75] whose fearsome skillset encompassed observational science, architecture, mathematics, engineering, astronomy, geology, cartography, botany, history, sculpting, music and painting. The key point is that art and science did not sit in his brain as two hemispheres or cultures, but expertise in each of these disciplines cross-fertilized the other.

Will artificial intelligence ever create Coca Cola's *Holidays are Coming*?

Campaigns that stand the test of time are those that beguile and are embraced and remembered by people. Christmas ads such as Coca Cola's 1995 *Holidays are Coming* (global) and John Lewis's 2013 *The Bear and the Hare* (UK) are good examples of these. As analytics and artificial intelligence are increasingly employed not just to target, but also to make ads, is it conceivable that machines might make such emotionally resonant content? At this stage we can correctly say 'not now', but would anyone bet against the future? If so, on what grounds?

As depicted in Chapter 11, analytics and big data processing are increasingly able to infer emotional life, what we think, and how we feel about brands and products. Is it an entirely different proposition to suggest machines will be able to answer campaign objectives with emotionally resonant imagery and music optimized to elicit maximum emotional feedback? Although machines might not understand love, hate and emotional life, does this matter if they are able to push the right buttons in us?

In June 2015 *Marketing* ran the click-bait headline 'In ten years [sic] time your agency will be an algorithm' for an article about technology that can make the creative part of advertising cheaper for advertisers (by getting rid of expensive human creatives).[76] Dynamic creative optimization already allows for use of different templates within an ad based on how well it is performing. This allows change of headlines, images, video scenes, offers and even pricing based on how (or if) people are interacting with the ad (Clabiorne et al., 2015). As we have seen in this book, this is no longer restricted to programmatic techniques, but it is increasingly spilling onto our streets through out of home advertising. The next stage of this is use of algorithms to write intelligible ads that are relevant to the product and the audience. In reality, these will not replace creatives in the near future, but they will have an impact on non-creative digital advertising that lets us know about offers and sales.

Branding campaigns and ads for emotionally involving high-ticket items will still require the human touch. The value in dynamic and automated content is the ability for machines to alter the ads' content on the basis of where we are, language type (such as receiving ads in Japanese while visiting New York), time of day and our activity type (such as shopping, holidays or rushing to a meeting). For truly creative content to be realized, it would require that intelligent machines and robo-writers learn cultural codes, values, politics, aesthetics, typography, nuances of human language use and the multitude of ways that people are affected by all of this (or what we can cluster together as *contextual sensitivity*). Of course collectively we are not just one culture, but multiple groups that share different values and sensibilities. These would also have to be traced, tagged, ordered, put to work and constantly re-assessed for change. The best creatives in advertising are able to display sensitivity to these lifeworlds so as to be able to create contextually sensitive advertising. *If* it were conceivable to render all of culture into information, or for machines to learn contexts as people do, the creation of advertising would require a big data set of impossible volume, variety and velocity. It would need to encompass our collective mediation of lived life and culture (such as developing trends, politics, news stories, language use and popular culture); it would need to understand older cultural settings as well as more recent cultural formations (such as language use, religion, social habits, music and arts); it would need to be able to trace, compare and make sense of how the new formations are emerging out of old formations in real time; and it would have to be sensitive to nuances of expression where the slightest difference in a facial expression can move a smile from warmth to sarcasm. If such a mapping of human contexts and discourse were possible, these signs and cultural variables would still have to be depicted in an engaging way. This would entail the bisociation and combination of textual elements (images, sounds, music and words) to engage and win our attention. That is to say that an ad in this fleshed-out vision of automated advertising is an algorithmically arranged set of ingredients that are bisociated, coordinated and optimized for either maximum group and/or individual impact and reaction. A tall order? Yes, but given the introduction of evolutionary algorithms to advertising in 2014 and advances in deep learning, I hesitate to say impossible.

Beyond seduction: algorithmic creativity

It is fair to say that the creative department is safe for a while yet, although it may need to upskill to take advantage of new technologies. On the relationship between data and creativity, there are two main arguments. These are:

1. *Data hinders creativity*: this sees data-enhanced creativity as a contradiction. Data provides too much information with the net result being that ideas and campaigns are weak and lacklustre;
2. *Data is a catalyst for creativity*: this worldview is best expressed in the case examples for B-Reel (and others) in Chapter 7 where creatives made use of behavioural data and analytics and applied the insights from this information at an executional level.

Both of these views presuppose that the purpose of advertising is seduction, or to ensnare potential consumers in values, signs and stimuli that elicit feelings and emotions for products. What artificial intelligence, programmatic logic, behavioural sensitivity and heterogeneous advertising invite into the debate is the possibility that the principal aim of advertising is not beguiling consumers, but *fulfilling* their needs and expected wants. Persado, for example, is a persuasive language company based in San Francisco. Its aim is not artful copywriting, but short copy under 600 characters for email marketing messages, display ads, tweets, text messages and push notifications. The principle is actually less about persuasion than information, although the mention of 'emotional language' in the quote below from David Atlas, the chief marketing officer of Persado, is noteworthy: 'We start to break down the language, organise it, looking at emotional language, descriptive language and functional language, and in this way you can start to calculate, swapping in, using a whole bunch of artificial intelligence technology ...'.[77] Connecting with the earlier quote from *Wired*'s Chris Anderson on the importance of data, correlation and faith in the capabilities of analytics, Persado's Atlas says, 'There are no ethics, there are no aesthetics, there is math and efficiency, and a knowledge of what works'.

This is a different way of thinking about advertising. It is to move the principle of advertising from one that promotes (by leveraging and biosociating every cultural resource it can to stimulate feelings) to one that serves. This principle exists elsewhere in the media environment as automated journalism is increasingly being used by respected news agencies such as the Associated Press as a means of providing detail-heavy news that does not require human context, interpretation or analysis. For example, Associated Press (2014) estimated it was reporting the quarterly earnings coverage for about 300 companies. Now it automates 4,400 such reports each quarter by means of its Automated Insights journalism. This frees journalists to do more analytical work on the implications of these figures and reports (Associated Press is also keen to highlight that no jobs have been lost as a result of introducing Automated Insights). If advertising is seen as a utility or service industry for consumers, so they are aware of the latest and best deals, and new products they might be interested in, this changes things. One might retort and say this is what advertising has always done. This is true to an extent, but one forgets behavioural and programmatic logic, filtering, heterogeneity and the principle of relevance that is synonymous with digital advertising. Google is emblematic of this as it is low in mediation and it filters which ads get to consumers so their mediascapes are not littered with irrelevant content. The advertising landscape looks somewhat different when depicted this way because it means that behavioural and programmatic logic is the principle means of doing advertising (as opposed to homogenous and widely targeted advertising such as that done through televisual and broadcast media).

This is not to suggest that branding is not required. What branding does is present ready-made understanding of what a product is and what a company stands for. Historically, like a black hole, the advertising part of the business of branding is to condense values, aspirations, politics, product function and how an object connects with the broader fabric of our lives into a singularity that appeals to us. This is why creatives are so keen to highlight the connection between storytelling and advertising: stories depict contexts, character, values and propositions in interesting and condensed ways. Stories are imaginative and entail creation of self-referential worlds. This involves generation of significance, meaning, essences, emotional relevance and connection. To speculate, what data-driven advertising represents is an unfettering of creativity from both mass media and the need to provide consumers with information (just as with automated journalism). Persado's David Atlas makes a similar point, highlighting that 'It doesn't put writers out of business. It just eliminates the drudgery of what is very often pretty repetitive fast turnaround writing'. Rather than bemoaning the rise of programmatic logic, this behavioural shift frees creatives to consider brand communication in the widest possible sense. Think of it this way: societies have long harboured concerns about the rise of machines, post-industrial culture, automation and robots doing our jobs. However, the corollary of this vision is that people are emancipated from drudgery to engage in higher forms of culture and intellectual enquiry. Similarly, the rise of programmatic logic means that creative departments will not be tasked with delivering information. After all, people are quite capable of looking for information themselves (or their virtual personal assistants will do it for them). Instead, creative advertising graduates (transcends?) from dressing information in attractive ways to being able to more purely engage with values and the affective dimension of branding. We are already seeing evidence of this in the rise of branded entertainment, sponsored films, viral content, games and sponsored communication that defies categorization into traditional media silos. Rather than seeing programmatic logic as the enemy, it is a blessing for creative departments in that heterogeneous and real-time media can provide live brand updates and creatives can get to work on the phenomenology of branding which means rich experiences, bigger stories, infinite worlds, intense significance, deeper affect, more emotion, and finding means to make us even more passionate about brands. Automation is potentially a blessing for Adland.

Fuelling the machine

At the time of writing this conclusion in 2016 programmatic is principally about low quality ad placement, but the technical and economic logic of programmatic is clear in that it seeks to make maximum use of online networks to harness as much data as is possible to target people in real time. One key objective is to serve advertising, but the more fundamental aim is to influence and modify behaviour at key moments when we are most susceptible or receptive (depending on one's viewpoint of these practices). This rich data is also useful for long-term branding strategies, market positioning and creating the right overall message to be communicated to people. Although the commercial intention is to collect all of the data all of the time, we are not there yet. However, the recent activities of data management platforms and the mega-tech corporations depicted in this book portend an advertising environment that is intelligent, reactive and sensitive to our behaviour, histories, locations, bodies, gaze, intentions and emotions; and critically is able to automatically fashion advertising in real time to be more effective. What of people in this equation? How does consent figure in this picture? Do we have the right laws and regulations in place to ensure we are not informationally exploited?

What is clear is that parts of the digital advertising industry are avaricious for data, would like to see regulations on data protection weakened, and have a clear interest in accessing more intimate information about emotions and bodies. This is logical because all advertising practitioners understand that emotions play a principal role in behaviour, purchase decisions and how we feel about brands (and the services and material objects they represent). Although I am consistently keen to avoid dystopian narratives, the advertising enterprise is an attempt to control what people think, feel and do. For this to be achieved, data is required and the answer to the question, 'Who fuels the machine?' is of course 'you and me'. I will leave the reader to decide whether the business of influence is innately wrong, but from the point of view of data, the ethics are clearer. If someone wants to collect and generate data about a person, they should explain what they want to do and ask if the individual is OK with that. This should be done before collection starts and no personal data should be obtained without meaningful consent. To reiterate, the pro-privacy position of this book is not one based on seclusion, locking away information, or having something to hide. It is the opposite: privacy is about being open as well as closed, having control regarding whom we share data with, and having a loud say about what happens to our bodies, information and reputations. At heart, privacy is about dignity and respect for others, and what they wish to share, allow access to, or reveal. Advertising can be part of this but it should be respectful, and explain in meaningful terms to individuals what data it wants to make use of and what it wants to do with it. For advertising to respond positively it needs to recognize personal and informational self-determination. This means only making use of personal and/or intimate data that has been obtained through meaningful consent.

The advertising industry maintains that behavioural advertising and existing opaque consent mechanisms are necessary for many online services, sites and apps to survive, and that a truly opt-in situation would be terminal. My view on this remains the same as in the first edition of this book, in that people should be in control of what data they share, they should not be tracked without their knowledge and consent, and that a more upfront approach is healthier for all concerned. Advertising *is* very useful as a means of keeping much online content free and we should work towards maintaining this. A diverse set of news sites, for example, are supported by advertising and it is good that people do not have to pay to access this because it is healthy that all income brackets have access to a diverse range of viewpoints. Further, not only is advertising beneficial as a means of supporting publishers and therefore free content, but the best of advertising can be useful, valuable, amusing and insightful. What is required is greater transparency about both personal and non-personal data collection and processing. As we touched upon in Chapter 5, DDB's Bill Bernbach once said that we have to recognize the power of mass media and the various ways in which it might influence society, and that creators of advertising could either brutalize society or raise it to another plane. The same applies to our digital media environment today. Currently our media technologies are being abused, but it is within the power of Adland to contribute to a healthier data environment. This should not be an impossible task for the advertising and data industry: after all, people like free content, people like buying things, people like knowing about new things and people like creative ads. Surely an opt-in approach is not that hard?

Further regulation is vital, not least because we already have significant experience with how online data trackers abuse connectivity in digital life. The logic of data exploitation is too firmly embedded into the DNA of both digital advertising and the data industry for self-regulatory techniques to be effective. My call for regulation is less about limiting, hindering or impeding than ensuring that we are growing the right types of innovation with data. Only national and transnational regulators have the clout to keep industries in check and while my natural political inclination is towards less regulation, individuals should not be left to fend for themselves against a data industry that stacks the cards in its favour through unreadable terms and conditions, and opaque third party practices. However, this is not a doom-and-gloom narrative. Our position should not be anti-technology, but one that disallows the abuse of technology. My outlook on technology is positive in that it provides more benefits than drawbacks. To achieve a better quality of connected life we should analyse the data industries, publicize our findings to all who will listen, apply pressure on our regulators, and support organizations campaigning to ensure that companies behave in accordance with laws and regulations. Indeed, those within the advertising industry (creatives and data acolytes alike) who have misgivings might be more vocal in promoting genuinely ethical uses of data.

Adland, already keen to stave off excessive regulation, could lead on a more positive approach by setting up ethics committees involving politicians, industry figures, technologists, academics, privacy groups and lay citizens. A trade association such as the Internet Advertising Bureau might arrange this. This means that as we move towards increasingly aware environments, we do so in an informed manner. We should strive towards a time when all people understand the data/services value exchange; when consent is meaningful; when our regulatory system can cope with the profusion of sensors slowly but surely entering everyday life; and when the advertising industry is incentivized not to misbehave due to increased levels of trust, transparency and high quality data willingly shared.

Notes

1. Online communication pre-dates the Internet. Howard Rheingold offers the best coverage of this in his 1993 book *The Virtual Community: Homesteading on the Electronic Frontier*, published by MIT.
2. This is well illustrated by Carolyn Marvin's 1988 *When Old Technologies Were New: Thinking About Electric Communication in the Late Nineteenth Century*, published by Oxford University Press.
3. *Wired* has an article still online from 2000 that documents the crash well, available from: www.wired.com/2010/03/0310nasdaq-bust/.
4. Warc.com is an online service offering advertising research, accounts of best practice, evidence and insights from the world's leading brands. It also publishes leading academic journals on advertising, not least the *Journal of Advertising Research* and the *International Journal of Market Research*.
5. This total of 98% is in the original IAB document cited. I assume this is a rounding error.
6. American import Black Friday arrived in the UK in 2013 and reshaped pre-Christmas consumption. For example, on the day (29 November 2013) John Lewis saw a huge spike in site visits from midnight onwards, selling one iPad every ten seconds.
7. Webpages are written in a language called HTML. By using "tags" this allows the writer of pages to create and control different pieces of content in a webpage (for example, titles, headings, pictures, files, links and so on).
8. Named after Google co-founder Larry Page and not after web*page*.
9. Available from: www.iab.net/guidelines/508676/508767/ad_unit.
10. Available from: www.thesun.co.uk/sol/homepage/features/6410 544/Sun-Investigation-Adverts-for-major-British-brands-appear-on-paedo-websites.html
11. These are available from: https://developer.apple.com/app-store/review/guidelines/.
12. Candy Crush Saga is a free-to-download mobile game, but users pay extra for more moves to improve their score. It started on Facebook, but moved to mobile devices in 2012. According to developer King.com, by the end of 2014 it was played more than a billion times a day.

13. See, for example, the report generated for the Belgian Privacy Commission by ICRI/CIR in cooperation with iMinds-SMIT analysing Facebook's revised policies and terms: www.law.kuleuven.be/icri/en/news/item/facebooks-revised-policies-and-terms-v1-2.pdf.

14. Note that the root of amateur is "lover of" and, while unpaid, amateurs may be both passionate and skilled.

15. See Katz, E. and Lazarsfeld. P.F. (1955) *Personal Influence*. New York: Free Press.

16. Article available from: www.campaignlive.co.uk/article/creativity-defined/1342573.

17. See www.ddb.com/bernbach.html for a full list of these.

18. The principle is well evident in some of our oldest writers who have pushed and crossed the line of censorship. Perhaps the Marquis de Sade's *Philosophy in the Bedroom* (1965 [1795]) illustrates best that a life lived creatively will come up against censorship.

19. In addition to publishing books, Dave Trott also blogs for *Campaign* at http://davetrott.campaignlive.co.uk/.

20. Draycott, R. (2012) '"Marketing is Dead" says Saatchi & Saatchi CEO', *The Drum*, www.thedrum.co.uk/news/2012/04/25/marketing-dead-says-saatchi-saatchi-ceo.

21. Cassetteboy achieved success and notoriety with parody mash-up videos of celebrities such as David Cameron.

22. Research slides available from: www.happiness.coca-cola.com/uk/en/coca-cola/why-teens-choose-happiness.

23. This is a point I discuss at chapter length in *Creativity and Advertising* (2013). I draw upon phenomenology, which is a philosophy that deals with experience. It is a method and approach interested in how things come to be rather than in what they are. Essences are not found, but they are disclosed. Reading creativity in advertising this way, advertising is not just about promotion but linking products and icons with very basic human experiences of reality. It is the steering of perception.

24. See, for example, Negus, K. and Pickering, M. (2004) *Creativity, Communication and Cultural Value*. London: Sage.

25. See Cannes Creative Data Lions at: www.canneslions.com/lions_innovation/awards/creative_data/introducing_creative_data/.

26. A truism acknowledged by the marketing and advertising industries. See *Marketing*, for example, and the article 'The truth about trust, hate and brands' at www.marketingmagazine.co.uk/article/1340158/truth-trust-hate-brands.

27. The study carried out by Nielsen was based on more than 28,000 Internet respondents in 56 countries.
28. Available from: www.youtube.com/watch?v=ckiQV_0RXyU.
29. Available from: www.youtube.com/watch?v=OTcdutIcEJ4.
30. Campaign available at: http://listenforyourself.tumblr.com/#!/.
31. Tweet available at: https://twitter.com/waynerooney/status/153471328018640896.
32. Event details and précis of Mark Field's talk available at: www.iabuk.net/events/library/digital-britain-conference-manchester-2015.
33. Available from: www.buzzfeed.com/virginmobilelive/celebrities-posing-with-the-old-versions-of-themselves#.yfrQyk2K5P.
34. Available from: www.buzzfeed.com/lidl/ways-to-be-a-frugal-foodie.
35. Available from: www.buzzfeed.com/cornettouk/stages-of-developing-a-crush#.pyr8JLbDl.
36. Available from: www.buzzfeed.com/googleuk/animals-with-privacy-issues-1k7c6#.pbmdz9Q7M.
37. See coverage of campaign at: www.campaignlive.co.uk/thework/1355319/.
38. See the TMWLimited and Durex campaign video at: www.tmwunlimited.com/our-work/case-study-durex-earth-hour.
39. 4chan is an image-board website where people may post anonymously. Because of few rules, it is notorious for being edgy, obscene, idiotic, brutal, but also brilliantly funny. Rick-rolling, lolcats and many other internet memes began here.
40. Available from: www.youtube.com/watch?v=_-fLV28SkZ8&feature=player_embedded.
41. Cited in an article for inc.com available from: www.inc.com/magazine/201206/josh-dean/b-reel-changing-advertising.html
42. *The Wilderness Downtown* was named Best of Show at the South by Southwest Interactive Awards, won the Grand Prix in the Cyber category at the Cannes Lion Awards, and was named Site of the Year by the Favourite Website Awards (FWA).
43. This is a complex campaign and story, possibly best understood by seeing the project video: http://yellobrick.co.uk/case-study/reverie/.
44. Public companies report their performance on the basis of a quarterly filing, typically in January, April, July and October. Reports follow soon after. Included in earnings reports are items such as net income, earnings per share, earnings from continuing operations and net sales.
45. Available from: http://techcrunch.com/2015/06/07/adblocking/.

46. Internet World Stats for 2014 Q4 records US levels of internet penetration at 86.9 per cent.
47. Acceptable Ads Initiative: https://acceptableads.org/en/.
48. See law in full here: www.legislation.gov.uk/ukdsi/2008/978011 0811574/contents.
49. Business-to-business advertising is covered by the Business Protection from Misleading Marketing Regulations (2008). In addition to being accurate and honest, advertisers must not make misleading comparisons with competitors. That includes: using a competitor's logo or trademark, or something very similar; comparing your product with a competitor's product that's not the same. See: www.legislation.gov.uk/uksi/2008/1276/contents/made.
50. Both broadcast and non-broadcast advertising codes can be found at: www.cap.org.uk/Advertising-Codes.aspx.
51. Available from: www.education.gov.uk/publications/standard/ publicationDetail/Page1/CM 8078.
52. Available from: www.gov.uk/government/uploads/system/uploads/ attachment_data/file/203333/Bailey_Review_Progress_Report.pdf.
53. See BBC story on vlogging and promotion at www.bbc.co.uk/news/ uk-30203816.
54. See Chapter 3 for distinctions.
55. See Tyler Vigen's *Spurious Correlations* at: www.tylervigen.com/ spurious-correlations.
56. List of data sources available from: http://datasift.com/platform/ datasources/.
57. Gnip, now owned by Twitter, also has access to data from the largest social networks other than Twitter (such as Facebook, Instagram, Tumblr, Foursquare, YouTube, Google, Reddit and more).
58. Available at: http://mutualmind.com/category/social-command-center/.
59. Available from: www.piqora.com/.
60. Along with Union Metrics, Curalate, Adobe and Spreadfast.
61. First shown 1.30 am, 25 July 2015.
62. Full list of Adobe's analytics and on-site personalization services at: www.adobe.com/privacy/analytics.html?f=2o7.
63. Available from: www.linkedin.com/pulse/undying-death-privacy-daniel-solove.
64. Available from: https://play.google.com/store/apps/details?id=com. jeanmarcmorandini.

65. Available from: https://play.google.com/store/apps/details?id=com. eurosport.player&hl=en_GB.
66. Available from: www.xiti.com/en.
67. This principle was coined and developed by the psychologist Martin Seligman (1975) through his work on depression.
68. First revealed by UK's *The Guardian*, the XKEYSCORE program collects data about people's internet searches, emails, documents, usernames and passwords, and other private communications.
69. See *The Drum*, 14 May 2015, www.thedrum.com/news/2015/05/14/ dont-sack-your-copywriter-yet-are-machines-set-take-over?
70. See for example Campaign, 16 July 2015, www.campaignlive.co.uk/ news/1355981/.
71. See for example Campaign, 10 July 2015, www.campaignlive.co.uk/ news/1355070/.
72. Will Sansom of Contagious Communications speaking at the Cannes Lion Advertising festival in 2015. See *Marketing* article here: www.marketingmagazine.co.uk/article/1352673/ten-years-time-agency-will-algorithm.
73. Full text available from: https://archive.org/stream/advertpshy-cho00scotrich/advertpshycho00scotrich_djvu.txt.
74. This campaign idea by Diesel has many executions that can be found at: www.creativeadawards.com/diesel-be-stupid-advertising-campaign/.
75. That occurred between the fourteenth and seventeenth century and involved rebirth of interest in art, literature, observation and learning in Europe, and marked the transition from the medieval to the modern world.
76. Available from: www.marketingmagazine.co.uk/article/1352673/ ten-years-time-agency-will-algorithm.
77. Interviewed for *The Drum*, 14 May 2015, www.thedrum.com/ news/2015/05/14/dont-sack-your-copywriter-yet-are-machines-set-take-over?

Appendix
(A-Z of Key Terms)

Adblocking: the use of software to remove ads placed by third parties.

Ad exchange: similar to a stock exchange in that it auctions impressions to the highest bidder.

Ad fraud: serving ads that have no potential to be viewed by a human user.

Ad networks: have access to ad spaces on publishers' websites. They marry available stock from web publishers with demand from advertisers for spaces in which to place their advertising.

Affect: to arouse feelings and emotions and stimulate the body.

Algorithms (in advertising): mathematical procedures created to sort and process data about people and their behaviour.

Analytics (in advertising): the ways in which data is collected, analysed and put to work to understand audiences and target advertising at people at a time when they will be most receptive.

Attribution: the attempt to understand and quantify what aspects of advertising influence people, when influence occurs and to what degree.

Behavioural advertising: ads targeted by the sites we visit and our interests, online habits and purchases.

Big data: refers to volume of data; velocity by which data moves and needs to be reacted to; and the variety of forms it comes in.

Biometric: refers to the analysis of human body characteristics.

Bisociation: blending elements from different domains for creative effect.

Classifieds: a form of advertising where readers post their own ads. It is called classified advertising because it is generally grouped under headings classifying the product or service being offered (such as cars, property or jobs).

Click fraud: when a person or machine repeatedly clicking on ads and drives up costs, sabotaging an advertiser's digital ad campaign.

Combinatorial creativity: combining elements for novel and strategic effect.

Cookies: small text files stored on a user's computer by a web browser that identifies our computer to a web server.

Correlation: identification of trends, patterns and links between different pieces of data.

Creativity (in advertising): the process of communicating the strategy of an advertising campaign in an attractive and influential manner.

Culture hacking: intentional manipulation of signs for effects beyond what they were intended to convey.

Data management platforms (DMPs): these collect, store, manage and put to work large volumes of data gathered from online and offline sources.

Data mining: the process of analysing databases to find relationships of value to the database owners.

Dynamic creative optimization: the automatic altering of an ad to fit the viewer and context in real time.

Earned media: relies on people to forward messages and content.

Emotiveillance: typically machinic acts of monitoring emotion with a view to influencing and managing people.

Empathic media: the capacity for media technologies to sense, interpret, understand what is significant for people, act on their emotional states, pre-empt behaviour, and make use of their intentions and expressions.

Ideas (big): turning advertising strategy (what message is to be communicated and to whom) into a memorable, convincing, palatable and potentially enjoyable advertising experience. They act as a rallying point for the brand because they express their values in a simple way.

Ideas (small): these are tactical and reactive, and are employed to cope with and take advantage of fast-paced media environments/current affairs.

Impressions: used in relation to display advertising, impressions are the unit for how many times an ad is served.

Influencers: thought leaders of people's peer groups. They are used by Adland to curry credibility and reach audiences.

Integrated marketing communication: the business of maintaining brand presence consistency across traditional and non-traditional communication channels.

Inventory: this is the stock of ad slots that an advertiser's ad might be inserted into.

Machinic verisimilitude: the way by which devices and technologies appear to understand what we think and feel.

Marketing funnel: the path from awareness of a product to purchasing it.

Media hacking: innovative use of media technologies to create content and campaigns.

Mixed reality: makes use of digital/virtual media and the real world.

Native advertising: sponsored content online that integrates itself into the context in which it is being delivered.

Net neutrality: where every person or organization's internet data is treated equally and neither restricted nor prioritized.

Non-interruptive advertising: advertising that does not rely on interruptive hard-sell techniques, but attractive content that is sought and subsequently shared.

Optimization: in advertising this refers to how websites are altered to maximize chances of higher placing on search engine results.

Personal data: data which relates to a living individual who can be identified from a given data set, or by means of other information which a person or machine is likely to come into the possession of.

Privacy protocol: refers to what otherwise might be phrased as privacy norms, rules of interaction, codes of behaviour and expectations from both human and machinic others.

Profiling: generating information about individuals and groups, and turning that information into knowledge that is useful in some way.

Programmatic: a form of display advertising based on the premise of using data from all sources possible (online and offline) to both deliver advertising and create the advertising content. It often makes use of **real-time bidding**.

Programmatic logic: this represents the intention to use artificial intelligence and big data processes to map the entire context of our lives.

Publishers: in the same way that there are book, magazine and news publishers, there are also web publishers. They make websites, apps and digital content where advertising is placed.

Real-time bidding: this allows buyers to determine the potential merits and value of an online ad space in the time it takes a webpage to load. Done by machines, this is automated media buying achieved through bidding for inventory.

Relevance: germaneness to the context in which people find themselves (for example type of site, location, time and interests).

Retargeting: the automated act of carrying out specific follow-ups (typically with emails and targeted banners) with web users who have visited a website and not purchased a product or service.

Scalability: recognizes that the internet and the web are incomplete technologies. This is not negative, but precisely the opposite, because it allows for continual growth and development.

Sentiment analysis: the use of digital means to extract understanding and meaning from group behaviour, people's preferences and what we say and post on social media.

Strategy (in advertising): this consists of knowing the target market, how the advertisement should speak to the target market (for instance, tone of voice), and the media best suited for reaching that target market. It is the *what* is to be communicated rather than the *how*.

Storytelling: translation of facts and information into character and narrative form.

Telepresence: the sense of being at a location other than where the physical body is located.

Third-party ads: ads served on a web publisher's behalf.

Third-party data: information bought and sold in an open market environment to build a rich and comprehensive view of consumers.

Transmedia storytelling (in advertising): where aspects of an advertising campaign are dispersed and fragmented across different media.

Value exchange: in a digital context, this is the transaction of swapping rich data for better experiences.

Viral: whereby content is shared through personal networks.

Reference List

33across.com (2016) *Take CTRL*, http://33across.com/, accessed 10 May 2016.

Adobe (2015) *Adobe Privacy Center/Analytics and on-site personalization services*, www.adobe.com/privacy/analytics.html?f=2o7, accessed 16/05/15.

Advertising Age (2003) *History: 1990s*, http://adage.com/article/adage-encyclopedia/history-1990s/98705/, accessed 19 April 2015.

Advertising Age (2015) *2015 Marketing Fact Pack*, http://brandedcontent. adage.com/mic/regform/index.php?&referal_id=124&msg=Please +register, accessed 29 January 2015.

Alexa (2015) *The Top 500 Sites on the Web*, www.alexa.com/topsites, accessed 6 February 2015.

Altman, I. (1975) *The Environment and Social Behaviour: Privacy, Personal Space, Territory, Crowding*. Monterey, CA: Brooks/Cole.

Anderson, C. (2008) The End of Theory: The Data Deluge Makes the Scientific Method Obsolete, *Wired*, http://archive.wired.com/science/ discoveries/magazine/16-07/pb_theory, accessed 22 September 2014.

Arden, P. (2003) *It's Not How Good You Are, It's How Good You Want To Be*. London: Phaidon.

Article 29 Data Protection Working Party (2011) *Opinion 15/2011 on the Definition of Consent*, http://ec.europa.eu/justice/policies/privacy/ docs/wpdocs/2011/wp187_en.pdf, accessed 30 September 2014.

ASA (2014) *Spotting Online Ads*, www.asa.org.uk/~/media/Files/ASA/ Hot%20Topics/Spotting%20Online%20Ads.ashx, accessed 25 June 2015.

Associated Press (2014) *A Leap Forward in Quarterly Earnings Stories*, https://blog.ap.org/announcements/a-leap-forward-in-quarterly-earnings-stories, accessed 10 May 2016.

Aurora Creative (2014) *The Company*, www.aurora-creative.com/com pany.html, accessed 23 November 2014.

Bailey, R. (2011) *Letting Children be Children: Report of an Independent Review of the Commercialisation and Sexualisation of Childhood*, www. gov.uk/government/uploads/system/uploads/attachment_data/ file/175418/Bailey_Review.pdf, accessed 15 July 2015.

Banet-Weisner, S. (2012) *Authentic TM: The Politics of Ambivalence in a Brand Culture*. New York: New York University Press.

Barry, P. (2008) *The Advertising Concept Book*. London: Thames and Hudson.

Beniger, J.R. (1986) *The Control Revolution: Technological and Economic Origins of the Information Society*. Cambridge, Mass.: Harvard University Press.

Berners-Lee, T. and Cailliau, R. (1990) *WorldWideWeb: Proposal for a HyperText Project*, www.w3.org/Proposal.html, accessed 20 January 2015.

Bluekai (2014) *Going Global: Programmatic Audience Development Around the World*, www.bluekai.com/going-global/going-global.pdf, accessed 28 May 2015.

Boden, M.A. (2010) *Creativity and Art: Three Roads to Surprise*. Oxford: Oxford University Press.

Bullmore, J. (2003) *More Bull More: Behind the Scenes in Advertising* (Mark III). Henley-on-Thames: Warc.

Caillois, R. (2001 [1958]) *Man, Play and Games*. Urbana and Chicago: University of Illinois Press.

Calcutt, A. (1999) *White Noise: An A-Z of the Contradictions in Cyberculture*. London: MacMillan Press.

Campaign (2015a) *Does Too Much Data Stifle Creativity?*, www.campaignlive.co.uk/news/1355070/, accessed 15 July 2015.

Campaign (2015b) *Brian Cox: 'Data is Never Bad'*, www.campaignlive.co.uk/news/1353191/brian-cox-data-bad/?_ga=1.261620749.180822648.1427713562/, accessed 15 July 2015.

CAP (2015) *Video Blogs: Scenarios*, www.cap.org.uk/Advice-Training-on-the-rules/Advice-Online-Database/Video-blogs-Scenarios.aspx#.VdS2zSxVikr, accessed 20 August 2015.

Chartered Institute of Public Relations (2015) *What is PR*, www.cipr.co.uk/content/careers-cpd/careers-advice-and-case-studies/what-pr, accessed 3 February 2015.

Clabiorne, A. Stephenson, C., Atkinson, C., Holden M., Florence, M., Bishop, W. and Wiseman, W. (2015) *Sentience: The Coming AI Revolution and the Implications for Marketing*. Kindle: PHD.

Cracknell, A. (2011) *The Real Mad Men*. London: Quercus.

Davis, A. (2013) *Promotional Cultures*. Cambridge: Polity.

DDB (2012) *Bill Bernbach said…*, http://www.ddb.com/BillBernbachSaid/Slideshow/, accessed 11 June 2016.

De Sade, M. (1965 [1795]) *The Marquis de Sade: The Complete Justine, Philosophy in the Bedroom and Other Writings*, trans. R. Seaver and A. Wainhouse. New York: Grove Press.

DFC Intelligence (2014) *DFC Intelligence Forecasts Global Video Game Industry to Reach $96B in 2018*, www.dfcint.com/wp/?p=358, accessed 10 December 2014.

Digiday (2014) *Confessions of a Fake Web Traffic Buyer*, http://digiday.com/publishers/confessions-bot-traffic-buyer/, accessed 21 August 2015.

Doubleclick (2005) *The Decade in Online Advertising*, www.doubleclick.com/us/knowledge_central, accessed 10 October 2014.

Dove (2015) *Dove Ad Makeover*, www.dove.co.uk/en/Tips-Topics-and-Tools/Latest-Topics/Dove-Ad-Makeover.aspx, accessed 10 October 2014.

The Economist (2006) *The Ultimate Marketing Machine*, www.economist.com/node/7138905, accessed 20 July 2015.

The Economist (2011) *All the World's a Game*, www.economist.com/node/21541164, accessed 15 August 2014.

Edge (2006) *The Making of Adventureland*, 162, pp. 104–107.

eXelate (2015) *Our Data Management Platform: A Unified Approach to Audience Based Marketing*, http://exelate.com/products/data-management-platform/, accessed 13 July 2015.

European Commission (2012) *Commission Proposes a Comprehensive Reform of Data Protection Rules to Increase Users' Control of their Data and to Cut Costs for Businesses*, http://europa.eu/rapid/press-release_IP-12-46_en.htm?locale=en, accessed 16 October 2014.

Google (2010) *Search Engine Optimization Starter Guide*, http://static.googleusercontent.com/media/www.google.co.uk/en/uk/webmasters/docs/search-engine-optimization-starter-guide.pdf, accessed 20 January 2015.

Google (2014) *The Importance of Being Seen*, https://think.storage.googleapis.com/docs/the-importance-of-being-seen_study.pdf, accessed 03 July 2015.

Hackley, C. (2007) The Trouble with Creatives: Negotiating Creative Identity in Advertising Agencies, *International Journal of Advertising*, 26(1): 63–78.

Hegarty, J. (2011) *Hegarty on Advertising: Turning Intelligence into Magic*. London: Thames & Hudson.

Hildebrandt, M. (2008) Defining Profiling: A New Type of Knowledge, in M. Hildebrandt, M. and S. Gutwirth (eds), *Profiling the European Citizen: Cross-Disciplinary Perspectives*. Dordrecht: Springer.

Holliday, R. (2015) Media and Popular Culture, in V. Robinson and D. Richardson (eds), *Introducing Gender and Women's Studies* (4th edition). London: Palgrave.

Hopkins, C. (1998 [1923]) *My Life in Advertising & Scientific Advertising*. Chicago: NTC Business Books.

Huizinga, J. (1955 [1938]) Homo Ludens. Boston: Beacon.

IAB (2011) *Gaming Britain*, www.iabuk.net/blog/10-uk-video-game-audience-stats, accessed 9 May 2016.

IAB (2012) *Consumers and Online Privacy 2012 – Bitesize Guide*, www.iabuk.net/sites/default/files/Consumers%20and%20Online%20Privacy%202012%20-%20Bitesize%20Guide.pdf, accessed 20 April 2014.

IAB (2014a) *IAB / PwC UK Digital Adspend Study – H1 2014*, www.iabuk.net/research/library/Online-adspend, accessed 20 January 2015.

IAB (2014b) *IAB / PwC UK Digital Adspend Study Full Year 2013*, www. iabuk.net/research/library/2013-full-year-digital-adspend-results, accessed 20 January 2015.

IAB (2014c) *The Programmatic Handbook*, www.iabuk.net/resources/ handbooks/the-programmatic-handbook, accessed 10 January 2015.

IAB (2015) *15% of Britons Online are Blocking Ads*, www.iabuk.net/about/ press/archive/15-of-britons-online-are-blocking-ads, accessed 1 July 2015.

IAB/YouGov (2014) *Trading Places: Cars, Jobs and Homes*, www.iabuk. net/blog/trading-places-cars-jobs-and-homes, accessed 2 January 2015.

ICO (2012) *Guidance on the Rules on Use of Cookies and Similar Technologies*, https://ico.org.uk/media/fororganisations/documents/1545/cookies_ guidance.pdf, accessed 14 June 2015.

The Intercept (2015a) *Secret 'BADASS' Intelligence Program Spied on Smartphones*, https://firstlook.org/theintercept/2015/01/26/secret-badass-spy-program/, accessed 20 July 2015.

The Intercept (2015b) *XKEYSCORE: NSA's Google for the World's Private Communications*, https://firstlook.org/theintercept/2015/07/01/nsas-google-worlds-private-communications, accessed 20 July 2015.

IPA (2011) *UK and International Awards Ceremonies*, www.ipa.co.uk/Content/ UK-and-International-Awards-Ceremonies, accessed 1 December 2011.

Jenkins, H. (2006) *Convergence Culture*. New York: New York University.

Jones, J.P. (2004) *Fables, Fashions, and Facts About Advertising: A Study of 28 Enduring Myths*. Thousand Oaks: Sage.

Katz, E. (1957) The Two-Step Flow of Communication: An Up-to-Date Report on an Hypothesis. *Public Opinion Quarterly* (21): 61–78.

Katz, E. (1973) Television as a Horseless Carriage, in G. Gerbner, et al. (eds), *Communications Technology and Social Policy*. New York: Wiley.

Katz, E., Blumler, J.G. and Gurevitch, M. (2003 [1974]) Utilization of Mass Communication by the Individual, in V. Nightingale and K. Ross (eds) *Critical Readings: Media and Audiences*. Maidenhead: Open University Press.

Katz, E. and Lazarsfeld. P.F. (1955) *Personal Influence*. New York: Free Press.

Koestler, A. (1970 [1964]) *The Act of Creation*. London: Pan Piper.

Kosta, E. (2013) *Consent in European Data Protection Law*. Leiden: Martinus Nijhoff Publishers.

Laney, D. (2001) *3D Data Management: Controlling Data Volume, Velocity and Variety*, http://blogs.gartner.com/doug-laney/files/2012/01/ad949-3D-Data-Management-Controlling-Data-Volume-Velocity-and-Variety.pdf, accessed 15 April 2015.

Langville, A.H. and Mayer, C.D. (2006) *Google's PageRank and Beyond: The Science of Search Engine Rankings*. New Jersey: Princeton University Press.

Lazzarato, M. (2004) From Capital-Labour to Capital-Life, *Ephemera* 4 (3): 187–208.

Lazzarato, M. (2014) *Signs and Machines: Capitalism and the Promotion of Subjectivity*. Los Angeles: Semiotext(e).

Livingstone, S. (1997) The Work of Elihu Katz, in J. Corner, P. Schlesinger and R. Silverstone (eds), *International Handbook of Media Research*. London: Routledge.

Livingstone, S. and Helsper, E.J. (2006) Does Advertising Literacy Mediate the Effects of Advertising on Children? A Critical Examination of Two Linked Research Literatures in Relation to Obesity and Food Choice, *Journal of Communications* 56 (3): 560–584.

Lysyj, L. (2015) Your Agency Hates You and You Don't Even Know It, *Advertising Age*, http://adage.com/article/viewpoint-editorial/agency-hates/299532/, accessed 20 July 2015.

Manovich, L. (2003) *The Language of New Media*. Cambridge: MIT Press.

Marshall, D. (ed.) (2010) *Understanding Children as Consumers*. London: Sage.

Mazzarella, W. (2006) *Shovelling Smoke: Advertising and Globalization in Contemporary India*. Durham and London: Duke University Press.

McStay, A. (2011a) *The Mood of Information: A Critique of Online Behavioural Advertising*. New York: Continuum.

McStay, A. (2011b) Profiling Phorm: An Autopoietic Approach to the Audience-as-Commodity, *Surveillance and Society*, 8(3): 310–322.

McStay, A. (2013) *Creativity and Advertising: Affect, Events and Process*. London: Routledge.

McStay, A. (2014) *Privacy and Philosophy: New Media and Affective Protocol*. New York: Peter Lang.

McQuail, D. (2000) *Mass Communication Theory*. Sage: London.

Mediative (2014) *The Evolution of Google Search Results Pages & Their Effects on User Behaviour*, http://pages.mediative.com/SERP-Research, accessed 2 February 2015.

Meng, T.K. (2015) *The Plot Quickens*, www.campaignlive.co.uk/news/article/1339894/the-plot-quickens/, accessed 28 March 2015.

Millward Brown (2010) *Neuroscience: A New Perspective*, www.millward brown.com/docs/default-source/insight-documents/points-of-view/MillwardBrown_POV_NeurosciencePerspective.pdf, accessed 14 April 2014.

Morley, D (1980) *The Nationwide Audience: Structure and Decoding*. London: BFI.

NAI (2015) *Understanding Online Advertising*, www.networkadvertising.org/faq, accessed 12 July 2015.

Negus, K. and Pickering, M. (2004) *Creativity, Communication and Cultural Value*. London: Sage.

Nielsen (2012) *Nielsen: Global Consumers' Trust In 'Earned' Advertising Grows in Importance*, www.nielsen.com/us/en/press-room/2012/ nielsen-global-consumers-trust-in-earned-advertising-grows.html, accessed 13 April 2015.

Nissenbaum, H. (2010) *Privacy in Context: Technology, Policy, and the Integrity of Social Life*. Stanford: Stanford University Press.

Oates, C., Blades, M., Gunter, B. and Don, J. (2003) Children's Understanding of Television Advertising: A Qualitative Approach, *Journal of Marketing Communications*, 9 (2): 59–71.

Ofcom (2015) *Adults' Media use and Attitudes*, http://stakeholders.ofcom. org.uk/binaries/research/media-literacy/media-lit-10years/2015_ Adults_media_use_and_attitudes_report.pdf, accessed 30 May 2015.

Ogilvy, D. (1985) *Ogilvy on Advertising*. New York: Random House.

O'Reilly, L. (2015) *This Ad Blocking Company has the Potential to Tear a Hole Right Through the Mobile Web — And it has the Support of Carriers*, http:// uk.businessinsider.com/israeli-ad-blocker-shine-could-threaten-mobile-advertising-2015-5#ixzz3dzOzg3I6, accessed 12 June 2015.

PageFair (2014) Adblocking Goes Mainstream, *PageFair*, http://blog. pagefair.com/2014/adblocking-report/, accessed 10 February 2015.

Pasquale, F. (2015) *The Black Box Society: The Secret Algorithms that Control Money and Information*. Cambridge, MA: Harvard University Press.

Peppers, D. and Rogers, M. (1993) *The One to One Future: Building Relationships One Customer at a Time*. New York: Currency Doubleday.

PewDiePie (2015) *This Book Loves You*. London: Penguin.

Phillips, D. and Curry, M. (2003) 'Privacy and the Phentic Urge: Geodemographics and the Changing Spatiality of Local Practice, in D. Lyon (ed.), *Surveillance as Social Sorting: Privacy, Risk and Digital Discrimination*. New York: Routledge.

PWC (2015) *Video Games*, www.pwc.com/gx/en/industries/entertain ment-media/outlook/segment-insights/video-games.html, accessed 11 May 2016.

Ray, B. (2014) Ad Tech Isn't a Threat to Agencies, It's an Opportunity, *Advertising Age*, http://adage.com/article/guest-columnists/ad-tech-a-threat-agencies-opportunity/294557/, accessed 19 July 2015.

Ritzer, G. and Jurgenson, N. (2010) Production, Consumption, Prosumption, *Journal of Consumer Culture*, 10(1): 13–36.

Ross, K. and Nightingale, V. (2003) *Media and Audiences*. London: Open University Press.

Scott, W.D. (2007 [1903]) *The Psychology of Advertising in Theory and Practice*. Boston: Small, Maynard & Company, https://archive.org/ stream/advertpshycho00scotrich/advertpshycho00scotrich_djvu. txt, accessed 20 August 2015.

Seligman, M.E.P. (1975) *Helplessness: On Depression, Development, and Death*. San Francisco: W.H. Freeman.

Shannon, C. and Weaver, W. (1949) *The Mathematical Theory of Communication*. Illinois: University of Illinois Press.

Shirky, C. (2008) *Here Comes Everybody: How Change Happens when People Come Together*. New York: Penguin.

Siebelink, R. and Belani, E. (2013) *10 Questions about Programmatic Buying ...and the Answers Marketers Need*, http://rocketfuel.com/downloads/10-Questions-About-Programmatic-Buying.pdf, accessed 20 January 2015.

Smith, E. (2010) *iPhone Applications & Privacy Issues: An Analysis of Application Transmission of iPhone Unique Device Identifiers (UDIDs)*, www.pskl.us/wp/wp-content/uploads/2010/09/iPhone-Applications-Privacy-Issues.pdf, accessed 20 July 2015.

Smythe, D.W. (1977) Communications: Blindspot of Western Marxism, *Canadian Journal of Political and Social Theory*, 1 (3), 1–27.

Starch, D. (1914) *Advertising: Its Principles, Practice, and Technique*, www.archive.org/download/advertisingitspr00stariala/advertisingitspr00stariala.pdf, accessed 20 July 2015.

Stringer, N. (2015) *EDAA Annual Report: On the Path to Greater Consumer Trust*, www.iabuk.net/blog/edaa-annual-report-on-the-path-to-greater-consumer-trust, accessed 8 May 2015.

TNS Omnibus (2012) *TNS Omnibus Surveys of Parents of Children aged 5–16 in the UK and of Children and Young People aged 7–16 in GB for the Bailey Review*, www.gov.uk/government/uploads/system/uploads/attachment_data/file/202918/Bailey_Review_Comparing_Baseline_and_Repeat_TNS_Omnibus_Survey_Results.pdf, accessed 13 July 2015.

Trott, D. (2009) *Creative Mischief*. London: Loaf.

TRUSTe (2013) TRUSTe 2013 *Great Britain Consumer Confidence Privacy Report: What Consumers Think, Business Impact, and Recommended Actions*, www.iabuk.net/research/library/member-research-truste-2013-great-britain-consumer-confidence-privacy-report, accessed 6 May 2015.

Tungate, M. (2007) *Adland: A Global History of Advertising*. London: Kogan Page.

Vico, G. (2001 [1725]) *The New Science of Giambattista Vico*, trans. D. Marsh. London: Penguin Books.

Vigneri, L., Chandrashekar, J., Pefkianakis, I. and Heen, O. (2015) *Taming the Android AppStore: Lightweight Characterization of Android Applications*, http://arxiv.org/pdf/1504.06093v2.pdf, accessed 3 May 2015.

Warc (2015) *Warc 100: The World's Best Digital Agencies*, www.warc.com/warc100/topdigitalagencies2015.100, accessed 20 September 2015.

White Ops (2014) *The Bot Baseline: Fraud in Digital Advertising*, www.whiteops.com/, accessed 21 August 2015.

xAd/telmetrics (2015) *Mobile: Path to Purchase 2014*, www.mmaglobal.com/files/documents/mobile_path_to_purchase_2014_overview_us_whitepaper.pdf, accessed 23 June 2015.

Young, J.W. (2003 [1940]) *A Technique for Producing Ideas*. New York: McGraw Hill.

Y&R (2016) *Who Are We?* www.yr.com/about, accessed 21 May 2016.

Zeisler, A. (2008) *Feminism and Pop Culture*. Berkeley, CA: Seal Press.

Index